Global Rage after the Cold War

Global Rage after the Cold War

Frank Louis Rusciano

Rider University

First published in 2006 by
PALGRAVE MACMILLAN™
175 Fifth Avenue, New York, N.Y. 10010 and
Houndmills, Basingstoke, Hampshire, England RG21 6XS.
Companies and representatives throughout the world.

PALGRAVE MACMILLAN is the global academic imprint of the Palgrave Macmillan
division of St. Martin's Press, LLC and of Palgrave Macmillan Ltd. Macmillan® is a registered
trademark in the United States, United Kingdom and other countries. Palgrave is a registered
trademark in the European Union and other countries.

Library of Congress Cataloging-in-Publication Data

Rusciano, Frank Louis, 1954-
    Global Rage after the Cold War/Frank Louis Rusciano.
        p. cm.
    Includes bibliographical references and index.
    ISBN 1-4039-6499-8
        1. Culture conflict. 2. East West. 3. International relations. 4. Islamic
    conutries—Foreign public opinion. 5. Developing countries—Foreign public
    opinion. 6. Mass media and public opinion. I. Title.
HM1121R87 2006
303.6'095'0956'090511—dc22   2005051249

A catalogue record for this book is available from the British Library.

Design by Macmillan India Ltd.

First edition: April 2006

10 9 8 7 6 5 4 3 2 1

Printed in the United States of America.

To my parents, Frank Joseph and Philomena Susan, and to Elisabeth,
scholar, teacher, friend

Those who teach us teach our children as well . . .

Contents

List of Figures

List of Tables

Preface

This book began the last time I taught our Department's Senior Seminar in Political Science. The course was a workshop analyzing world opinion. Students were required to do content analyses on articles and editorials referencing world opinion in a wide range of international newspapers. I gave an introductory lecture on how various world newspapers reflected different perspectives on international public opinion. I then assigned them to research topics on the agenda for world opinion and come in one week later for class with suggestions on what we might study.

That first class met on September 5, 2001; a week later, on September 12, 2001, there was no longer any question regarding the topic of our study.

I had initially planned a larger book-length project in which I would extend the analysis of world opinion past the initial three months of the study. As I delved deeper into the subject, however, I found that the fundamental questions of why the attacks on 9/11 occurred were not being answered adequately. I also found echoes of analyses I had done, some almost a decade earlier, on the rise of nationalism and ethnic violence in the post–Cold War era. I realized that the phenomenon of global terrorism and the rise of nationalism and ethnic violence were symptoms of the same problem—the loss of identity and global status that various nations and peoples felt in the aftermath of the Cold War. Their violent responses were part of a pattern of *global rage* that threatened any possibility of a post–Cold War "order."

This book is divided into three parts. Part I examines world opinion in the international press on 9/11 and the construction of identity among Muslim and non-Muslim nations. Not only was the process similar in both contexts, the potential failures to create identities that led to pride promoted various forms of violence in both areas as well. Part II examines violent actions by state and non-state actors in Germany, China, India, and the United States—actions driven not just by physical threats but by threats to the identities of citizens of these nations. Part III proposes solutions to the problem by attacking the roots of despair that promote such violence.

Although this is a book about rage, it attempts also to be a book about hope. I recall reading the local newspaper in my wife's hometown of Rutland, Vermont during a visit in 1984. A letter to the editor spoke of how the world would be a "paradise" if the Soviet Union and Communism did not exist. The Soviet Union is gone, and Communism is generally viewed as a failed ideology. Yet the serpents of nationalistic violence and "ethnic cleansing" in the 1990s and global terrorism in the new century have found their way into this imagined Eden. We cannot, and need not, wait to see the next manifestation of global rage—and while the world will never be a paradise no matter how many of our demons we dispel, I believe that there is a chance for creative leadership to stem the tide of this pandemic of anger.

This book would not have been possible without the talents and help of many people. I would acknowledge first my students in the Senior Seminar, with whom I worked on the initial analyses—Jennifer Bottorff, Danielle Cannis, Kamni Kahn, Nikoi Kotey, Juan Nunez, Lisa Puchon, Amber Railey, Jennifer Shamy, and Sheila Wiatr. Their spirit and work during that difficult time showed that the search for knowledge, and the sharing of it with others, can have healing effects for all of us. Similarly, my research assistants Frishta Sharifi and Adaluz Veloz were responsible for the research on the Iranian and Dominican newspapers, respectively, in Chapter 6; their work was invaluable and made that section possible. The other group of individuals to whom I owe an enormous debt are the "SPAR" people at Rider—my wife, Roberta Fiske-Rusciano, and colleagues, Jonathan Mendilow, Minmin Wang, James Castagnera, Bosah Ebo, Barbara Franz, Yun Xia, Lucian Frary, and Barry Seldes. These colleagues, who form our research seminar at Rider University, were kind enough to tear my work apart unmercifully in order to make it better. I trust that the final result is worthy of their efforts.

I would be remiss if I did not acknowledge my editor at Palgrave, David Pervin. David provided the inspiration for this book when he approached me about it at the Harvard University symposium where I first presented the 9/11 study. He also went over various approaches to the subject in great detail through numerous consultations with me. Finally, he proved to have the incredible patience and persistent pressure that ensures such projects will go to fruition. There would not have been a book without him.

Finally, I want to extend specific thanks to Roberta Fiske-Rusciano and Minmin Wang, for allowing me to use the analyses that we performed together on China in Chapter 4, and to Roberta Fiske-Rusciano and Christopher Hill for allowing me to use similar analyses from Chapter 6. Given that we initially worked together on the analyses and use of this data, these chapters belong to them as much as me, although I claim all responsibilities for any material (and especially lapses in argument) contained therein.

Part I

9/11 and Global Rage

Introduction: World Opinion on September 11, 2001—If the World Doesn't Hate Us, Why Would Someone Do This?

What perceived grievance could motivate individuals on the other side of the world to plot and carry out suicide attacks within the United States? The common response points to American policy in the Middle East, particularly toward the Israeli-Palestinian conflict. Other explanations reference the ongoing decline of Muslim countries, rifts between secular governments supported by the West, and fundamentalist forces in the Middle East. All of these explanations have credence, and provide pieces of the puzzle. But analysts have neglected the relationships among the events of September 11 and other forms of religious and ethnic violence since the fall of the Berlin Wall. Understanding the roots of global rage in the post–Cold War era requires a global perspective that elaborates, without necessarily negating, the other explanations.

In the aftermath of the attacks on September 11, 2001, an editorial writer stated in the *International Herald Tribune* that these events heralded the first blow in a "clash of civilizations"—Western versus Muslim. At the same time, he also asserted that the events were an affront to world opinion and the international community.[1] Inadvertently, he was employing two contradictory perspectives, each implying very different discourse conventions, meanings, and ultimately, actions.

The allusion to a "clash of civilizations" refers to Samuel P. Huntington's assertion that in the post–Cold War era, the major conflicts have been between different "civilizations," or primordial groupings based around the complex of ethnicity, religion, and culture. Huntington dismisses the term "international community" as a "euphemistic collective noun (replacing 'the Free World') to give global legitimacy to actions reflecting the interests of the United States and other Western powers."[2] Further, he rejects the notion of "world opinion" on the grounds that it is based upon "argument[s] that a universal culture or civilization is now emerging . . . none of

which withstands even passing scrutiny."³ Huntington's argument represents
a step forward and a step backward historically. It moves forward by recognizing that identity could have referents beyond the boundaries of the
nation-state. It moves backward by assuming that these referents would be
"civilizations" based upon ancient associations that combine region, culture,
religion, and ethnicity.

Global opinion theory, by contrast, argues that nations advance interpretations of "world opinion" whose structure and content are favorable to
their interests and values. A process of negotiation then ensues among the
involved nations to resolve these interpretations. Nations that violate any
resulting consensus risk isolation from the "international community."
The global opinion approach combines previous studies of world opinion
theory with notions of "international society" derived from the English
School of international relations theory.⁴

Global opinion theory shares with the English School of international
relations theory the notion that shared opinions supported the origins of
the nation-state and that the nations of the world constitute a societal unit.
Regarding the first, Mayall notes how a general consensus had to undergird
even the existence of the nation-state, since "if sovereign authorities are to
conclude agreements, they must recognize one another as sovereign."⁵
Similarly, global opinion theory argues that "the first genuine 'world opinion' may have been the consensus among countries that nation-states were
legitimate groupings for the organization of human activities."⁶
Regarding the second, Mayall notes

> Anyone who has ever tried to discuss the general context of international
> relations has been forced, sooner or later, to *use some collective noun*
> [emphasis added]. Some have opted for the community of mankind, others
> for the society of states, yet others for a states-system, or world society, or a
> series of international regimes.⁷

Global opinion theory similarly includes the notion of the "world as a
unit," employing such phrases as "world community," "world public," or
"civilized nations"⁸ as synonyms in its analyses.

Global opinion theory departs from the English School by stressing the
influences of *communication* and *world opinion* in the creation and maintenance of international society, rather than power and the imposition of values by one set of nations (as in Europe). Hence, an international community
defined by world opinion "tends to appear when the 'imagined community'
of nations, constructed from common linguistic usages, becomes integral to
the administration of scarce resources beyond the nation-state."⁹

I will argue that a common element unifying many of the past decade's
incidents of ethnic and religious violence is a rage caused by global status

dislocations after the end of the Cold War. These processes are all part of a post–Cold War version of *identity politics*—defined here as the construction and projection of a nation's or a people's identity in a manner compatible with its citizens' values and acknowledged generally by the rest of the world. But therein often lies the problem, as the values certain nations or groups wish to project, or the identities they find acceptable, do not achieve for them the international reputation in world opinion that they desire. Acts of frustration and hatred accompany such failures.

For this reason, the differences between the "clash of civilizations" and the "global opinion" theories are more than academic. If global rage has its sources in primordial differences that predate the modern era, and the Cold War was merely an interruption in this conflict (as Huntington implies), then there is little to be done to alleviate the problem. We must simply accept it as fact and endeavor to project our civilization's values as preeminent in the world. If, however, global rage has its sources in a loss of international status among certain peoples and nations, then global opinion theory suggests a different approach to the problem. Since world opinion, like public opinion, can be changed, it follows that it may be possible to alleviate the loss of international status without resorting to violence. Under these circumstances, for the United States or other powerful nations to project their values as preeminent in an overly aggressive fashion might be counterproductive. Such actions would only underscore the relative weakness and lost status of other regions, exacerbating the problem.[10]

This chapter tests the applicability of the "global opinion" and "clash of civilizations" theories following the attacks of September 11, 2001 by analyzing how several international newspapers conceptualized world opinion toward the United States and this event. International newspapers offer one means of gauging media perspectives on world opinion. Since global status is the subject here, newspapers of record are critical forums through which messages about a nation's or people's global reputation are disseminated. The conflicts surrounding 9/11 could only result in a "clash of civilizations" if an international consensus interpreted the conflict as civilizational—that is, if world opinion generally supported this explanation.

The newspapers were chosen to represent the major "civilizations" Huntington describes. They included the *New York Times*, the *London Times*, and Israel's *Ha'aretz Daily* (Western civilization); the *Arab News* (Islamic civilization);[11] the *China Daily* (Sinic civilization); the *Times of India* (Hindu civilization); the Argentinean *Nacion* (Latin-American civilization); the Nigerian *Guardian* (African civilization); and *Pravda* (Slavic-Orthodox civilization). The *International Herald Tribune* was added as an example of a newspaper that aspires to an international perspective. All the newspapers are independently published, with the exceptions of the *China Daily* and the

Arab News, both of which are government controlled. The analysis was done in English, using translated versions of the newspapers where needed, except for the *Nacion,* which was analyzed in the original Spanish edition. With the exception of "Western civilization," all of the other regions are represented by only one newspaper. The newspapers in the former included *Ha'aretz* because it was appropriate to use an Israeli newspaper given the relevance of the Middle East to the issue, and because it was also useful to include another newspaper not published in or from the United States. It is, of course, debatable whether the *Arab News* is a valid "representative" of "Muslim civilization." Huntington's analysis begs that classification, however, since the "clash of civilizations" thesis assumes implicitly a great degree of issue coherence within, but not between, the regions he defines. It will be useful, no doubt, for some future project to include a number of Muslim newspapers, but availability and time and language constraints limited the present study to one paper.[12]

These media analyses follow Herman and Chomsky's assumption that newspaper discourse tends to reflect the dominant ideological and regime interests of the nation of origin.[13] While the newspaper's national origin does not *determine* its discourse, it does provide clues to how certain issues are discussed and how certain terminologies are framed. It is clear that a sample of ten newspapers cannot actually measure world opinion, or even elite opinion, for that matter. Different newspapers within the same country, state, or region may have very different editorial positions. However, analyzing newspapers of record does give some general guidance about elite perceptions of world opinion. Because this study examines changes in perceptions of world opinion over time, it demonstrates how these perceptions change as different events occur. Since these are influential publications, the shifts they record can be interpreted as both *reflecting* and *affecting* world opinion, to some extent.

The Agenda for World Opinion following September 11, 2001

In the seven weeks of the study, 287 references to world opinion on the September 11 attacks appeared in the ten newspapers. Consistent with its claim to being "the world's newspaper," the *International Herald Tribune* contained the most references (25 percent of the total, or 72 references), more than twice that of the second-highest number of references, from the Nigerian *Guardian* (12 percent, or 34 references). The rest followed with 11 percent (*Ha'aretz*), 11 percent (the *New York Times*), 9 percent (*Nacion*), 8 percent (the *Arab News*), 8 percent (*Pravda*), 7 percent (*London Times*), 5 percent (*China Daily*), and 5 percent (*Times of India*).

In the sample, 67 percent of the references appeared in editorials and the rest appeared in reports. It was found that "world opinion" was more likely to be referenced implicitly (as it was in 91 percent of cases) rather than explicitly. Explicit references included the phrase "world opinion" or some equivalent, such as "international opinion," "world public opinion," "international public opinion," and so on. Implicit references referred to the attribution of some judgment or reaction to the world, such as "worldwide shock," "world outrage," and a "complete political and ideological isolation of terrorists through international cooperation." Other implicit references attributed actual expressions of opinion to the world or to the international community, noting, for instance, how "the world had ignored" support for terrorism, that "the world will not forget," and that "the world was appalled" by the attacks.[14]

Does "the World" Hate the United States?

From discussions of opinions on "the Arab street" to American news-magazine covers asking "Why Does the World Hate Us So Much?" the attacks of September 11, 2001 have stimulated interest about how the world thinks of the United States, or how *world opinion* regards it. Raising this question refocuses our attention toward whether "the world" does indeed "hate" the United States, or more generally, how the rest of the world perceives the nation. Beyond certain anecdotal evidence, however, this issue has been difficult to address. Polls that attempt to assess responsibility for the attacks, in the narrow sense of the term, do not really capture the meaning of this question for Americans.

Perceptions of "how the world feels about the United States" are as diverse as the newspapers and regions of the world studied. Contrary to critics of the United States, positive evaluations of the nation outweighed negative ones by a margin of 27 to 23 percent[15] during the period studied. As figure I.1 indicates, however, these assessments varied somewhat according to newspaper—in the Nigerian *Guardian*, Russian *Pravda*, and, surprisingly, both the Saudi *Arab News* and Israeli *Ha'aretz*, negative evaluations of the United States outweighed positive evaluations. Positive evaluations outweighed negative evaluations in the other six newspapers.[16]

These findings are reflected in the reactions of leaders abroad. Two weeks after the attacks, a former German minister of economic affairs stated, "the United States enjoys a wave of sympathy and friendship around the world" (*New York Times*, October 1, 2001). Similarly, the Gulf Cooperation Council (representing six Arab Persian Gulf nations) stated that it was "willing to enter an alliance that enjoys the support of the international community to

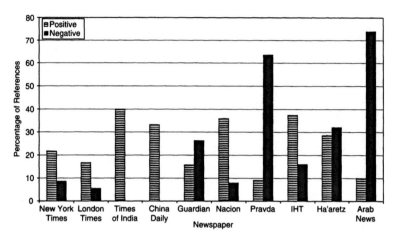

Figure I.1   Positive and negative world opinion on the United States, by newspaper

fight international terrorism and to punish its perpetrators" (*Arab News*, October 1, 2001). despite the Saudi paper's negative evaluations of world opinion on the United States. It is notable that in the Israeli *Ha'aretz* and the Saudi *Arab News*, negative evaluations of the United States outweighed positive ones. Upon examination of the stories, however, it was found that these results occurred for different reasons. The Israeli paper generally held the position that after the attack, the United States, like Israel, understood how it felt to be under siege and surrounded by a hostile world. The Saudi paper took a different perspective, indicating that the attack on the United States was, in part, in response to world opinion about U.S. foreign policy, notably toward Israel and the Palestinians. In the first case, the negative evaluations of world opinion on the United States were an expression of empathy and fellow feeling; in the second, they were a criticism of American policies.

These results do not tell the entire story, however. As figure I.2 illustrates, perceptions of world opinion toward the United States shifted in the newspapers during the period under study. In the weeks up to October 3, positive evaluations of world opinion far outweighed negative evaluations. But in the following week, negative evaluations outweighed positive ones, and while the findings reversed themselves again in the week starting October 17, the high levels of international support did not repeat themselves. Indeed, the trend reversed itself again in the final week of the study, when the negative evaluations of world opinion on the United States outweighed the positive in the foreign press studied.

The likely reason for this shift was the American and British bombing campaign against Afghanistan, which began on October 7. When the United

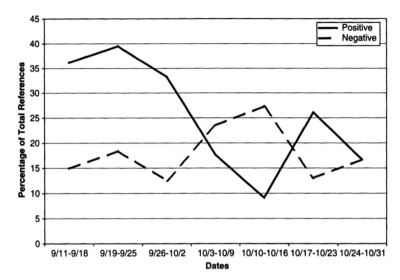

Figure I.2 Positive and negative world opinion toward the United States, from September 11 through October 31, 2001

States took military action in response to the attacks, its international image shifted from injured party to aggressor in certain foreign newspapers. Compare, for instance, these two quotations from the Nigerian *Guardian,* published approximately a month apart:

> Tuesday's terrorist attack on the United States of America must be condemned by the whole world. (September 13, 2001)
>
> Strained by heavy bombardment of Afghanistan, which entered its second week on Sunday, global support for the Anglo-American air strikes against the host of the prime suspect in September 11 terrorist attack on World Trade Centre and Pentagon is under the threat of snapping. (October 16, 2001)

However, the problem goes beyond the retaliation taken by the United States against the Taliban. For the very nature of terrorism for world opinion makes efforts at creating an international consensus in world opinion difficult.

Terrorism and International Reaction

In the newspapers' references to world opinion, "terrorism" was routinely condemned by all the nations studied. But problems arose regarding how to define "terrorism" beyond the horrible examples in New York and Washington, DC. Because terrorism is a *method*, rather than an ideology, a nation, or a leader, it is a difficult subject for world opinion: one may "know it when they see it," but generating a general description for all or even most nations to accept has proven elusive. If "terrorism" can be defined to include unintended civilian casualties in a military campaign, for instance, along with the intentional targeting of civilian populations, it becomes very difficult to reach an international consensus on the term's meaning or on legitimate responses to it. For instance, while terrorism is generally described as a weapon of the weak, this definition necessarily absolves the major powers from being accused of practicing it. Instead, such powerful nations are assumed to have sufficient resources to project power by other means, providing them with an ethical high ground in international affairs. But this assumption also circumscribes efforts to create a consensus on what constitutes "terrorism" and limits the ability to attack it.

In order to understand how the problem of defining terrorism impacts upon potential world opinion processes, one must examine the terminology used in the newspapers more closely. Previous research has revealed a consistent terminology for world opinion across several international newspapers.[17] This terminology includes the following basic components:

- the *moral component,* which refers to values shared by all nations in their judgments of world opinion
- the *pragmatic component,* which refers to interests shared by all nations in their judgments of world opinion
- the *power* of world opinion, which refers to its apparent influence on world events and nations' behaviors
- the *nation's image,* or *reputation,* in world opinion, as it is perceived by itself and other nations
- the *world considered as a unit,* such as an international community, which may judge and respond to other nations' behaviors
- the *threat of international isolation,* which operates as a potential punishment for nations that do not heed the dictates of world opinion.

The newspapers' discourse defines a *process* of world opinion involving these components. The *moral component* provides value-driven justification for condemning a given nation or action; the *pragmatic component* contributes to the *power* of world opinion to influence events by convincing nations that what is moral is often also consistent with the common interest. At stake for the subject country is the *nation's image,* or its reputation in world opinion; indeed, citizens tend to integrate their nation's international image into their construction of national identity.[18] Finally, errant nations or leaders are threatened, or punished, by *international isolation* from the world community, or some other entity that defines the *world as a unit.* One may summarize the global opinion process in a preliminary definition of world opinion: *"world opinion* refers to the moral judgments of observers, which actors must heed in the international arena or risk isolation as a nation."[19]

In past studies of world opinion, the moral component tended to be more common and more important than the pragmatic component.[20] The moral component partially explained the influence of world opinion over international affairs; indeed, morality tended to be central to discussion of the power of international opinion to influence events or the actions of leaders or nations. In this study, however, the moral component appeared in slightly fewer cases (42.2 percent) than the pragmatic component (44.3 percent). Further, the moral component was not correlated with the power or influence world opinion was assumed to have regarding the crisis (r = .038, significance = .521); by contrast, the presence of the pragmatic component was correlated with the power of world opinion (r = .164, significance = .005).

Given the difficulties involved in defining "terrorism," it appears that the *interests* nations were perceived to share, rather than moral concerns, were the driving force behind the judgments rendered regarding world opinion. Put another way, the newspapers generally acknowledged that even without a moral consensus regarding value judgments, attacks such as those on September 11 threatened the peace and security of all nations. This perspective was reflected in a number of newspaper reports and editorials, where the attacks were interpreted not just solely as being against the United States, but as an assault on the very notions of "civilization" or "civilized society." As General Assembly President Han Seung-soo of South Korea stated at the United Nations, "Terrorism is not a weapon wielded by *one civilization against another,* but rather an instrument of destruction through which small bands of criminals seek to undermine civilization itself" (*China Daily,* October 4, 2001; emphases added).

This view also appears affected by the United States' response to the attacks in the week of October 3–9. As shown in figure I.3, the percentages of references to the moral component of world opinion are fairly consistent over time during the study; at no time do they constitute a majority of the citations, making up instead between 34.7 and 49 percent of the references to world opinion. By contrast, the pragmatic component is more evident in the first three weeks of the crisis, appearing in a majority of cases in two out of the three weeks. This pattern shifts sharply after October 3, when the percentage of pragmatic citations drops below that of the moral citations; as with the positive references to the United States, the pattern recovers somewhat in

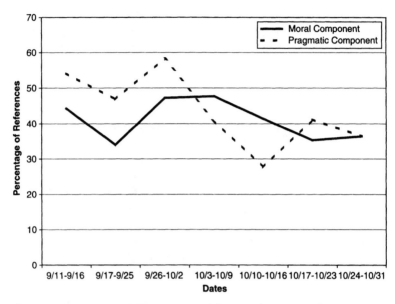

Figure I.3   Percentage of references containing moral or pragmatic components, by week

the week of October 17, only to fall below the percentage of references to the moral component in the final week of the study.

It seems reasonable that the patterns of positive references to the United States and of citations of the pragmatic component should appear so similar. Other nations could find common cause and a common interest with the United States when it was viewed as a victim of these attacks; all countries could identify with the threat such actions posed to world order. But once the United States took aggressive action in response, certain newspapers perceived that world opinion no longer reflected interests that were shared internationally, and instead focused upon the implications of seemingly unilateral action by the United States and Great Britain.

The changes in perceptions of world opinion over time do not appear to have been lost on the Bush administration. Prompted in part by the British, the administration released partial evidence linking bin Laden to the attacks on the United States, evidence that provided the basis for their suspicion that Afghanistan was harboring him. This effort to incriminate bin Laden continued past the dates covered by this study, with the release of videotapes that showed him discussing the attacks and rejoicing over the resulting loss of life. The American administration clearly intended to affect world opinion, indicating their belief that at least in the initial period after the attacks of 9/11, this strategy was important for battling terrorism.

Reconsidering the Results: A "Clash of Civilizations" or a Process of Global Opinion?

For the purposes of comparing the usefulness of the global opinion model versus the "clash of civilizations" model, the ten newspapers originally included in this study were combined into three groups. Since the "clash of civilizations" argument posited a conflict between the Western and Muslim civilizations in the aftermath of September 11, 2001, it was deemed appropriate to classify the nations in the following manner for purposes of comparison. The new categories included the West (the *New York Times*, the *London Times*, Israel's *Ha'aretz Daily*, and the *International Herald Tribune*); Muslim civilization (the *Arab News*);[21] and the other civilizations (the *China Daily*, representing Sinic civilization; the *Times of India*, representing Hindu civilization; the Argentinean *Nacion*, representing Latin-American civilization; the Nigerian *Guardian*, representing African civilization; and *Pravda*, representing Slavic–Orthodox civilization).

Figure I.4 shows the timing of references to world opinion in these three groups. Two results stand out. First, the timing of references in the Western and other civilizations' newspapers are strikingly similar; indeed, the η value for the relationship between dates for the two groups barely registers at .024. By contrast, the η values for the relationships between the Western

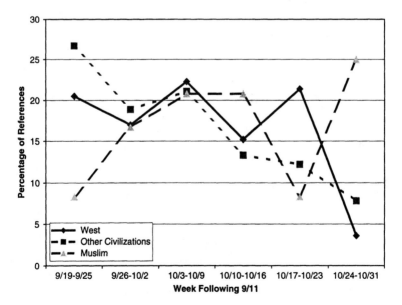

Figure I.4 References to world opinion, by Western, Muslim, and other civilizations ($N = 287$)

and Muslim newspapers (.167), and the other civilizations' and Muslim newspapers (.223) both indicate significant differences. Past research on media content regarding world opinion suggests that when the dates of references on a given issue *converge* among two or more media outlets, there is an apparent *consensus* on the agenda for world opinion in those media.[22] Conversely, when the dates of references to world opinion *diverge*, there is an apparent *disagreement* on the agenda for world opinion in those media. If the "clash of civilizations" thesis were correct, one would expect perceptions of the agenda in the Western and the Muslim newspapers to differ; however, one would not expect the perceptions of the agenda in other civilizations' newspapers to correspond with the Western perception of this agenda.[23]

There are also significant differences when one compares the evaluations of world opinion toward the United States across these categories. If the clash were primarily between civilizations, one would expect little or no correspondence between the content of world opinion from nations not involved in the conflict and the content of those that were. However, this is not the case. The percentage of positive and negative references to world opinion on the United States in the Western and other civilization groups are virtually the same. Positive references outweigh negative ones by 29.6 to 16.8 percent in the Western newspapers, and by 26.1 to 20.3 percent in the other civilizations' newspapers, respectively. In the Muslim newspaper, however, negative references outweigh positive ones by 73.7 to 10.5 percent. Further, a multiple-range analysis indicates that significant differences occur between mean evaluations in all the Western and Muslim newspapers, and in all the other civilizations' and Muslim newspapers;[24] by contrast, the Western and other civilizations' newspapers show significant differences in only one newspaper other than the *Arab News*.

When one examines the timing of positive and negative references to the United States, however, a surprisingly different pattern emerges. Figure I.5 shows the mean evaluations of world opinion on the United States in each group's newspapers, derived by coding positive references as 1, neutral references as 0, and negative references as –1, and adding and averaging the results. Two findings stand out. First, the *Arab News's* mean evaluations of world opinion on the United States are much lower than the other groups' evaluations. But a second critical pattern also emerges. The peaks and valleys of evaluations in the *Arab News* and the other civilizations' newspapers covary over time. When the *Arab News's* evaluations become more positive, the other civilizations' evaluations also become more positive; when the *Arab News's* evaluations become more negative, the other civilizations' evaluations also become more negative. The Western newspapers

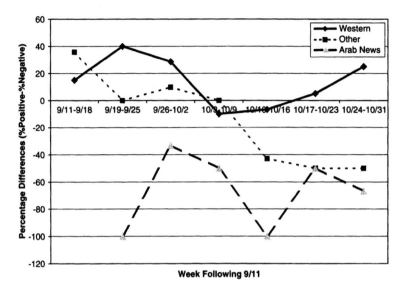

Figure I.5   Differences between percentage of positive and negative references to world opinion on the United States, by week and civilization

did not follow this model, but rather showed a comparably flat pattern over time, with values ranging from 0 to around .4. As a result, the timing of references to world opinion shows a weak negative correlation between the Western newspapers and other civilizations' newspapers (τ-b = −.138, p = .037); a weak positive correlation between the Western newspapers and the Arab newspaper (τ-b = .138, p = .042); and a strong positive correlation between the other civilizations' newspapers and the Arab newspaper (τ-b = .482, p = .000).[25]

While the previous findings may appear contradictory, they actually offer a possible insight into how world opinion is constructed. When a nation or group of nations is the object of negative world opinion, they generally do not tend to evaluate the ebb and flow of that opinion. When one looks at the general pattern of world opinion in this study, one finds that it is primarily sympathetic to the Western perspective; the general convergence of Western newspapers' evaluations and other civilizations' newspapers for all references to world opinion suggests this conclusion. However, when one focuses primarily upon the evaluations of the United States as a specific topic, there is an apparent covariance between the rise and fall of these evaluations in the Saudi and other civilizations' newspapers over time. As the object of world opinion changes, then, the object nations' newspapers may not perceive the ebb and flow of world opinion, even as other newspapers around the world appear to do so. A closer examination of the manner in which these three groups construct world opinion helps to explain this process further.

Disaggregating the Components of World Opinion in the Three Groups

World opinion functions best when it is focused upon a particular nation, leader, or action taken by some participant on the "world stage." Hence, while it was possible to condemn the Taliban regime in Afghanistan for harboring terrorists, it was far more difficult to pinpoint other possible targets against whom there would be an international consensus regarding responsibility for September 11. An example of this problem can be seen in an article in the *Arab News* from October 9, 2001. On the one hand, the reporter notes that after the attacks on Afghanistan,

> Bin Laden and his Taleban [*sic*] protectors vowed revenge and a holy war. But they looked *increasingly isolated* as most Arab and Muslim states remained circumspect—only Iraq and Iran openly denounced the US-led military action. (October 9, 2001; emphases added)

On the other hand, the choice of new targets was condemned in the paper's perception of world opinion:

> European diplomats said any attempt to extend the campaign by targeting Iraq, as some US officials have suggested, *would blow apart the global coalition against terrorism,* and alienate not only Arab and Muslim states but also key European partners including Russia. (ibid.; emphases added)

In such an atmosphere, the most visible actors involved in the conflict—in this case, the United States—became a natural focus for world opinion, both positive and negative. It is natural that American and Western newspapers in general might miss this focus; it is equally natural that newspapers from other regions of the world, Muslim and non-Muslim, would focus upon it.

In order to analyze the effects of the problems of defining terrorism, a factor analysis compared the ways in which the three groups of newspapers constructed this concept following September 11. This analysis was designed to reduce the six components of world opinion mentioned earlier down to the factors that generally composed the different newspapers' perspectives on world opinion. From these factors one may interpret the values and interests that each group of newspapers reflected as it constructed

Table I.1   Factor analyses of components of world opinion for three groups of newspapers

	Factor 1	Loading	Factor 2	Loading	Factor 3	Loading
Western newspapers						
	Moral	.711	Isolation	.806	Unit	.768
	Pragmatic	.768	Image	.603		
Arab newspaper						
	Moral	.917	Unit	.682		
	Pragmatic	−.758	Isolation	.787[a]		
Other civilizations' newspapers						
	Pragmatic	.761	Isolation	.787	Image	.845
	Power	.763	Unit	−.663	Moral	.616

[a] The force of world opinion was not included in the analysis of the *Arab News* because none of its references to world opinion included this component.

its perception of world opinion. The results, presented in table I.1, indicate that the different groups constructed their usages of and discourse on world opinion from its components in different ways.

The Western newspapers' factors were defined in the following manner:

- *opinion consensus factor*—consisting of the moral and pragmatic components, both with positive loadings. This factor illustrates that the Western newspapers perceived a close alliance between the value issues and the interest issues of all the nations in the world on terrorism in this instance.
- *image projection factor*—consisting of the threat of isolation and the nation's image, both with positive loadings. This factor illustrates that the Western nations believed that their very identities and images in world opinion were tied to the unambiguous stance against terrorism as they wished to define it, since those who disagreed risked the threat of international isolation.
- *unit definition factor*—consisting of just the world as a unit, with a positive loading. This factor indicates the role of the international community in the Western newspapers' perceptions in enforcing a consensus on terrorism.

Taken together, these three factors define a region whose perception of world opinion required them to link their very identities and images to the international community's condemnation of their definition of terrorism and to draw support for the actions they deemed necessary to combat it. An article in the *International Herald Tribune* illustrates how these factors are articulated in terms of the international status these nations created for themselves in the wake of 9/11:

> Parallel to the United States' campaign in Afghanistan against terrorism, Europe's leading countries—Britain, Germany, France . . . —are using their engagement in the American-led coalition *to strengthen their status in the world's hierarchy of power.*
>
> In the case of France, the stakes involve sustaining rather than widening a first-rank role in the strategic equation . . . For Britain, the goal was described as taking a new handhold on leadership in Europe . . . In German terms, Chancellor Gerhard Schroeder's pledge of willingness to take full military risks in combating terrorism beyond NATO's borders represented a gesture of emancipation from the limited international role the country has played since the defeat of Hitler . . . Germany . . . could feel free to move gradually toward a level of global political influence corresponding to its vast economic capacity. (October 12, 2001; emphases added)

Not surprisingly, the *Arab News* perceived the role of world opinion differently. Its references portrayed an awareness of the dangers of a Western scramble for international status in world opinion on this issue, as shown in the factors derived from the analysis:

- *opinion ambiguity factor*—consisting of the moral component with a positive loading and the pragmatic component with a negative loading. This configuration is common in cases where a nation's newspaper perceives a conflict between the interests and the values shared by the world. In this case, the Arab newspaper perceived that while it shared the values of fighting terrorism, it might not share the interests of other countries in how to go about this task.
- *community ambiguity factor I*—consisting of the world as a unit with a positive loading and the threat of international isolation with a negative loading. This configuration reflects the desire to be part of a global community, while not wishing to be threatened with international isolation if the conflict attached a stigma to Muslim nations.

In essence, the *Arab News* recognized the moral issue of terrorism, but was generally suspicious of the methods that might be used to combat it and wary of any resulting condemnation that might be directed toward Saudi Arabia or other Muslim nations as a result. This conflict is evident in a statement by the Imam of the Grand Mosque in Makkah, who called upon world leaders not to respond to the terrorist attacks against the United States on September 11 with violence:

> "We should exercise restraint and look at things very deeply, we should give priority to public interests and promote world peace and security" . . . Saudis

warned Muslims 'not to mix up the concepts of real terrorism and legitimate jihad (holy war)' which he said was governed by clear rules and ethics. [Those who practice terrorism] do not consider the grave dangers to the future of Islam and Muslims, especially Muslim minorities around the world," the Imam said. ("Officials in Islamic countries have voiced concern over an anti-Muslim backlash in the West after the September 11 attacks," September 29, 2001; emphases added)

The ambiguity of the value issues surrounding terrorism versus "legitimate jihad" creates a situation in which the interests of Muslim nations and those of the West risk divergence. Hence, the Arab newspaper perceived world opinion to be more ambiguous than the Western newspapers, and more likely to threaten Islamic nations if the "international community" were allowed to isolate actors or dictate other punishments.

The other civilizations' newspapers perceived world opinion as having influence in two ways: through the power of the interests it defined for all nations, and through the importance of taking a moral stance against terrorism to safeguard the nations' images. However, these newspapers also expressed mistrust about the threat of international isolation by the world community. The analysis identified the following factors:

- *interest protection factor*—consisting of the pragmatic component of world opinion and the power of world opinion, both with positive loadings. This configuration indicates that the other civilizations' newspapers perceived the common interests in fighting terrorism as constituting the influence world opinion had over their actions.
- *community ambiguity factor II*—a factor similar to the factor in the Arab newspaper, except that in this case, isolation had a positive factor loading and the world as a unit had a negative factor loading. This result indicates some mistrust, perhaps of the Western interpretations of world opinion regarding terrorism and the possible direction the threat of isolation might take.
- *image protection factor*—consisting of the nation's image and the moral component of world opinion, both with positive loadings. This configuration indicates the need these nations' newspapers felt to make a statement condemning terrorism, as a means of protecting their images and identities.

One can see in these results the power that world opinion has due to the interests nations share in combating terrorism, and the fear of not condemning the attacks and putting one's own nation's image at risk. As an editorial in the Nigerian *Guardian* stated:

When a thing like this happens, it is impossible for people to take a neutral position. It is either you support what has been done or you are against it.

And we have seen the outpouring of sympathy from all over the world that has greeted this tragedy.

There are several reasons why some people may choose to jubilate at the misfortune that has hit America . . . These are arguments which will make for scoring impressive points if one is writing a term paper at a university. However, the tragedy that took place last Tuesday was not an academic exercise. It is for real. (September 16, 2001)

The editorial states the necessity of making a clear statement about where one stands on this issue and the shared interests of all peoples in the world that gave the problem its prominence and power to influence world opinion. As Soh Chang-Rok, a South Korean specialist in international relations, was quoted as saying in the *International Herald Tribune*, "There's enormous international pressure to help out the U.S. So we have to keep silent" about the buildup of Japanese forces in their participation in retaliating against terrorism (September 28, 2001).

However, Rhuslan Khasbulatov argued in an editorial in *Pravda* that one must address the unequal divisions of wealth and power in the world, which reflect the colossal accumulation of inner antagonism between the different parts of this world community. He argues that we all must take account of opinions in the developing world, where world poverty is concentrated, as well as in the "Islamic sector" of the world community, and not just those of the countries of "the enlightened West" (October 26, 2001).

There is evident mistrust of any notion of a "world community" that does not work to treat all nations as part of a "single, integral organism" (ibid.). This mistrust is reflected in the conflict between the threat of international isolation and the view that the world is a unit.

From these analyses, one can hypothesize about how the different constructions of world opinion fit to reflect a process. For the Western newspapers, there was no ambiguity about the moral or interest issues involved in the fight against terrorism; Western nations endeavored to project their image as leaders as a means of gaining international status. For the Arab newspaper, there was considerable mistrust in the leadership being offered by the Western nations, and a fear that it might be directed against the interests of Muslim countries. The other civilizations' newspapers fell somewhere in between. They condemned terrorism, aware of the interests they shared in fighting terrorism and protective of their images, yet were wary that Western leadership might potentially define the international community in a manner that threatened them. The center position of the other civilizations' newspapers helps to explain why their references to world opinion in general followed those of the Western newspapers. But it also explains why, when the focus shifted to the United States and its leadership, their references to world opinion tended to correspond to the Arab newspaper's references over time and in content.

World Opinion and Afghanistan

While the attacks of September 11 do not appear to have prompted a "clash of civilizations," it is possible that the perpetrators of these horrible acts intended to create this result. In such a scenario, Huntington's thesis would still explain the motivations behind these actions, if not the actual outcome. Michael Doran explores the possibility that a "pragmatic fanaticism" actually motivates al-Qaida, as part of an overall strategy to disrupt alliances and advance the cause of militant Islam. The attacks thereby represented "a variation within a historical process"[26] in which the United States would be brought into direct conflict with Islamic populations. The bases of this strategy were circumstances that gave

> rise to a mode of *identity politics* that, for lack of a better term, I will dub "anti-Western brinksmanship," by which I mean the tendency of Middle Eastern actors to challenge the interests of a Western power directly, or indirectly, through one of its local allies in order to provoke the threat of Western intervention, if not the actual intervention itself. In these crises, Middle Eastern leaders adopt utopian nationalist and religious ideologies tailored to appeal to a number of disaffected groups simultaneously. These ideologies undoubtedly exploit transnational identities such as Arabism and Islam, which embrace the majority of people in the region.[27]

Clearly, challenging Western powers directly while appealing to "transnational identities" such as Arabism and Islam sets up the "clash of civilizations" that Huntington describes. Doran argues that the strategy apparently did not work—the U.S.-led attack on the Taliban did not result in a general uprising among the Islamic peoples, nor did it split American alliances or sink the United States into a quagmire, as happened to the Soviet Union. He credits this failure to bin Laden's "miscalculation of the strength of public opinion [and] . . . the intentions and capabilities of a superpower."[28]

While these statements are correct, they overlook the power of *international opinion* to affect the world's response to the Afghan campaign, including the response of the Arab nations. Analyses of the ten international newspapers regarding evaluations of Afghanistan after September 11, 2001 reveal an interesting pattern that helps explain why the American response did not promote a "clash of civilizations."

Figure I.6 shows the percentage of positive and negative evaluations of Afghanistan in world opinion over the two months studied. The references are overwhelmingly negative during this entire period. Negative evaluations

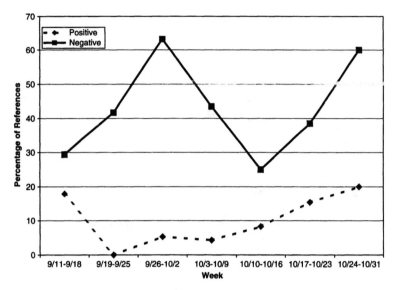

Figure I.6   Positive and negative references to Afghanistan, by week

reach as high as 63 percent and never fall below 25 percent; positive evaluations are all at 20 percent or below. To the extent that these references indicate world opinion about the country, the judgment is clearly negative.

There are few relevant variations among different newspapers when one divides the results up by "civilizations." Following the analysis in the previous section, newspapers were classified into groups representing the Western, Muslim, and other civilizations. The percentage of positive references to Afghanistan was then subtracted from the percentage of negative references for each group by week. Hence, percentages above zero in figure I.7 indicate a net negative evaluation in world opinion, while percentages below zero indicate a net positive evaluation in world opinion. The most obvious result is that there are no percentages below zero; the closest Afghanistan comes to a positive evaluation is among the other civilizations' newspapers in the first and sixth weeks, when the percentages of positive and negative judgments are equal. Among the Western newspapers, negative judgments outweigh positive ones through the entire period.

Another obvious finding is that the differences between the two groups' percentages follow a similar pattern. Although the Western newspapers' evaluations tend to be more negative, both groups display a double-peaked curve over the seven weeks, with the other civilizations sometimes showing a one-week lag behind the Western newspapers regarding when the peaks occur.

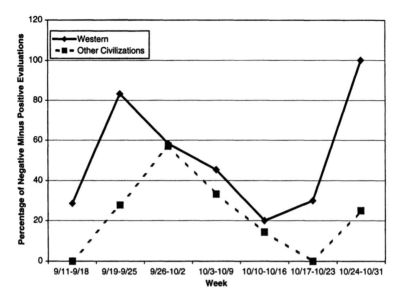

Figure I.7   Percentage of negative versus positive evaluations on Afghanistan, by week and civilization

But perhaps the most interesting result is what the graph does not show. The *Arab News* is not represented here; it included only one reference to Afghanistan, which was negative. This suggests two important conclusions. The Saudi newspaper was apparently silent on the issue of world opinion on Afghanistan because it knew that the Taliban were internationally isolated; the *Arab News* stated as such explicitly on October 9, 2001. A nation, leader, or group tends to fall silent when they fear becoming a global pariah by associating with the isolated party. It follows then, that the force of world opinion again asserted itself against a "clash of civilizations." Put bluntly, very few nations liked the Taliban internationally, and therefore they had few defenders when they were attacked, even among those whom al-Qaida might have perceived were their natural allies. The process of global opinion once again trumped the supposed bonds of "civilizations."

Conclusions

It is natural for citizens to react to a trauma like the attacks on September 11 by feeling that they are under siege in a hostile world. It is also natural to seek to partition the world into our allies and our enemies, those "for us" and those "against us." Absent the Berlin Wall, the borders—however loosely defined—of clashing civilizations that harbor either good will or bad will toward us could provide a comfortable means of ordering and understanding the world and its dangers.

But these reactions oversimplify the way other nations view the world's intentions toward the United States. World opinion about this country, or about any subject for that matter, is an ongoing process that potentially affects our international image and shifts it in response to events. While an international consensus might arise through a negotiation among the different perspectives on world opinion, the evidence here suggests that such a consensus eluded American efforts, at least through October 31, 2001. This does not herald an ongoing or impending "clash of civilizations," however. Indeed, several newspapers from different civilizations explicitly rejected this interpretation of the attacks. Consider this statement from the *Arab News:*

> The specter of the "Clash of Cultures" as predicted by Samuel Huntington should be treated like the work of a fortuneteller. His thesis is no more than Armageddon dressed up as social science. (September 28, 2001)

The Israeli *Ha'aretz* expressed a similar sentiment within a week of the Arab newspaper:

> Public debate was ushered down the wrong lane immediately after the attacks in the United States, the moment formulations such as . . . "clash of civilizations" took hegemonic hold. Thanks to these bin Laden notched up a major triumph: a terrorist gang that does nothing to help the population in the name of which it purportedly murders was transformed by the West and anointed the representative of a billion people. (October 4, 2001)

The problem was acute enough for Arab officials to meet in Cairo on October 29, 2001 "to discuss the threat of a 'conflict of civilizations' following the September 11 attacks on the United States." This effort was justified by the concern from delegates that "today the world is burning" and by their desire "to pour a little water on the fire" (*Arab News,* October 29, 2001).

Finally, a Pew Research Center global study released on December 19, 2001 showed that most people in the United States (52 percent), Western Europe (63 percent), and the Islamic nations (64 percent) rejected the idea that the attacks of 9/11 were a result of a "clash of civilizations" between Western and Muslim nations. This rejection was echoed by pluralities in nearly every region of the world surveyed.[29]

If potentially opposing sides in the conflict do not wish to have the attacks interpreted as a "clash of civilizations," and if the process of world opinion in the major newspapers here suggests the same conclusion, why does this danger persist? According to an *Arab News* article,

> the events of Black Tuesday do not reflect the clash of civilizations he spoke about. The reason for this is the speedy condemnation of the events by all Muslim countries. But the events themselves are very dangerous…and could lead to a clash of civilizations if the zealous on both sides chose confrontation. (*Arab News*, October 9, 2001)

The critical deciding point, then, appears to be the interpretations of the actors involved and the rest of the world that observes their actions. As David McDowell stated, "There is only a clash of civilizations if that is the way people wish to interpret recent events" (ibid.).

When all is said and done, interpreting the meaning of the September 11 attacks is a matter of choice and consensus internationally—that is, decisions to be rendered in *world opinion*. World opinion is the key factor determining the manner in which we construct the emerging global configuration; considerations such as a "clash of civilizations" or other interpretations become secondary to this force, and therein lies the danger when dealing with the issue of terrorism.

The preceding analysis suggests that an international consensus on terrorism had, until at least October 31, 2001, eluded nations in the world community for two reasons. A clear definition of terrorism must precede its condemnation, and such a definition had not been reached. In a related fashion, even the general condemnation of terrorism is directed against a *method*, not a nation, leader, or some other actor on the international stage. One must recall here our working definition of world opinion: the moral judgments of observers, which actors must heed in the international arena or risk isolation as a nation. When the actors are underground and not clearly associated with any nation, and the definition of the method becomes problematic, the influence of world opinion is likely to be limited, unless one addresses the underlying anger that prompts attacks by state *and* non-state actors. This strategy necessarily involves going beyond a mere definition of terrorism and its condemnation, to an analysis of the actual sources of weakness and frustration that make it appear a legitimate weapon, regardless of its definition.

Our argument so far has suggested that the antipathies between the West and the particular Muslim followers who attacked the World Trade Center and the Pentagon were not the result of a "clash of civilizations." But, to paraphrase Huntington, "if not civilizations, then what?"[30] We return to the question of motivations and grievances with which this chapter began.

Several surveys indicate that Muslims around the world generally disapproved of the attacks of September 11. However, there are undeniable problems in the relationship between the United States and the Islamic world. Bernard Lewis noted in "The Roots of Muslim Rage" that the reaction of Muslim nations to the West, particularly the United States, had changed from "admiration and emulation" to "hostility and rejection." He traced this change to

> A *feeling of humiliation*—a growing awareness, among the heirs of this old, proud, and long dominant civilization of having been overtaken, overborne, and overwhelmed by those whom they regarded as their inferiors ... [For] there is something in the religious culture of Islam which inspired, even in the humblest peasant or peddler, a dignity and a courtesy toward others never exceeded and rarely equaled in other civilizations. And yet, in moments of upheaval and disruption, *when the deeper passions are stirred, this dignity and courtesy toward others can give way to an explosive mixture of rage and hatred* which impels even the government of an ancient and civilized country ... to espouse kidnapping and assassination, and try to find, in the life of the Prophet, approval and indeed precedent for such actions.[31]

Many Muslim peoples are thus left only with a "war against modernity ... [through which] Islamic fundamentalism has given an aim and form to the otherwise *aimless and formless resentment* of the Muslim masses."[32]

A survey of nine predominantly Muslim nations conducted by the Gallup organization in December 2001 and January 2002 supports this analysis, revealing that while citizens in these countries viewed the United States with admiration, they felt that it did not return that sentiment, instead disrespecting their nations and the Islamic religion. Lewis attributes these sentiments to a "clash of civilizations" between the Islamic and Western worlds, but we have already rejected this explanation.

Why, then, would many Muslims feel such rage and humiliation? The answer lies in the loss of international status and identity their citizens and others have suffered following the end of the Cold War.

1

The Cold War World Turned Upside Down

On November 9, 1989, our era ended. The breaching of the Berlin Wall sounded the end of not merely the Cold War, but an epoch of global conflict that started with the assassination of Archduke Francis Ferdinand in June 28, 1914. Now with the twentieth century truncated, we are straining to discern the shape of the 21st.

—Robert L. Bartley[1]

Addressing the problems that led to the attacks on September 11, 2001 requires a perspective that looks beyond the Middle East or the Western and Muslim "civilizations" to the entire post–Cold War global configuration. A series of contingencies following the end of the Cold War affected the status of nations in the international society of states. These changes prompted a devaluation of collective identities for certain individuals; the failure of collective identity, in turn, affected their personal sense of worth. Acts of violence by state and non-state actors (sometimes referred to as "terrorists") are, therefore, not disparate events. Rather, they represent attempts to assert identities in a local or global context and to reclaim a status that specific nations or peoples feel they have lost.

At a conference on Europe in the new world order held at Georgetown University in 1991, the noted political theorist Shlomo Avinieri observed how "the institutions we have had until now, and which will have great difficulties adapting to the new situation, were based on the concept that the West had to be defended, and if possible, things should be . . . rolled back . . . in the East."[2] Observers are similarly unable to adapt to the new demands of analyzing political conflict in the post–Cold War era. Until the collapse of the Soviet Union and the Eastern bloc, political theorists were largely preoccupied with the operations and shortcomings of liberalism or Marxism as defining principles for states. The new conditions at the end of the Cold War have prompted, among other things, a resurgence of nationalism and political fundamentalism and a scramble to redefine national borders most observers had considered settled. To date, resurgent nationalism and fundamentalism have been viewed as latent syndromes previously suppressed by centralized control from the Soviet government, only to be unleashed once the center collapsed.

This explanation is incomplete in three ways. First, it assumes that the resurgence of nationalism or fundamentalism can be understood in the same terms as earlier nationalistic movements, and that centralized control represented only an "interruption" in history regarding such movements. Second, it overestimates the ability of centralized authorities to control nationalistic or fundamentalist movements, while ignoring the extent to which Soviet authorities (among others) used both as a means of advancing their own ends.[3] Finally, it ignores the general role national or group identity plays in the definition and maintenance of nations, and the reasons why this role has become important in the wake of the Soviet collapse.

This chapter attempts to present a three-part approach to these deficiencies. First, it studies the special circumstances for reconstructing national identity in the post–Cold War era. Second, it studies how national identities (and social reality in general) are constructed and how this construction is carried out in unique forms in the mass media within the post–Cold War context. Finally, it addresses the issue of the emergence of nationalism and fundamentalism in the emerging world order by studying the construction of national identity as a form of political communication that involves a social/psychological process and an ongoing process of international negotiation.

What follows is divided into three sections. The first section describes the processes that led to the need for a reassertion of national identity and new means to define it. The second section describes how the national consciousness and international image of a nation have become the primary factors in the negotiation of a nation's identity in world forums. The final section describes how these processes have operated in certain Muslim nations following the end of the Cold War, providing a fertile ground for recruitment of non-state actors willing to commit violent acts.

Defining the Post–Cold War Context

The post–Cold War context can perhaps be best understood by noting that prior to the economic and ideological collapse of the Soviet Union, analysts tended to divide the world into three parts: first-world nations (the major industrial powers), second-world nations (the Communist nations such as the Soviet Union, the Warsaw Pact countries, and China),[4] and third-world nations (the less-developed nations of Latin America, Africa, the Middle East, and Asia). In liberal economic theory, the stages of development are traditionally divided into preindustrial, industrial, and postindustrial levels, each characterized by such factors as the main occupation of a majority of the workforce and the economic and natural resources available to the nation.[5] However, the typology of nations and the typology of levels of development do not correspond directly: first-world nations may be industrial or postindustrial, second-world nations may be industrial or preindustrial, and third-world nations tend to be preindustrial. As such, the second-world overlapped the first and third worlds in this hierarchy of economic development. The reasons for this overlap can be ascribed to the ideological distinctions that formerly separated first- and second-world nations, which thereby provided alternative definitions of "national development" and "national identity."

Much of liberal theory rests upon the notion that economic activity and related issues such as growth and development are objective standards that lie outside the realm of politics. Marxist theory, however, particularly as it was applied in this context by the former Eastern bloc, locates economic activity and all related measures within the context of political definition.[6] This conflict in ideology delineates the division of nations into first-, second-, and third-world nations. For first-world nations, development was defined, and nations ranked, according to material satisfaction, measured in such terms as the per capita GNP and the subsequent division of wealth in the society.[7] For second-world nations, material satisfaction was a political construct in the Marxist framework, relating to goals or desires deemed appropriate by centralized authorities; as such, "development" was defined by a different standard, as nations were ranked according to their progress toward the ultimate end of historical or material development—that is, the Communist society. Third-world nations occupied different positions in the developmental hierarchy, depending upon which standard for development one used.[8] According to liberal theory, third-world nations occupied the lowest position. However, third-world nations were also potential battlefields upon which the clash of worldviews was pursued. Here, the West advanced the purely economic notion of development, wooing them with the promise of greater material wealth, a higher standard of living, and their attendant political liberties. The East pursued what J. L. Talmon describes as a "messianistic" interpretation of development, promising these nations that if they embraced Communism, they would become more advanced historically than their Western counterparts.[9]

The clash of these two visions had an impact on the issue of national identity, because, as Yael Tamir notes, "Aspiring to national self-determination is . . . bound up with the desire to see communal space not only as an arena for cooperation for the purpose of securing one's interests, but

[also] as a place for expressing one's identity."[10] National self-determination, or the claiming of a common culture leading to national identity, presents citizens with considerations of economic viability (how does citizenship serve my material interests?) and personal identity (what status do I derive from being a member of this nation?). The collapse of the second world portended the rise of nationalism and political fundamentalism because it removed a fundamental path by which nations could define their status in the world and defend their standing in a hierarchy of economic, social, and political development.

The status deficiency that results from the loss of a nation's favored position in one hierarchy promotes a need among citizens to search for alternative means of delineating their country's status. This need tends to be more subconscious than articulated. Still, the ideological collapse that accompanied the end of the Soviet Union's centralized control over the second world is arguably of equal, or greater, importance than the collapse of its power. The power collapse provided the opportunity for the emergence of nationalism in its present form, but the ideological collapse provided its impetus.

According to Liah Greenfeld, "*National identity is, fundamentally, a matter of dignity. It gives people reasons to be proud.*"[11] As such, it provides a means of avoiding the condition of *ressentiment*, which

> refers to a psychological state resulting from suppressed feelings of envy and hatred . . . and the impossibility of satisfying those feelings . . . the structural basis of envy itself . . . is the fundamental comparability between the subject and the object of envy, and the belief on the part of the subject in the fundamental equality between them . . . [However] the actual inequality . . . rules out practical achievement of the theoretically existing equality. The presence of these conditions renders a situation *ressentiment*-prone irrespective of the temperaments and the psychological makeup of the individuals who compose the relevant population. The effect produced by *ressentiment* is similar to "anomie."[12]

Such feelings apply to the group identities of non-state actors as well. When Greenfeld published her work on nationalism in 1992, the primary concern was over violence in the name of nationhood in such places as Bosnia and Germany. At present, the primary concern is over violence in the name of the group identity of non-state actors in such places as Afghanistan, Kenya, New York, and Washington, DC. The object of identity changes, but the underlying causes of violence and anger remain the same.

The collapse of the second world and the resulting loss of one path to national identity and status left both an assumption of equality and an actual inequality. In contrast to the Cold War era, in which the Western

and Eastern blocs often did not recognize (or respect) as legitimate various governments allied with the opposite side, regimes in the post–Cold
War order were generally to enjoy what O. Obasanjo refers to as "respect
for the sovereignty of nations."[13]

But the classification of nations as preindustrial, industrial, and postindustrial confers upon countries unequal standing in the world, which gives
rise to the invidious comparisons Greenfeld describes. First, there are clear
inequalities in resources and standards of living, exacerbated by "individual and collective expectations rising rapidly, especially as the world's rich
want more of everything and the poor desire what the rich already have."[14]
Second, there are the related inequalities in the "social value" of national
identity derived by nations, which depends on their position in the developmental hierarchy. The "social value" of national identity lies in its ability to accord pride to its citizens, to confer upon them a sense of dignity
and collective mission. However, within any hierarchy, only those occupy-
ing the top positions may derive status, and hence pride, from their station. By this international standard, the status of the most-developed
nations is defined, in part, by the fact that only a few countries may occupy
the highest rank at any given time. Fred Hirsch refers to this problem in
societies as "social crowding," since the top positions would lose their
social value as bases for national pride if all or most nations were able to
achieve these positions.[15]

Citizens of less-privileged nations may thus suffer from a "national status deficiency," as the alternatives to liberal theory, which offered these
countries a vision and a sense of collective mission and pride, have collapsed. Indeed, latent nationalist feelings probably hastened this collapse as
the alternative model lost credibility. But this syndrome need not be confined only to the less-developed nations; any nation that has undergone a
status dislocation due to structural changes in the post–Cold War era is
susceptible to the same psychological reactions from its citizens. Robert
Reich describes how such dislocations may arise from comparisons
between nations even in the midst of absolute gains in material well-being:

> Sociologists have long noted the phenomenon of relative deprivation,
> whereby people evaluate their well-being in light of others' wealth. The aver-
> age citizen of Great Britain is better than twenty years ago, but feels poorer
> now that the average Italian has pulled ahead. When I ask my students
> whether they would prefer living in a world in which every American is 25
> percent wealthier than now and every Japanese was much wealthier than the
> average American, or one in which Americans were only 10 percent wealth-
> ier but still ahead of the average Japanese, a larger number of people usually
> vote for the second option. Thus, people may be willing to forego absolute
> gains to prevent their perceived rivals from enjoying even greater gains.[16]

Thus, the restructuring of national identity in the post–Cold War era involves the struggle for citizens of a given country to define their status in the community of nations within the developmental hierarchy, as it now exists.

The Social Construction of Identity: From Propaganda War to Negotiated Construct

Since the end of the Cold War, the elements that go into the structuring of national identity have become bases for conflict. As *ressentiment* rises among nations, the tangible and intangible aspects of their national identity become issues in the struggle for status. The tangible aspects include the exact borders of the nation, its economic condition, and the peoples over which it has legitimate authority. The intangible aspects include a shared historical memory, a common cultural heritage, and a common ethnicity. But all of these factors are social constructions.[17] This section derives the elements involved in the generation of national identity and analyzes the manner in which these elements have emerged in the presence of a post–Cold War configuration.

In order to perform such a derivation, one must first examine the sources of "nationhood" as they have previously existed. Gyorgy Csepeli notes that

> groups identifying themselves and others in terms of a national category are the products of a relatively recent historical development. The word "nation" is definitely not new but its uses as a category for self-identification for a particular assembly of people was unknown before the French revolution of 1789 . . . In this period the modern values of liberty, property, equality and the establishment of institutions aimed to realize these values (such as parliamentary democracy, the market and class society) invalidated previous categories of self-identification as successful means of social legitimation.[18]

As such, "national identity as a modern means of self-identification can be analyzed as a set of affective and cognitive components."[19] Also, changes in the institutions created to realize certain values—such as the transition from a socialist economy to a market economy and its attendant values—should be expected to affect the nature of national identity and, in turn, the psychological state associated with it.

But there is more to identity than the citizens' cognitions. For the social construction of identity to take place, the "national dreams and dangerous myths"[20] that make up national identity must be communicated to others. The individual cognitive "map" of identity is therefore translated into national identity when it is shared and ultimately accepted or rejected by others within and beyond the national society; the social construction of the concept depends upon discourse between those who wish to create an identity and those who must acknowledge the identity for it to have legitimacy.[21] The construction of national identity thereby involves the interaction between individual psychology and political discourse. As Eric Waddel notes,

> group identity does not exist in isolation, but rather is based on the notion of culture difference, and hence, organized around boundaries and interactions across boundaries . . . In such a dialectical context, group identity is both self-ascribed (by those within the group) and ascribed by those beyond the boundary (the other group).

> The degree of concordance between ascription and self-ascription and, indeed, the very recognition of one or the other group depends upon the relations of power existing between the two.[22]

When the primary conflict over national identity involved the competition between two notions of development, political communication served mainly as a platform for the propaganda battle between East and West. A variety of (often anomalous) structures resulted as the two sides created borders for nations that served this conflict. Entities that shared ethnic and historical identities, such as Germany and Korea, were divided; at the same time, other entities that shared few discernible characteristics, such as the Soviet Union, Czechoslovakia, Yugoslavia, and many countries in Africa and the Middle East, were created without regard for historical or ethnic identities.

In the post–Cold War era, the elements involved in the structuring of national identity have changed as the propaganda battle has receded. This change requires that we reconsider the processes by which identity in general, and national identity in particular, are constructed.

Like individual identity, national identity is defined "in the context of a relationship."[23] Identity consists of the notion one has of oneself and the recognition of that notion by others. Similarly, national identity arises from a negotiation between the idea citizens have of their nation (their self-image, or *Selbstbild*) and their nation's image among citizens and leaders of other nations (their international reputation, or *Fremdbild*).

If national identity is to provide a sense of dignity for individual citizens—that is, if it is to have some "social value" to those who claim it—it must command the respect of others. This respect must necessarily arise out of a process by which citizens' perceptions of their country are reconciled with other nations' images of it. Hence, national identity grows out of an interactive process, a negotiation between national consciousness and international image that is conducted in world forums such as the United Nations and global media outlets. National identity clearly serves the material and psychic needs of the citizens or leaders associated with it. But what defines a nation's international image and, hence, its status? In individual societies, public opinion and reputation define the status of particular objects and the individuals associated with them.[24] In the global community, world opinion and the international reputation of a nation define the basis for this status and the citizens and leaders associated with it.

World opinion no longer conforms to the structures set by the ideological conflict in the Cold War; a nation does not automatically command status with a significant portion of the world merely by declaring itself Communist or democratic. Instead, world opinion has become a more free-floating phenomenon, whose meaning for each nation must be negotiated.

Thus, since the end of the Cold War, the construction of national identity—an element so essential to a citizen's dignity and sense of self since the beginning of the twentieth century has become a process involving an often-subtextual negotiation between a nation's *Selbstbild* (national consciousness, or the image a nation's citizens have of themselves) and its *Fremdbild* (international image in world opinion, either actual or as perceived by its citizens). At the same time that so many nations were losing status internationally, their identities were being tied more than before to their international image. This process has resulted in a feeling of dislocation and a loss of identity, and has ultimately fueled a rage that makes individuals wish to strike out at those they perceive responsible for their loss of status. The United States, at the top of the status hierarchy globally, becomes a likely target of this rage. But other nations or individuals may choose targets closer to home in an attempt to assert their identities in a manner the world will acknowledge.

These processes are all part of a post–Cold War version of *identity politics*—defined here as the construction and projection of a nation's or a people's identity in a manner compatible with its citizens' values and acknowledged generally by the rest of the world. But therein often lies the problem, as the values certain nations or groups wish to project, or the identities they find acceptable, do not achieve for them the international reputation in world opinion that they desire. Acts of frustration and hatred accompany such failures.

The major variable in a nation's success in asserting its own vision of its national identity is its ability to convince other nations, particularly the major powers, that this vision does not conflict with the norms or interests of the international community. "International image" is therefore primarily determined by the moral and pragmatic components of world opinion regarding a nation's identity. The moral component of world opinion deals with "*values* which relevant nations [are] supposed to share, where issues are discussed in terms of right and wrong behavior," thereby referencing the norms of the world community. The pragmatic component of world opinion deals with "*interests* which relevant nations are supposed to share, where issues are discussed in terms of practical costs and benefits" to the nations involved, thereby referencing the *interests* of the world community. Most of the activity concerning world opinion primarily includes leaders (and sometimes citizens) of the various nations involved in the negotiation of a country's identity in various world forums.[25]

Four hypotheses regarding the resurgence of nationalism and political fundamentalism in the post–Cold War era, and the resulting dynamics of the negotiation of national identity, are described below. In the next section, these hypotheses will be applied to the case of non-state actors in Muslim nations. They will then be used to examine other instances of similar rage by state and non-state actors in subsequent chapters.

Hypothesis 1   There exist feelings of *ressentiment,* or status anxiety, resulting from the direct and indirect effects of the Soviet Union's and the Eastern bloc's collapse, even in nations that were not included in this alliance.

Hypothesis 2   This sentiment is reflected in a resurgent nationalism or political fundamentalism that is associated with anomie, renewed assertions of national or group identities, and an increased potential for violence by state or non-state actors.

Hypothesis 3   A relationship exists between citizens' perceptions of their national or group consciousness (i.e., their *Selbstbild*) and their nation's or group's international image (i.e., their *Fremdbild*).

Hypothesis 4   These individual-level negotiations between *Selbstbild* and *Fremdbild* parallel macro-level negotiations of national identity carried out by political leaders, intellectual elites, and citizens and are directed toward a national and international audience through the media and other world forums.

Before proceeding with the analysis, however, it is necessary to define the terms used thus far:

National consciousness: This term includes citizens' national pride and other affective reactions to national symbols such as the flag and the national anthem. It also includes opinions on what holds the nation together and what constitutes national characteristics. This term is also referred to as *Selbstbild*, or literally, the self-image individuals have of their nation.

International image: This term includes (a) the affective reactions of other nations to the country or group in question; and (b) the reputation of the country or group in world opinion as perceived by the country's citizens. This term is also referred to as *Fremdbild*, or literally, the actual and perceived reputation of a nation or group in world opinion.

Ressentiment: This term, in the present usage, refers to feelings of powerlessness and hopelessness that are linked to negative feelings about one's country or about the country's standing in the world. Also included in this notion of international status deprivation are feelings of anomie, which are linked to a suspicion of outsiders, especially if they threaten the citizens' sense of national consciousness or the country's standing in world opinion.

Political fundamentalism: This term refers to a movement that offers a political and a religious identity to state or non-state actors. These movements typically espouse unique interpretations of history and economic development as part of their appeal.

The Muslim World and the Roots of *Ressentiment*

The history of the Muslim people begins with the Ottoman Empire. This dynasty, born under the religious and political leadership of the prophet Mohammed, once enjoyed a proud hegemony over significant portions of the world. The Ottomans considered themselves the most civilized and enlightened of civilizations, for they were directed by a dominant religion, triumphed on the battlefields, and made significant advances in the sciences and other areas. One is therefore tempted to attribute the rage many Muslims now feel toward the West, especially the United States, to resentment due to this empire's fall from power, an anger at being overtaken economically and politically by people they consider "infidels."

Because of the ancient roots of Middle Eastern civilizations, every analysis of this region begins with history. But oftentimes, the historical examples evoked have little explanatory power beyond the realm of mythmaking. This is not to say that the passing of the "Golden Age" of Islam centuries ago has no bearing upon the feelings of dislocation many Muslim nations presently experience. But it is the symbol, rather than the legacy, of this period that holds sway over the imaginations of many of the peoples we will discuss.

For the account of the Islamic decline from power fits other civilizations as well. The Asian peoples of China, for instance, also ruled over significant portions of the world, and excelled in their times in areas such as science and mathematics. They similarly dismissed other peoples as "barbarians" with whom they had little desire for contact, and from whom they had little to learn. Indeed, this attitude explains much of the decline of this civilization, and others, in the recent centuries.

Carlos Fuentes once observed that "cultures that exist in isolation perish, and only cultures that communicate and give things to one another survive."[26] Interactions and communication explained for him why the Greeks were able to repel invaders while the Aztecs were "paralyzed" by the arrival of the Spanish Conquistadors. While neither the Muslim nor the Asian cultures have perished, they have fallen behind in large part owing to a propensity toward isolation and a belief that there is little to be learned from outsiders, be they infidels or barbarians. Bernard Lewis notes how it was not until the eighteenth century that the Ottoman Empire even attempted to establish embassies in different nations. When Muslim rulers had something to say to the leaders of other nations, they dispatched an envoy to deliver the message, with the understanding that the envoy would return as soon as this was done.[27]

Western culture, by contrast, especially as it is represented in the United States, constantly borrows from other cultures with a relentless acquisitiveness. It collects ideas, music, scientific advances, literature, and other influences, remakes them into forms both compatible and useful, and disseminates them, usually for profit. In this sense, Westerners are somewhat deserving of the labels other cultures have attached to them. We do borrow from others with a *barbarity* that pays little attention to the symbolic meanings of the things we take as we adapt them to our own needs. We do display an *infidelity* to the origins and significance of what we borrow, and in fact, to any creed of our own that might limit what we take from other regions. Further, we often export the results of these transformed products as cultural goods to the very people from whom we borrowed them. While such actions may produce resentment, they may also help to explain the Western edge in political and economic development over the past two to three centuries.

Using the decline of the Ottoman Empire to explain Muslim *ressentiment* implies that these peoples have not tried other means to instill a sense of pride in the intervening years. This assumption is false. Instead, the failure of these other alternatives helps to explain why many citizens of Muslim nations experience a sense of lost status in the post–Cold War era. The history of this failure goes back only a few decades.

Pre- and Post–Cold War History and the Muslim World

The Ottoman Empire's decline began at the end of the First World War, when they were defeated along with Germany and the Austro-Hungarian

Empires with which the had allied themselves. From the 1940s through the 1970s many Muslim nations, notably Egypt and others, followed a secular, anticolonialist ideology with pan-Arab nationalistic overtones.[28] Such ideologies seemed ideally suited to the global position of these nations within the context of the East–West struggle. Anticolonial ideologies allowed nonaligned nations to play each side against the other without allying formally with either. Nationalism further enabled these countries to assert their identities as unique actors on the international stage. While both the Western nations and the Soviet Union could reasonably be charged with colonial aspirations, the term "colonialist" was usually applied to the West and the former colonies held by Britain, France, and other European nations, and was also used to characterize the "imperialist" ambitions of the United States. Marxist ideology provided a critique of the colonial imperative, and even while many Muslim nations were loathe to embrace an alliance with the Soviets, socialism provided a convenient vehicle to explain and leverage their disadvantaged positions in the world. Lewis notes how

> the victory of the Soviet Union in 1945 suggested a different solution—a return to the economic explanation of Western success, but with a socialist shortcut . . . Various forms of socialism, sometimes called Arab socialism, sometimes called scientific socialism, were adopted.[29]

However, these experiments "ended in disastrous failure . . . Most people in the regions have by now decided that socialism—or their experience of it—is neither Arab nor scientific."[30]

Goldstone similarly documents the failure of socialism, as even many of the Muslim nations with significant oil reserves remained underdeveloped and essentially under the economic control of their former colonial masters.[31] The number of countries in which Western intervention and influence was evident is daunting—Iran, Egypt, Saudi Arabia, and Iraq are but a few examples. It is no coincidence that the first truly Muslim theocratic state founded in the Middle East was Iran, where American intervention had installed the Shah several years earlier.

The Marxist model also proved unsuitable as an anticolonial ideology for other reasons. The political turmoil in Afghanistan in the late 1970s pitted Communists in that government, who "wanted to aggressively modernize the country under government control on the model of the Soviet Union," against "the Islamists, who wanted to halt those aspects of modernization that mostly impinged on family organization, local tribal authority and clerical control."[32] The Soviets then had to send troops to support a friendly government that had little support among the Afghan people. The quagmire into which the Soviets settled, in part due to the

United States' support of the Islamist guerilla movement against the Russian occupiers, is well known. However, the organization of this movement gave shape to a political fundamentalism that had formerly existed primarily in reaction to Communist attacks on traditional mores. The military movement, which drew support from other Islamic countries in terms of arms and personnel, was matched by a growing political movement motivated and directed by Islamic fundamentalist ideals.

The Russian withdrawal from Afghanistan, the subsequent collapse of the Soviet Union, and the general refutation of Marxist ideology left the Islamic nations in a conundrum. The invasion of Afghanistan dispelled any illusions among Muslims that Marxist ideology might be a useful means of asserting their national identities against the former colonial powers. But losing faith in one alternative did not draw these countries closer to the Western capitalist model. The triumph of the West in the battle against Communism left these nations, as well as much of the rest of the world, in a subordinate economic and political position, "dependent upon foreign investment and assistance." At the same time, modernization had also created a college-educated youth "acutely aware of the subordinate position of their countries and their cultures in global affairs."[33] The presence of an educated elite within a subordinate culture provides a significant seedbed for the spread of radical political alternatives.

Redefining a nation's present economic position and relief from these feelings of status anxiety on a global level necessarily require views of history and development that provide alternatives to the ideologies individuals perceive dominate them. The Russian attack upon Islam in Afghanistan made a reaction against Marxist ideology a *fait accompli* even before the collapse of the Soviet Union. Part of Marxism's attraction lay in the belief that a country's or a people's disadvantaged economic position relative to other nations was just temporary, and in fact, served as proof that they were on the right side of history. For decades, Communist states (and their primary theorists) supported their arguments by asserting that the true nature of their creed would only become evident when the entire world was ordered according to Marxist ideology. When this myth failed for the Soviet Union and the Arab experiments in "scientific socialism," Islamic political fundamentalism filled the gap with its own interpretation of Muslim and world history. This was a natural substitution, especially since the materialist elements of Marxism were never a good fit with the religious tenets of Islam.

Timur Kuran summarizes the interpretation of history that took hold among these "Islamists" in the wake of the Soviet collapse following the 1980s:

> The march of history, Islamists are also trained to believe, is going their way. Earlier generations of Islamists had predicted that the two major economic systems of the modern era, capitalism and communism, were doomed to

fail, because in their own way they bred injustice, inequity, and ineffi-
ciency . . . capitalism will self-destruct when its vulnerability finally shows
through. Capitalism has failed humanity because it breeds emptiness, mistrust, dissatisfaction, and despair even among the materially successful.[34]

"Material success" is therefore devalued so that the comparative global
economic circumstances of Muslim nations become an indicator of their
superior moral and historical positions. Kuran goes on to note that the
political fundamentalists have offered, as an alternative to capitalism, the
model of an Islamic economic system that includes specific banking operations they interpret as more in keeping with their religious traditions.
However, given that attempts to create such a system in countries such as
the Sudan, Iran, and Pakistan have failed, he questions how a model
adapted from fourteen centuries ago during a supposed Islamic "Golden
Age" could be expected to function in a global environment.[35]

The answer lies in part in the particular *function* one assumes the model
performs:

As Pierre Bourdieu observed, social structures never have a disembodied
reality; they are always negotiated by individuals in their own strategies for
maintaining self-identity and success in life. Such institutions are legitimized by the "symbolic capital" they accrue through the collective trust of
many individuals. When that symbolic trust is devalued . . . this devaluation
of authority is experienced not only as a political problem but as an
intensely personal one, as a loss of agency.[36]

Individuals are likely to attribute these systems' failures to the corrupt
nature of the global economic environment, which therefore provides an
impetus for change, by violent means if necessary.[37] The refrain is familiar
from our previous experience with Marxist analysis—the ideology promises that its system will work when, and only when, the entire world conforms to its model. The creed functions to sustain, and indeed elevate,
individuals to ward off feelings of *ressentiment.* The appeal of such ideologies is seldom measured by what they accomplish, but in what they promise; in fact, their failure is often perceived as proof of the sinful nature of
the rest of the world. It is an unfortunate historical fact that individuals
will often commit the most heinous acts rather than abandon a promise
that has sustained them and their identity.

The Islamist model of history and development, then, is *functional,*
albeit not in the material sense we generally use to judge such systems.
Kuran understandably judges the Islamic system of banking, for instance,
according to the capitalist standards of development, economic growth,
and the material well-being of its adherents. But the Muslim model also

allows its adherents to avoid the *ressentiment* associated with a perceived devaluation of their national or group identities. It sustains them through a past characterized by a fallen empire, colonial and postcolonial experiences, failed experiments with Arab socialism and nationalism, and the emergence of a dominant Western capitalist paradigm that grants them a diminished international status.

These thoughts lead to actions. With the correct provocation, the rage that often accompanies *ressentiment* can be directed toward the vulnerabilities of one's perceived "enemies." Such acts are not just fueled by hatred or strategic considerations; they also provide the opportunity for the individuals involved to project their identities in a manner the world will notice. It is no accident that figures like Osama bin Laden find recruits among the young, college-educated individuals that Jack Goldstone has described. Those who perceive a gap between their deserved place in the world and the one their people occupy are likely candidates for political fundamentalism and an alternative view of history that grants them the status they crave. As Juergensmeyer notes:

> Activists like . . . Osama bin Laden . . . have imagined themselves to be defenders of ancient faiths. But in fact they have created new forms of religiosity: like many present-day religious leaders they have used the language of traditional religion in order to build bulwarks around aspects of modernity that have threatened them, and to suggest ways out of the mindless humiliation of modern life.[38]

Ressentiment and Political Violence: Anomie, Identity, and Reaction

There are indicators of the crisis in Islamic identity politics in opinion surveys of Muslim countries. *Ressentiment* is a form of anomie, a feeling of helplessness in the present and pessimism about the future that is linked to one's sense of national identity. To the extent that national or group identity provides a source of pride, *ressentiment* creates one avenue for the avoidance of these feelings. To analyze this further, information from the 1995–1997 World Values Study was used to identify measures of these attitudes that correlated with national pride, allowing one, in turn, to use these questions to measure *ressentiment*.[39]

The analysis begins with two questions to measure levels of anomie:

> "Taking all things together, would you say you are: Very happy, Quite happy, Not very happy, Not at all happy?" (coded into 0 and 1, with the split at the median value for the sample).

"All things considered, how satisfied are you with your life these days?" (1 = Dissatisfied, 10 = Satisfied; coded into 0 and 1, with the split at the median value for the sample)

To measure national pride, a standard question was used:

"How proud are you to be _____ (substitute your own nationality)? (Very proud, Quite proud, Not very proud, Not at all proud)."

The answers to both of the anomie questions correlated with the answers to the questions about national pride. The greater a respondent's sense of national pride, the more happy they were likely to be (Gamma = .247) and the more satisfied they were likely to be with their lives (Gamma = .187). But when the responses were broken down by regions of the world, certain striking differences between Islamic and other nations emerged.

For this portion of the analysis, nations were classified into three categories, drawn in part from Huntington's classification of "civilizations" as interpreted by Norris and Inglehardt.[40] The categories included Western nations, Islamic nations, and the Other nations in the study.[41] The two measures of present *resentiment*—happiness and life satisfaction— were broken down by region of the world. The results, as shown in figure 1.1, indicate that the Islamic nations lagged behind the Western nations in overall happiness, and behind the Western and Other nations in life satisfaction; these differences were significant at the .000 level.[42]

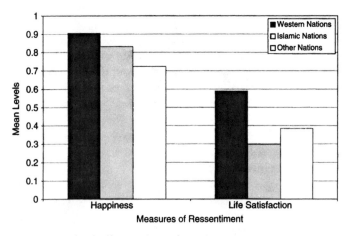

Figure 1.1   Mean levels of *ressentiment,* by region

However, an interesting result was obtained when a future measure of *ressentiment* was analyzed for the different regions of the world. For this analysis, the following measure of anomie was used:

> "For . . . the following pair of statements, please tell me which one comes closest to your own views: Humanity has a bright future OR Humanity has a bleak future?"

Responses to this question correlated positively with national pride (Gamma = .125). But the mean value for Islamic nations was higher than the mean value for both the Western and Other nations in the sample. Despite a generally dimmer view of the present, then, citizens of the Muslim nations generally envisaged a future characterized by lower levels of *ressentiment* than other citizens in the sample.[43]

We have already discussed the power of an alternative view of history and development to present hope to peoples in a disadvantaged global position. This measure allows us to view the flip side of that equation. For there is a correlation between a belief that the future is bleak and the belief that political violence is justified among the Islamic nations (Gamma = .401). This relationship does not exist for the other two groups of countries (Gamma = .090 for the Western nations and Gamma = .035 for the Other nations). The results are consistent with the previous analysis. When feelings of *ressentiment* about the future emerge because national or group identities fail to provide a sense of pride, political violence is a likely consequence.

Within the Islamic nations there are also perceived targets for this hostility. Three questions generally used to measure tolerance for unpopular groups in a society were used here to test the connection between anomie and approval of political violence. Respondents were first asked to name which group they "liked the least" from a list; regarding this group, they were asked the following questions:

> "Do you think [THE LEAST-LIKED GROUP] should be allowed to hold public office?" (Yes/No).
> "Do you think [THE LEAST-LIKED GROUP] should be allowed to teach in our schools?" (Yes/No).
> "Do you think [THE LEAST-LIKED GROUP] should be allowed to hold public demonstrations?" (Yes/No).

Tolerance measures such as these are often used as indicators of anomie within given societies[44] in order for them to be considered measures of *ressentiment*, however, they must be correlated with national pride, and here an interesting result occurs. None of these measures correlated with national pride for the Western or Other nations in the sample.[45] By contrast, all of these measures correlated with national pride for the Islamic nations.[46] These results suggest that for the Islamic countries, the measures of anomie also serve as measures of *ressentiment*. A similar result was obtained regarding the tendency to approve of political violence. Among the Western and the Other nations, none of these measures correlated with approval of political violence.[47] Among the Islamic nations, all of these measures correlated with approval of political violence.[48]

The results paint a portrait of citizens in Muslim countries who have lower expectations of the present, but higher expectations of the future, when compared with citizens in the West. At the same time, though, they show a propensity toward political violence if their view of the future is bleak, and they differ from the other regions in that the intolerance associated with *ressentiment* also correlated with approval of political violence. Taken together, these results provide clear evidence that in the case of the Islamic countries, our first two hypotheses about the roots of rage are supported. One finds tendencies toward *ressentiment* in the post–Cold War period that are associated with national pride and political violence.

The potential results when these factors are combined are chilling. If political fundamentalism links the future to an unworkable model of development and economic growth for many of these citizens, their vision of the future will almost invariably become bleak. Following upon the failure of these models and the dreams associated with them would probably be violence directed against those whom the citizens "like the least" both within and without the society, who then become convenient scapegoats for the failure.

Aspirations deferred can bring tragic results. The costs of failing to address *ressentiment* have been painfully evident over the past decade. Consider the negotiations that allowed the following statement by Ismail Ibrahim Abuyayy, a Palestinian speaking after the historic 1993 Oslo Accords, which seemed to portend the creation of a Palestinian state:

> For 40 years I have no identity. I am pushed from here to there. I am shunned by the world . . . But when I hear this news, I lift my head. Today I am a citizen from Gaza. (New York Times, 1993; emphases added)

Abuyayy's words eloquently illustrate the third and fourth hypotheses in our analysis. The lack of recognition from a world that "shunned" this man for 40 years deprived him of an identity. The Oslo Accords and the careful negotiations of identity among the elites afforded him the opportunity for an identity that fit a time and place; no longer would he be "pushed from here to there"—instead, he was "a citizen from Gaza." The acknowledgement of world opinion (*Fremdbild*) and his own perception of birthright (*Selbstbild*) had combined to define his identity in a manner that conferred a newfound pride.

The tragic denouement of this case has filled televisions and newswires for the past several years. When the accords fell apart owing to Yasser Arafat's outright rejection of an Israeli offer that granted nearly all of the Palestinians' demands, a wave of violence began that escalated to the present day. The burden of Arafat's failure ultimately fell upon his people as *ressentiment* translated into circumstances where "the suicide bomber may become a metaphor for the whole region."[49] Certainly, the suicide bombers of September 11 were symptomatic of this global disorder. The continual failure of their political and social systems to deliver on promises has prompted citizens to search for scapegoats in a local, national, or global context. This, in turn, provides a fertile ground for the recruitment of state and non-state terrorists. As James Baldwin once observed, "the failure of belief is not the same thing as ceasing to believe";[50] too many *ressentiment*-prone individuals are unwilling to exchange or modify a creed even when its tenets appear unworkable.

The challenge presented by violent expressions of identity sensitizes the observer to the limits and possibilities of the power of world opinion. Some theorists have envisioned that international public opinion might be able to restrain extreme nationalistic tendencies and the atrocities that so often accompany them. The reality is more sobering. World opinion actually plays a complex role in the emergence of nationalism and political fundamentalism; it supplies the international status that *ressentiment*-prone individuals seek in their construction of national identity. The "social value" of citizenship is measured by its capacity to grant status to individuals internationally.

But do these tendencies exist generally in the world, or are they peculiar to the Islamic nations? If the failures of national or group identity to ease *ressentiment* and the negotiation of identity from *Selbstbild* and *Fremdbild* are indeed global phenomena, they must apply to nations outside the Islamic world. There is evidence of these negotiations of identity and the potential status deficiencies they might cause in the present global configuration. The construction of identity, and the accompanying challenge of achieving global significance, occurs in a surprisingly consistent manner across several nations and cultures.

2

How We Come to Be Who We Are: Constructing Identity around the World

Creating a "usable" national identity in the post–Cold War era places extraordinary stress upon political systems. Observers once assumed that this process was a matter of choice, that citizens and leaders were the sole judges of the historical and cultural characteristics they would build into their perceptions of national consciousness.[1] In the post–Cold War era, however, the additional burden of considering world opinion and international reputation often strains nations to the point where rage appears to be the only reaction to a demanding international community. This symptom is not limited to the Islamic world; the negotiation of identity and its associated problems arise in a similar manner in other countries as well.

The problems arise because national identity is not rightfully considered as a *thing* or a *single belief*, but rather as a *complex of relationships* among affective reactions to a society and its institutions. At the center of these feelings is pride. When Greenfeld asserts that "*national identity is, fundamentally, a matter of dignity. It gives people reasons to be proud,*"[2] she implies that national pride must be maintained at sufficient levels, however defined, for a "usable" national identity to exist.

Greenfeld is not alone in asserting a link between national identity and self-esteem. Spinner-Halev and Theiss-Morse explore this connection in a review of writers they describe as liberal supporters of nationalism.[3] Their analysis, like Greenfeld's, disputes the notion that nationalism is solely a major cause of conflict—an idea that draws from the example of Nazism during World War II, among others. Instead, nationalism has positive characteristics that link together the individual, the nation, and the world. Spinner-Halev and Theiss-Morse note, for example, that

> Tamir . . . highlights the connection between the individual and the nation: "Membership in the nation is a constitutive factor of personal identity. *The*

self-image of individuals is affected by the status of their national community [emphases added]."[4]

Similarly, individual and national image are connected:

Kymlicka says . . . one key reason why national cultures are so important is that "people's self-respect is bound up with *the esteem in which their national group is held* [emphases added]."[5]

Finally, other writers raise the implicit question of where the source of national esteem, and hence, self-respect, lies:

Margalit and Raz . . . appeal to the apparent facts about the world when they argue for the connection between nationality and self-respect: "People's sense of their own identity is bound up with their sense of belonging to encompassing groups and . . . *their self-respect is affected by the esteem in which these groups are held . . . individual dignity and respect require that the group, membership in which contributes to one's identity, be generally respected and not be made a subject of ridicule, hatred, discrimination or persecution* [emphases added]";[6]

while

Taylor [states] "The modern context of nationalism is also what turns its search for dignity outwards." *We gain this dignity when others recognize our nation, particularly when our nation is recognized as equal to other nations* [emphases added].[7]

All of these statements link self-esteem and national pride, which in turn depend upon the recognition of one's nation or group as deserving of respect. This begs the question of the source from which this respect is derived. The first clue is that all signify the need to be held in esteem by individuals or entities *outside* the nation as a prerequisite for achieving dignity. In most cases, however, the authors do not specify further where or from whom this respect originates. Taylor comes closest to an attribution when he states that "our nation" must be recognized as "equal to other nations," but he is not specific regarding how one measures such equality.

The triangular relationship between individual self-esteem, national identity, and external status implies the importance of international recognition to self-esteem. There are also other factors that impact upon the efficacy of national or group identity to provide self-esteem. Any *model* of national or group identity is correctly understood as a system capable of maintaining pride in the midst of external challenges. Such challenges must include any threats to a nation's international status as well as other potentially damaging changes. Further, declines in factors contributing to national pride must be met with a compensatory increase in other supporting forces, if national identity is to remain viable.

Bacova notes that national identity is best understood as having both "primordial" and "instrumental" elements that support pride. The former refers to cultural ties based upon ethnicity, while the latter refers to ties based upon loyalty to the state:

> According to C. Geertz (1963) primordial attachments are . . . created at the social level when a community shares ideas of (also assumed) blood ties, the same race, speech, territory, religion, customs, and traditions . . .
> Individuals' attachments to communities that are of instrumental character . . . [are those] which are beneficial to them or bring them practical advantages (mostly economic and political). They are based on rational awareness, not closeness, but the need for protection of common interests.[8]

Bacova argues that Western culture tends to emphasize the instrumental elements over the primordial ones.[9] The problem with this is that it provides a convenient hierarchy of "rational" versus "irrational" notions of national identity. This thesis is convenient, and indeed comforting, for those who propagate a clash between Western and Islamic civilizations. It contrasts an enlightened, rational Western culture with a repressive, fanatical Islamic culture. It suggests that whereas Western nations are based upon common political and economic goals that bind a plurality of groups in an instrumental social contract, Muslim nations are based upon ethnic and religious beliefs that exclude those outside their respective primordial groups.

This argument ignores the complex realities and challenges of identity formation in all nations. Not only do Western nations also incorporate primordial elements into their ideas of identity, they turn to these elements to hold their nations together when crises threaten the instrumental performance of the polity. When countries face economic, political, or military crises, citizens of all nations are generally quick to raise questions of who "rightfully belongs" in their nation.

A better assessment of why Western nations are often able to sustain the myth that their nations rely upon instrumental ties lies in their general success in providing their citizens with acceptable levels of international economic, political, or military status. When a people are generally satisfied with their government's instrumental performance, the primordial aspects of their identity tend to remain somewhat dormant. Once a nation encounters stress that threatens their identity in the form of a challenge to their global economic or political status, the primordial aspects of identity often emerge with a vengeance. The reaction often takes the form of rage, focused upon some symbolic object or people, rightly or wrongly chosen. As we examine the elements affecting the construction of identity in a sample of primarily Western nations, we are guided by two controlling ideas. The first is that the instrumental and primordial elements exist side by side in this process, and provide alternative supports for national pride. This combination assumes that a nation's place in a hierarchy of international development affects its citizens' national pride. The stress resulting from comparisons to other nations can therefore have an invidious effect upon global order if citizens perceive their country as deficient in status relative to other countries.

The second is that any model of national identity must ultimately be evaluated in terms of the factors that affect national pride. This notion of dignity defines the core of a "usable national identity."

Constructing National Identity: Evidence from Twenty-Three Nations

It is commonly held that "we have few studies of how people set about [the] task of identity construction and maintenance."[10] It is further assumed that "comparative studies of the actual *negotiation* of national identity are virtually non-existent."[11] The reasons for these lacunae are that mapping the construction of national identity, particularly as it relates to dignity, is daunting:

> First, the relationship between national identity and self-respect is considerably more complicated than the self-respect theorists admit. Second, self-respect theorists usually focus only on the positive effects of group identification, even though there are negative ones as well.[12]

Creating a *general model* that describes the negotiation of national identity requires defining affective attitudes that influence national pride across a broad sample of nations. The result will be a complex of related factors that together constitute our sense of national identity. Further, even though the factors bolstering national identity may have positive effects on citizens' self-esteem, a failure or decline in these factors may have the opposite effect, encouraging a rage directed toward regaining the loss of self-esteem by whatever means necessary.

I begin with the two-part model of *Selbstbild* and *Fremdbild* elaborated in the previous chapter. The data for this analysis is from the International Social Survey, 1995: National Identity.[13] The initial measures for *Selbstbild and Fremdbild* were derived from a factor analysis involving five questions.

Respondents (henceforth, "R") were asked, "How proud are you of [R's country] in each of the following?":

1. the way democracy works[14] (Very proud, somewhat proud, not very proud, not proud at all);
2. its political influence in the world (Very proud, somewhat proud, not very proud, not proud at all);
3. its social security system (Very proud, somewhat proud, not very proud, not proud at all);
4. its armed forces (Very proud, somewhat proud, not very proud, not proud at all);
5. its fair and equal treatment of all groups in society (Very proud, somewhat proud, not very proud, not proud at all).

The analysis also included the following two statements:

1. There are some things about [R's country] that make me feel ashamed of [R's country] (Agree strongly, agree, neither agree nor disagree, disagree, disagree strongly).
2. For certain problems, like environmental pollution, international bodies should have the right to enforce solutions (Agree strongly, agree, neither agree nor disagree, disagree, disagree strongly).

The first five questions appear as one factor and were added together to form a PRIDE measure; the higher one's score on the scale, the greater one's pride in their nation. This index is taken as an initial measure of citizens' *Selbstbild*, or their positive perceptions of their nation. One might object that a citizen's degree of pride in his or her nation does not tell the whole story about how they perceive the country. In response, it must be kept in mind that while *Selbstbild* is not equivalent to national identity, it is a significant component of it. Further, while pride does not summarize all of one's feelings about one's nation, in its most critical embodiments, identity is (as Greenfeld asserts) "a matter of pride and dignity." Pride is not sufficient as a measure of national identity, but it is a necessary one.

The other two statements appear as a different factor; interpreting this factor demands that one take a closer look at global opinion theory, especially as it relates to the notion of the world considered as a unit and a nation's fear of international isolation. Following our previous definition of world opinion as "the moral judgments of observers which actors must heed in the international arena, or risk isolation as a nation," we understand how the second factor measures citizens' perceptions of their country's international image. Shame about one's national characteristics or actions implies a sensitivity (or fear) of others' judgments; these judgments are necessarily rendered by some means by other nations or their citizens, since a respondent might assume that fellow citizens also shared the feelings of shame. Shame also carries with it a moral dimension beyond sensitivity. The statement regarding shame thus speaks directly to the moral component of world opinion and the threat of isolation.

The second statement tests whether respondents are willing to give up national autonomy to an international body to enforce solutions to global problems and whether they desire to be part of an international community (as indicated by their willingness to adhere to other nations' judgments in collective endeavors).

These two statements combine to indicate an awareness of *world opinion about the international reputation or image of the respondent's nation*. As such, the two variables were combined into an index, referred to here as IMAGE1, which serves as the first measure of a nation's *Fremdbild*. The higher a respondent's score on this scale, the more negative the perception of their nation's image in world opinion.

The correlation between PRIDE and IMAGE1 is negative; the Pearson's r (-.204, with a significance level of .000) indicates that as PRIDE increases, reservations about the international image of one's nation diminishes, and vice versa. The result illustrates the *negotiation* between opposing vectors of forces—one inner-directed, and emphasizing one's national consciousness; and the other outer-directed, and emphasizing a concern about how the world perceives a country. National identity lies between these two poles of influence. National pride is tempered, and hence partially decided, by international forces of world opinion and reputation, particularly if citizens are concerned about a negative global image that could be a source of *shame*.

One might object, however, that it is self-evident that shame for one's nation and national pride are conflicting feelings; there might be no need for a global interpretation of these results. However, the variable also includes the question about whether the respondent's country should give up national autonomy to participate in international efforts; this question links feelings of shame with a willingness to forgo unilateral action for action that would bolster the nation's international involvement and reputation. There are other indicators that pride is linked to citizens' perceptions of their nation's relative position in the world. The next measure, IMAGE2, was constructed by combining responses to the following two statements:

1. The world would be a better place if other countries were like [R's country] (Agree strongly, agree, neither agree nor disagree, disagree, disagree strongly).

2. [R's country] is better than any other country (Agree strongly, agree, neither agree nor disagree, disagree, disagree strongly).

The first statement involves a value judgment regarding the condition of the world if the respondent's nation were an example to be followed. The second statement tests whether respondents would rank their country above all others in some qualitative hierarchy of nations. The responses to these statements indicate how citizens feel their nation "stacks up" against other nations and are a measure of *Fremdbild*. IMAGE2 is positively correlated with PRIDE ($r = .405, p = .000$), suggesting that the negotiation of identity also depends upon where one perceives one's nation in the international hierarchy of countries.

Previously, we hypothesized that the collapse of the Soviet Union and the general refutation of Marxist interpretations of history and development had basically left the capitalist model as the sole standard for international status. Put another way, the higher a nation's economic development, the higher its status in the international community should tend to be. To investigate this assumption, we correlated the measures of PRIDE, IMAGE1, and IMAGE2 with the per capita GDP, in dollars, of the respondents' nations. For example, the per capita GDP for Hungary was $6000, so all Hungarian respondents had a value of 6000 for this measure. GDP correlated positively with PRIDE ($r = .328, p = .000$) and IMAGE2 ($r = .173, p = .000$); it did not correlate with IMAGE1 ($r = .029, p = .000$). Pride in one's nation and the perception of one's standing in an international hierarchy of nations does appear to be related to the relative economic standing of the country. GDP does not appear to be related to perceptions of the moral judgments about one's country in the world. Since the moral component of world opinion is important for judging nations, this finding complicates the model, while adding an important insight—that is, that economic factors alone do not affect one's perception of one's international standing. As such, this opens the door to other approaches or models of identity that may prove to be a source of national pride and dignity relative to other nations.

Earlier, we noted that Western nations tended to emphasize instrumental aspects of their national identity because of their polities' general economic and political successes relative to other nations in the world. There is considerable variance in the PRIDE/IMAGE2 relationship across nations; it ranges from a low of $r = .174$ in Sweden to a high of $r = .490$ for Japan.[15] If our assumption is correct, national pride should be more closely related to IMAGE2, or the positive comparisons to other nations, in countries with a higher per capita GDP. To test this hypothesis, we correlated the Pearson's r for the relationship between PRIDE and IMAGE2 with the per capita GDP for the nations in the sample; these values are significantly correlated ($r = .282$, $p = .000$). Instrumental success in the economic realm correlates positively with a nation's tendency to relate its national pride to its perceived ranking relative to other nations. This finding supports the hypothesis that nations are more likely to emphasize the instrumental aspects of national identity if they have achieved relative success in the developmental ranking of countries. It also suggests that a decline in instrumental performance could adversely affect the relationship between pride and rankings relative to other countries, requiring other factors to fill the gap. Here, the primordial aspects of national identity might be likely to come to the fore. It is no accident that xenophobia tends to erupt in instances where a country's economic status is threatened, particularly if that challenge comes from foreign competition.

State, Nation, and Pride: Elaborating *Selbstbild*

A fundamental question regarding expressions of national pride is whether they are directed toward a state, considered as a set of governmental institutions and arrangements; or a nation, considered as an ethnic or religious entity. This question recalls the notions of instrumental and primordial identity, respectively, as explicated by Bacova. The former is related to the instrumental performance of the state and how well it performs its duties—guaranteeing contracts and providing collective goods. The latter is related to the primordial character of the nation and how a nation defines ethnicity, religion, and other ethnographic factors that figure into its collective identity. For the measure PRIDE, the results suggest that both forces are at work.

The scales for nation and state were derived from questions regarding the components of citizenship. A factor analysis was performed on responses to the following seven questions. Respondents were asked to tell how important they considered each of the following factors in determining who is "truly [a person of R's nationality]":

1. to have been born in [R's country]
2. to have [R's country's] citizenship
3. to have lived in [R's country] for most of one's life
4. to be able to speak [dominant language in R's country]
5. to be [of dominant religion in R's country]
6. to feel [as a person of R's nationality]
7. to respect [R's country's] political institutions and laws

The analysis generated two factors, with all variables having positive-factor loadings.[16] The first factor, which was combined additively into an index named NATION included the first six variables. This variable includes the components of primordial identity—birthright, citizenship, length of time lived in the country, language, religion, and feelings of identification. The second factor, which served as an index named STATE, included only the seventh variable. This variable describes one's attachment to the institutions responsible for the instrumental performance of the state.

The relationship between respondents' ethnographic characteristics in NATION and political allegiance in STATE is relatively strong; the Pearson's r equals .313, with a significance level of .000. The PRIDE index is similarly correlated with the STATE and NATION indices (Pearson's r equals .233 and .189, respectively, with significance levels of .000). Loyalty to the state's political institutions, ethnic and religious identification, and pride in one's nation thus form a nexus of relationships that further define a country's *Selbstbild*.

Immigration and International Image: Elaborating *Fremdbild*

Modern open societies in a globalized world find themselves increasingly challenged by the pressures of immigration. These pressures occur because societies with actual or de facto liberal immigration policies often tend naturally to become more diverse. The challenges that result affect both the instrumental and primordial aspects of nationhood.

As a practical matter, open societies are predicated upon liberal values that endorse diversity and celebrate at least certain forms of immigration as a positive influence on the polity. In actuality, though, open societies and open borders often make for a volatile combination. Modern democracies with thriving economic systems are often attractive to impoverished immigrants, who bring with them a strain upon social services and educational systems, real or imagined. Even in a nation of immigrants such as the United States, individuals understand the need for limitations on immigration. It is therefore no surprise when the realistic need for immigration policy sometimes becomes expressed as a xenophobia toward recent immigrants from citizens whose ancestors were immigrants a scant generation or so ago.

Similarly, while diversity is celebrated in theory as contributing to the richness of open societies, it also may produce real or imagined strains on the instrumental performance of the polity. An oft-asked question is, How much diversity of belief can be tolerated in an open society, particularly if certain traditions interfere with the functioning of governmental institutions? The issue of whether Muslim girls can wear their scarves to school in France is but one instance of this problem. Indeed, in the United States, women wearing the burka who refused to reveal their faces were ruled ineligible for drivers' licenses on the grounds that their pictures needed to be taken for identification purposes.

If the instrumental challenges of immigration are often vexing, the primordial challenges are potentially far worse. It is often asked how much even the most open of societies can absorb immigrants from all over the world before it must yield its basic sense of nationhood. If differences of religion, race, ethnicity, language, and birthright are to be ignored in defining who is part of a "nation," what is left? The common response in modern open societies is that such questions are irrelevant, since the real issues underlying immigration and diversity are instrumental, and therefore matters of policy subject to rational discussion and compromise. Sadly, while such assertions are comfortable to embrace, they are often useless, especially in times of crisis.

Attitudes toward the effects of immigration encapsulate both of these pressures. Respondents in the survey were asked about the degree to which they agreed with the following two statements:

1. Immigrants increase crime rates (Disagree strongly, disagree, neither agree nor disagree, agree, agree strongly).
2. Immigrants take jobs away from people (Disagree strongly, disagree, neither agree nor disagree, agree, agree strongly).

Responses to these questions were added together to form the variable IMMIGRANT. Not surprisingly, positive attitudes toward immigrants were negatively related to the primordial aspects of national identity represented in the NATION variable ($r = -.425$, $p = .000$). Similarly, positive attitudes toward immigrants were also negatively related to national pride ($r = -.279$, $p = .000$). Even in a sample of democratic polities, immigrants are perceived as a threat to both citizens' sense of nationhood and national pride.

The seven factors discussed thus far—PRIDE, IMAGE1, IMAGE2, GDP, STATE, NATION, and IMMIGRANT—combine together in the complex model shown in figure 2.1.

The model underscores an uncomfortable lesson within the liberal theory of nationalism—even though national pride can be viewed as having a positive effect within a polity, the attitudes that correlate with pride often reveal xenophobic, racist, or ethnocentric components. This realization is made more alarming when one examines how all the factors combine in their effects upon national pride, for a decline in one factor implies that another must emerge to compensate. A variety of disruptive phenomena can easily follow.

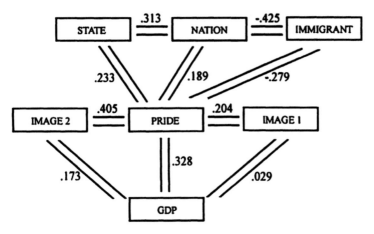

Figure 2.1   Model of national identity, with correlations among factors

A Model of National Identity

We have noted the tendency within liberal theory to emphasize the instrumental aspects, and ignore the primordial aspects, of nationhood. The incongruity of this tendency is compounded by the celebration of national pride as a source of self-esteem, and hence, a means of identity that binds the citizen to the state. Effective attitudes are never based solely in rationality; hence, anything that provides self-esteem and a sense of belonging to an individual has a downside should it begin to fail. Insults to dignity that follow often far outweigh the utilitarian interests of the individual who senses his or her identity is under attack. When these people lash out in rage, as individuals or as a group, too often the response of outsiders is one of shock and disbelief—how can these individuals violate their clear interests, they ask, by taking actions that in the final analysis will only hurt them. The list of examples is seemingly endless, from Lebanon to Kosovo and elsewhere—the war of all against all appears to only celebrate irrationality to observers who ask why these people are just "slitting their own throats."

One must recall that the model of national identity has as its center national pride in order for these types of behavior to become comprehensible. This model is easily represented, although obviously not completely captured, in a statistical analysis using the previous variables in our model. For this section, the variables IMAGE1, IMAGE2, GDP, NATION, STATE, and IMMIGRANT were regressed upon the variable PRIDE, which represented the core value determining the capacity of national or group identity to confer dignity upon individuals. The multiple R value for the resulting equation equaled .538, with a multiple R^2 value of .289. The resulting equation, using standardized Beta coefficients, is listed below:

$$.321 \text{ GDP} + .259 \text{ IMAGE2} + -.199 \text{ IMAGE1} + .144 \text{ STATE}$$
$$+ .098 \text{ IMMIGRANT} + .061 \text{ NATION} + -17.46 = \text{PRIDE}$$

This equation necessarily raises the methodological question of the level of national pride necessary to sustain a nation and provide its citizens with dignity. However, addressing this question in such a manner overlooks the utility of the model for this analysis. For our purposes, it is not important to view the equation as a formula for producing the "adequate" levels of national pride. Rather, it is designed to illustrate several hypotheses regarding national identity:

1. GDP, which we have chosen as a measure of the level of a country's development relative to other nations, not only has a strong positive effect on national pride in the post–Cold War era, but is also the least likely to change quickly over time. Barring unforeseen events, countries do not tend to "leap-frog" over several other nations to move up or down the global hierarchy of development.
2. The IMAGE1 and IMAGE2 variables suggest that any damage to a nation's international image will have to be compensated for by comparative increases in the other factors. Again, one must keep in mind that GDP is an unlikely compensatory factor in the short run.
3. The instrumental aspects in the STATE variable, which relate to respect for institutions of politics and law, and the primordial aspects of the NATION variable, may likely increase in importance if there are downward pressures on other variables affecting pride. Similarly, the anti-immigrant attitudes represented in the IMMI-GRANT variable may come to the fore if other factors affecting national pride decline.

The construction of a "usable" national identity cannot be reduced to an equation. Instead, the regression model provides a guide for analyzing challenges to national identity that might provoke violence or rage. If one begins with the assumption that a suitable level of national pride is necessary to sustain a country's identity, and that there are factors that affect pride in positive or negative ways, one may generate a qualitative model of potential crises. A positive international image, a strong sense of primordial ties, and a strong commitment to the legitimacy of political institutions and the law all affect national pride in a positive manner. Negative attitudes toward immigrants also affect pride positively. A negative international image, by contrast, affects pride negatively. Finally, a country's level of development, as reflected in its per capita GDP, may have a positive, negative, or neutral effect on its pride, depending upon whether the nation is toward the top, the bottom, or the middle relative to other nations, respectively. This qualitative model is illustrated in figure 2.2.

Given the relatively fixed position of GDP over short periods of time, the flexible portions of the model are defined by the other five factors. If there is a decline in a factor that affects pride positively (say, for instance, a good international image or a strong primordial sense of nationhood), one might expect a corresponding decline in national pride. Since pride must be maintained at a suitable level, however defined, for the polity to survive, other factors affecting pride positively must compensate. Either the state or its people will assert or unleash compensating forces to meet this challenge to identity. When primordial ideas of the nation are in question, for instance, it is often the case that anti-immigrant attitudes and violence become more common. An analogy to this process might be an inflated balloon, where if one puts pressure on one side by squeezing it, the other side must expand in order for it not to explode. The other areas expand to compensate for the portion that is squeezed, allowing the air to occupy the new space. In much the same manner, when national pride is under pressure due to one factor, other positive factors must increase in order to keep the system intact.

This response may result in violence in two ways. The strategies necessary to relieve pressures on national pride must be commensurate with the perceived level of threat directed toward it. Asserting political values often involves the projection of power that begets violence, with the violence increasing the greater the threat. But violence may also result from

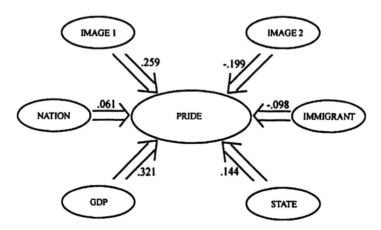

Figure 2.2 Regression model on national pride, with standardized betas

frustration, when an attempt to redress a decline in national pride by other means fails. In this case, violence is less an assertion of values and more an expression of despair—and again, the greater the challenge, the greater the level of despair and corresponding reaction.

This equation therefore provides a general framework for the rest of the analysis. As a seedbed for hypotheses, it suggests that the post–Cold War configuration has certain characteristics that place whole groups or nations in danger of status deficiencies, due to the relative immobility of the developmental hierarchy. The refutation of Marxist interpretations of history and development thereby created a structural decrease in one element of national pride. In addition, the shift in power relationships that erased the idea and power position of "nonaligned" nations created a similar structural decrease in national pride. Compensation must come from other factors in the model or from some other sources if rage and violence is not to result. In the following chapters, we will examine several examples where the alternatives to rage tragically failed.

All of the factors that define national pride are attitudinal variables, save one—the nation's per capita GDP. The distinct qualities of this variable are twofold. First, per capita GDP is an indicator of a country's ranking in the global hierarchy of development. Second, as has been shown, it correlates both with national pride directly and with the relationship between national pride and a positive image in other countries. As such, it implies that the higher a nation's instrumental success, at least in the economic realm, the greater a nation's tendency to link national pride with economic performance. This conclusion is consistent with the earlier point that Western nations—which typically outperform other nations economically (with the exception of Japan)—also tend to emphasize instrumental elements of national identity.

Several implications follow. First, since shifts in per capita GDP relative to other nations seldom tend to occur quickly, changes in the instrumental positions of nations in the global status hierarchy will be correspondingly slow.[17] Second, nations at the lower end of the economic hierarchy must "make up" for their international status deficiencies through some adjustment of the other variables in the model. While one cannot attach a numerical value to the level of national pride that citizens find sufficient to support a usable national identity, it is reasonable to assume that the need to express these other attitudes in a manner the world will recognize often results in violence or other varieties of destabilizing behavior. It also follows that a nation that experiences a sudden drop in economic status will be more likely to initiate destructive international actions.

Finally, and perhaps most frighteningly, if the nation is still unable to generate a usable national identity that stimulates pride, non-state actors might fill the void by offering an alternative identity. It might have been difficult once to imagine non-state actors with sufficient power to compete alongside the nation-state as a player in world politics or as an agency offering individuals a sense of pride with limited resources. Even the poorest state generally has far more resources at its disposal than even well-supported non-state actors. Non-state actors would therefore have to commit acts more spectacular than those often imagined by states to become participants on the world stage and stimulate pride among their followers—acts like flying planes into the World Trade Center and the Pentagon, restructuring American foreign policy as a result; or blowing up trains in Madrid, effectively ending Spain's participation in the war in Iraq. Tragically, our imaginations are no longer limited to the vagaries of state whims in pursuit of national pride.

Destructive expressions of nationalism, state actions designed to bolster national pride that offend the world, terrorist attacks by non-state actors—all are linked by the search for pride and status in a globalized post–Cold War world. Ten years ago, political observers were embroiled in discussions of the destructive effects of resurgent nationalism. Today, many of those same individuals are occupied with the horrors of global terrorism. Both are symptoms of the same disease, and unless we see them as such we cannot address them—or the next horrible manifestation that is likely to occur a decade or so hence. As we will see in the following chapters, expressions of violence cross the boundaries of "civilizations" easily, and are as likely to occur within nations as between them.

Part II

Rage and Reaction—Challenges to National Identity around the World

Introduction: National Identity as a Personal and Global Concept

The pandemic of global rage has its roots in the manner in which we construct identity. Although this book concentrates primarily upon national identity, the processes remain more or less the same for all levels of identification. Individual identity is constructed with an eye to the relevant reference groups in a person's life: "Identity is a phenomenon that emerges from a dialectic between the individual and society."[1] Reference groups change depending upon the relevant contexts in which one participates at any given time. Individuals may be in contact with several reference groups, each providing separate messages about their identities. Thus, "people have levels of identity" so that a resident of Rome is at once "a Roman, an Italian, a Catholic, a European, a Westerner."[2]

In a similar manner, public opinion is constructed with reference to specific groups, or "publics." A continuing controversy in public opinion research is the exact nature of interactions between specific publics and the opinions expressed by their members, This issue is directly relevant to the construction of identity at all levels—national, group, familial, etcetera. If public opinion involves the communication of attitudes, norms, and beliefs among specific reference groups, it becomes the primary means by which identity is disseminated, shared, and enforced within those groups.

The problems that past researchers have tended to encounter when investigating these relationships between identity and public opinion are twofold: first, How does one describe the dialectic of interaction between individual and group identity as a *process?* and second, What is the primary group that generates an individual's identity and determines the process within which he or she will participate? This section responds to these questions in the following manner. First, it argues that the process of public opinion, which guides the construction of identity, tends to be the same regardless of the reference group one considers. Second, it argues, following John Zaller's thesis, that since opinions are not be fixed, identity need not be fixed either. Instead, when the relevant reference groups clash in their interpretations, identity is "negotiated."[3] Further, this negotiation follows a pattern determined by the public opinion processes, which structure the construction of identity on any given level. This section will emphasize the potential clashes between a country's national consciousness (or *Selbstbild*, the image its people have of themselves) and its international image (or *Fremdbild*, the image other nations have of it). The negotiation between these two forces, if it is successful, produces a "usable" national identity for the countries involved. However, other factors from the regression model in Chapter 2 will be considered where appropriate.

The Construction of Identity and Public Opinion: The Controversies

Karl Deutsch argues that national identity is a form of social communication.[4] One may expand this observation, since all forms of social identity—familial, national, ethnic, or global—are constructed as forms of social communication between the individual and a reference group. We define this communication process as part of the general process of public opinion. Noelle-Neumann describes public opinion as those opinions that an individual can or must display in public in order to avoid social isolation.[5] Although certain critics take issue with this definition, it is generally accepted that any process of public opinion involves interactions between the individual and a group. According to Price and Oshagan:

> The social psychologist interested in public opinion seeks fundamentally to explain how "opinion" is modified by the fact that it is "public"—to explain, in other words, the various ways in which ideas and opinions are shaped and altered through interaction among people and the social groups they constitute.[6]

These authors also note that writers who defined this tradition, such as James,[7] Baldwin,[8] and Mead,[9] assumed that "a person's very identity is a product of social interaction(s)" such as those described above.[10]

Describing the interaction between the individual and the relevant "public" on any level, then, is key to understanding how identities are formed. At all levels, "macrolevel information exchange [occurs] within 'interpretive communities,' which in turn exercise the control of public opinion and culture that plays a role in ... hegemonic models" such as those defining national or group identity.[11] In the following chapters, we advance a theory about the process of opinion formation within the nation and the "world public" with regard to national identity. We also suggest that the way in which media define the boundaries and interpretations of national identity may be partially explained by this theory. The first step to understanding this process, then, is to study the process of world opinion as it has been delineated by past research.

World Opinion as Concept and Process

World opinion refers to "the moral judgments of observers which actors must heed in the international arena, or risk isolation as a nation."[12] This definition indicates a relationship between individuals within a nation and observers outside of it, operating in a "public" realm where world opinion is developed and where national identities are observed and defended. The "process of world opinion" occurs in several steps. First, an agenda of issues with which world opinion will be concerned emerges; this agenda has been shown to be remarkably consistent across newspapers from a variety of nations.[13] Second, a consensus forms regarding the "moral" position on the issue, and this consensus is transmitted internationally; national leaders and citizens reinforce this judgment by supporting it publicly and keeping dissenting opinions private.[14] Finally, when a nation's interests, actions, or public opinion conflict with this moral judgment, that nation may be threatened with international isolation. This threat may cause actors to temper the pursuit of actions that could lead to such condemnation.

The issue of apartheid in South Africa offers an example of this process. During the mid-1980s, the condemnation of the apartheid system held a prominent position in the global media. It was generally accepted that the system was immoral, and South Africa was isolated in tangible ways (such as being barred from participating in the Olympics) and intangible ways (such as having a negative international reputation). Other nations were reluctant to be associated with South Africa during this period, for fear of being isolated themselves; their public statements and actions condemned apartheid, even while some countries tried to maintain private transactions with the South African government. Ultimately, the isolation of South Africa was viewed as one of the major factors leading to the demise of the apartheid system.

Here, one observes an interaction between an individual nation's actors and an international "public" that affects the nation's reputation and ultimately causes it to heed the judgments of other nations. In many ways, this process parallels the "spiral of silence" process that Noelle-Neumann describes within individual societies. This process also proceeds in three steps: (1) individuals become aware that opinion is strengthening or weakening on a particular issue, guided in part by messages from the media; (2) individuals react to these changes with more confident speech in support of the emerging position, or silence in opposition to it; and (3) individuals fear isolation, which causes them to heed the emerging opinion in the society.[15]

The parallels between these two processes suggest that the interactions between the individual and the group are similar regarding the threat of isolation, the role of media, and individual reactions, regardless of whether one operates on the national or international level. If, however, "public" is defined as exposure to the judgments of others, as Noelle-Neumann first asserted, and as the definition of world opinion implies, which group is the relevant one for defining the individual's opinion? This question is particularly relevant with reference to national identity, a concept that has currency and meaning both within nations and among them. How does one define the group that has the primary influence upon this critical form of identity?

National Identity as a Construct within Opinion Processes

This issue does not just concern national identity. Individuals interact with a plurality of groups that may affect their opinions and identities:

> We can conceptualize interpersonal relations as constituting smaller opinion publics that may work in concert with or against the larger, systemic debate over policy issues. In such a confluence of *potential* normative forces, only certain ones will become operative over the course of an individual's social interaction concerning a given issue. An important empirical issue to be sorted out is the determination of which particular norms become salient for various people.[16]

Researchers have identified various "smaller opinion publics" that affect an individual's attitudes on specific issues. These reference groups include communities,[17] ideological groups,[18] and the small experimental groups used by Asch[19] and referenced by Noelle-Neumann.[20] The opinion processes, including the fear of isolation and the tendency of individuals to heed the opinions of others, operate even as the reference groups change. Hence, a common criticism of theories describing the spiral of silence and world opinion is that neither proves that the national or global society, respectively, is the relevant public to which the individual is responsive. Individuals come in contact with multiple reference groups; it seems arbitrary to argue that any given group is solely responsible for affecting an individual's opinion or identity.

The model necessarily becomes more complicated when an individual encounters two or more levels of reference groups at the same time. For instance, ethnic identity is not formed solely with reference to one reference group in a given nation; the national society also has an image of the ethnic group that affects the way in which its members view themselves. As such, ethnicity is relevant on at least two levels. Opinions about the individual's ethnic background may be complementary or conflictual on these two levels.

But such anomalies assume that opinions or identities are fixed once they are defined, so that one may trace their source back to a particular reference group. Our analysis argues that norms or identities that emerge from public opinion processes are not fixed. Rather, they vary with the time and context that define their influence. This approach follows Zaller's thesis that individuals do not have fixed opinions; instead, they carry within them varying "considerations" about an issue that reflect the social circumstances in which they find themselves at that time. As Zaller notes: "Response variation is rooted in an important substantive phenomenon, namely the common existence of ambivalence in people's reactions to issues."[21] This "ambivalence" is affected by reference groups and the "priming effect of media."[22] Both reference groups and media interact in a manner one may measure in the potential conflict between national consciousness and world opinion regarding national identity.

The notion of "ambivalence" suggests this interpretation etymologically: "ambi" refers to "both," while "valence" refers to "the capacity of an entity to unite or interact" with another. Ambivalence in attitudinal structures thus implies a suspension between potentially conflictual forces (such as reference groups or media, or reference groups mediated by media), all of which have the capacity to attract and influence the individual's attitudes. When the attitude or opinion studied concerns national identity, this "ambivalence" reflects the interaction of individual opinions with national and global reference groups, among others. In this section, I study the possible effects of these national and global reference groups whose perspectives are reflected in the print media and public opinion surveys) where available. The manner in which media and survey results present perspectives on world opinion on an issue pertinent to citizens' national identities may be explained in terms of the negotiations that aim at settling this "ambivalence."

National identity has relevance within both national and global "societies" for two reasons. First, world opinion legitimizes the very notion of national identity;[23] second, it determines the prestige value or status of a citizen's identification with a particular nation. The successful construction of national identity thus involves a negotiation among all of the factors we described in the previous section. In this chapter, we emphasize the negotiations between a nation's *Selbstbild* and its *Fremdbild*. However, understanding the expression of and reaction to rage will necessarily involve more factors from the model.

3

Fences Make Good Neighbors: Who Is "German" without the Wall?

In the film *Goodbye Lenin*, a mother who has faithfully served the East German state collapses in the street from a heart attack after seeing her son beaten up by police in a pro-democracy demonstration. She falls into a coma just before the collapse of the Berlin Wall, and remains unconscious until after German reunification has occurred. Her son, fearful for her delicate condition, brings her home and devises elaborate ruses to make her believe that the East German state still exists. The film serves as a metaphor for the construction of national identity, its vulnerability (symbolized by the woman's fragile condition), and its connection to personal identity.

National identity, past and present, is a common theme for reflection and argument in Germany. The place that symbolized the end of the Cold War became one of the first breeding grounds for the global rage that would follow. One might not expect rage and terrorism to occur in a country such as Germany, given its privileged structural status in the post–Cold War hierarchy of economic development.[1] But the country's unique condition—as a divided nation reunited but not clearly integrated—made it the scene for some of the earliest instances of violence spurred by disruptions to national self-esteem.

This chapter looks at the resurgence of nationalism and its contribution to global rage in Germany in the post–Cold War era and the resulting dynamics of the negotiation of national identity. We outline and analyze four steps in this process between 1991 and 1992:

1. The feelings of *ressentiment*, or status anxiety, resulting from the direct and indirect effects of the Eastern bloc's collapse on Germany
2. The manner in which this sentiment is reflected in a resurgent nationalism associated first with anomie and leading to new assertions of national identity

3. How citizens come to realize the relationship that exists between perceptions of their national consciousness and of their nations' international image

4. The resulting individual-level negotiations between *Selbstbild* and *Fremdbild* carried out by political leaders, intellectual elites, and citizens, and directed toward a national and international audience through the media and other world forums in order to address the damage done to Germany's international image and national pride.

Nation Building, Stage I: The Fall of the Eastern Bloc and the Links to *Ressentiment*

Perhaps no nation carries with it more negative historical baggage regarding the assertion of national feeling than the Federal Republic of Germany (FRG). Both within and outside this country, assertions of German national pride are always viewed suspiciously through the lens of the Nazi experience. As such, the postwar history of the German nation has been marked, in part, by a search for a "masterable past," an interpretation of the Nazi era that would allow the expression of national consciousness freed from the specter of a Nazi revival.[2]

Despite these concerns, reunification was initially greeted by German citizens with increased optimism; in 1989, 1990, and 1991 the percentage of German respondents stating they faced the new year "with hope" reached post–Cold War highs of 68, 56, and 56 percent, respectively. These results were clearly linked to feelings about reunification. In a 1991 survey, 61.2 percent of those who viewed reunification "with joy" were hopeful about the coming year; by contrast, only 36.7 percent of those who viewed reunification as a problem were hopeful about the coming year (*Allensbach Survey* 5055).[3]

A closer examination of the individuals who were worried about the effects of reunification (about 30 percent of the sample) reveals a link between these fears and classic measures of anomie. "Anomie," as defined in this case, refers to feelings of concern about the future and helplessness and powerlessness regarding one's ability to affect government or society. The measures of anomie used here are the same or similar to those typically used to measure such feelings in survey research.[4] The following results illustrate the relationship between such feelings and concerns about German reunification. Individuals who were worried about reunification were more likely to believe that:

1. Democracy could not solve the nation's problems (by a margin of 26.6 to 13.5 percent).

2. The government was run in the interests of the few (50.5 to 27.7 percent).

3. The government was run according to special interests (48.6 to 30.9 percent).
4. The politicians do not care what people like me think (71 to 56.9 percent).
5. People like me have no influence over what government does (60.1 to 49.5 percent).
6. One cannot trust most people (50.4 to 36.1 percent).

Negative feelings about reunification were also linked to another factor traditionally associated with anomie: the citizens' views about the economic situation in the country. Fifty-seven percent of those who viewed reunification with joy felt that the economic situation in Germany was "very good" or "good," as compared with only 34.6 percent of those who viewed reunification negatively (*Allensbach Survey*).

These measures of anomie are linked to misgivings about the newly constituted nation. Indeed, respondents who expressed concerns about reunification tended to believe that most Germans still had a "wall in their head," by a margin of 63.2 to 40.7 percent (*Allensbach Survey*). This result reflects the extent to which Germans felt their fellow citizens accepted the "idea" of a unified Germany, or whether they still thought of the country as two separate nations. Just over 53 percent of respondents took the latter view, indicating significant doubts among citizens about the newly constituted nation. Moreover, these doubts were also related to feelings of anomie similar to those measured previously.

Individuals who answered that German citizens still had a "wall in their head" were more likely to believe that:

1. Democracy cannot solve the nation's problems (by a margin of 21.2 to 14.3 percent).
2. The government is run in the interests of the few (45.2 to 26.8 percent).
3. The government does not work in the interests of the people (44.8 to 30.6 percent).
4. Politicians do not care what people like me think (67.7 to 51.8 percent).
5. Politics is too complex for people like me to understand (57.4 to 47.9 percent).
6. People like me have no influence over government (57.1 to 48.9 percent). (*Allensbach Survey*)

Finally, the lingering "wall" in German citizens' perceptions of their nation was also linked to their evaluations of the FRG's economic state. Only 43.4 percent of respondents who felt that the two nations were still separate rated the economy as "very good" or "good," as compared with 56 percent of respondents who did not feel this continued separation.

The results suggest that negative feelings about the new nation, so constituted, were linked to feelings of anomie. This relationship suggests the presence of *ressentiment*, or a feeling of powerlessness that is linked to negative feelings about one's country. This relationship is confirmed by one more finding from the survey. The percentage of individuals who felt that a "wall still existed in Germans' heads separating East from West" increases from 43.7 percent for those who were "very proud" to be German, to 47.8 percent for those who were "somewhat proud," to 53.9 percent for those who were "not very proud," to 57.8 percent for those who were "not at all proud." This inverse relationship between national pride and the feeling that East and West were still distinct entities provides more evidence of the relationships between a lack of national pride, nonacceptance of the re-created nation, and anomie.

These feelings were especially evident in the former Eastern sectors of the nation. In spite of the celebrations after the Wall came down, persons living in the East were more likely to believe the Wall still existed "in the heads" of citizens than those living in the West, by a margin of 58.1 to 48.8 percent. It is not surprising that the feeling of separation should be especially acute in the former Eastern sector.

M. Lane Bruner argues that "national identities are *always* contested, *always* political, and *always* a choice between narratives."[5] The peculiar problem of Germany involved the almost total rejection of one narrative (the Marxist narrative) in favor of another (the Western capitalist narrative). Harry Pross notes the contrasting ideas about development that existed in the East and the West prior to the German Democratic Republic (GDR)'s collapse:

> As far as the loss of state unity was concerned, the GDR forecast its recovery once the final stage of true socialism envisioned by Marxist theory had been reached. Similarly, in a distant, more just world, material living conditions would also have improved . . .
>
> On the other hand, the Western state declared itself a provisional construct from the start . . . Here, unity was not associated with a distant vision of satisfied economic needs. The state's role was seen as that of policing the market and of trying to ensure the immediate and repeated satisfaction of contemporary needs.[6]

The loss of identification with the Eastern model of development removed a source of pride that had formerly served as an alternative means of status. As Konrad Jarausch notes, in the wake of reunification, "toughest of all was psychological reconciliation. Easterners struggled with a loss of identity."[7] Jurek Becker links this loss of identity with the changed status of the former Eastern sector since reunification:

> Almost every single East German standard was abolished, not because it proved in each individual case to be inferior, but because it had been in force on the wrong side of the border . . . In a part of the world that called itself, with involuntary openness, the "Socialist camp," a proud idea has been so discredited that none of us will live to see an attempt to resurrect it.[8]

Other evidence suggests that a significant gap in perceptions of the two systems existed even following reunification. In 1990, for instance, citizens in the former Eastern sector overwhelmingly blamed poor leadership, rather than a general failure of socialism, for the collapse of the GDR, by a margin of 67 to 20 percent; by contrast, citizens in the former Western sector split about evenly on this question (45 to 41 percent, respectively).[9]

The dominant narrative of history also promoted specific ideas regarding the German past, making for further inconsistencies between the two sectors. Lane argues that the Cold War version of West German history, articulated by Ronald Reagan, Helmut Kohl, and Friedrich von Weizsäcker, painted the German people as victims of Hitler. Indeed, von Weizsäcker lists as "victims" of World War II "the dead of the war," "the six million Jews that were murdered," "widows," "homosexuals," "all nations who suffered in the war," "gypsies," "members of the resistance," and "German compatriots who died as soldiers (or during the air raids at home, in captivity, or during expulsion."[10] It was therefore a small leap when Reagan, upon visiting a cemetery where SS officers were buried, proclaimed, "They were victims, just as surely as the victims in the concentration camps."[11] It goes without saying that citizens of the former Eastern sector had been presented with a different version of history, one that viewed National Socialism as a logical outgrowth of capitalism. No doubt, these conflicting narratives provide a basis for conflict in a nation where the question of German history still remains controversial.

It is important to note, however, that there are a few differences in the relationships between anomie and concerns about unification between the former Eastern and Western sectors. Where there are doubts about the effects of reunification, this form of powerlessness is present. The reasons for *ressentiment* differed, though, for citizens in the two regions. Citizens in the former Eastern sector felt threatened by different changes than citizens in the former Western sector.

These differences are reflected in the characteristics that correlated with national pride for the Eastern and Western sectors. In the former Eastern sector, decreased national pride tended to correlate with anomie; in the former Western sector, this relationship was much more ambiguous. For this analysis, the following measures of anomie were broken down according to citizens' responses regarding their pride in being German:

Question 1: Do you face the coming year with hopes or fears? (Percentages indicate respondents who answered "with hopes.")

Question 2: Do you believe the government is run in the interests of the few? (Percentages indicate respondents who answered affirmatively.)

Question 3: Do you think the government acts in the interests of the whole population, or according to special interests? (Percentages indicate respondents who answered "in the interests of the whole population.")

Question 4: Agree or disagree: "Politicians don't care what people like me think." (Percentages indicate respondents who agreed with this statement.)

For questions 1 and 3, a lower percentage indicates a higher level of anomie among respondents; for questions 2 and 4, a higher percentage indicates a higher level of anomie. For citizens living in the Eastern sector, anomie is inversely proportional to feelings of national pride on all four questions: as national pride decreases, anomie increases. This finding supports the thesis that for many citizens of the former Eastern sector, reunification brought a form of disorientation and powerlessness that one associates with a diminished sense of national identity. Their weaker sense of national pride in the new setting correlates with increased pessimism and mistrust of government.

The results are different for the former Western sector. For questions 1 and 2, there are no clear patterns related to national pride; results increase or decrease and then converge. Questions 3 and 4 do follow, to some extent, the pattern one would expect if anomie and a lack of national pride correlated; however, these relationships are considerably less dramatic than those reflected in the results from the Eastern sector. Citizens in the former Western sector understandably did not experience the sense of disorientation and powerlessness that citizens in the Eastern sector felt after reunification.

However, another factor correlates more strongly with national pride in the former Western sector than in the former Eastern sector: the performance of the economy. I compared the percentage of respondents from the former Eastern sector describing the FRG's economic situation, and their own economic situations, as "Very Good" or "Good," broken down within categories of national pride. In both cases, the relationship between the economy and pride is questionable for respondents in the East; the percentage of respondents is almost as high among those who were

"Somewhat Proud" to be German as among those who were "Not at All" proud to be German. By contrast, in the Western sector, the lower the percentage of positive evaluations of the economy, the less pride citizens had in being German. For respondents in the former Western region, economic performance was more tied to national pride than for respondents in the former Eastern region.

This contrast is underscored by results from a 1990 survey fielded just prior to reunification. East Germans who expressed worries about reunification were more likely to doubt that the East and West had the same national character than East Germans who expressed joy, by a margin of 51.3 to 25.6 percent. West Germans who expressed worries about reunification were more likely not to view reunification and currency union as an achievement than West Germans who expressed joy, by a margin of 60.6 to 31.1 percent (*Allensbach Survey* 5040). Even prior to the formation of a newly unified Germany, East Germans were concerned about differences in national consciousness, while West Germans were concerned about the financial ramifications.

These results describe a situation where the economic dislocations caused by reunification threatened the status of former West German citizens. These individuals saw their nation's position as one of the preeminent economic powers possibly undermined by the costs of change. Not surprisingly, the economic results of reunification were viewed much more positively in the former Eastern sector than in the West. A majority of citizens in West Germany in 1990 did feel that reunification would have positive economic effects, by a margin of 55 to 27 percent; however, this expectation was more widely held in the East, by a margin of 78 to 10 percent.

The findings therefore suggest several relationships between the misgivings about a reunified Germany and feelings of anomie or a feared loss of economic status. These results indicate the presence of *ressentiment* (or feelings of helplessness), which correlates with a negative image of one's nation. A weakened pride in being German correlated with anomie in the former Eastern sector; the same weakened pride correlated with economic concerns in the former Western sector. Status dislocations of different sorts in the two regions resulting from reunification promoted sentiments of *ressentiment* among German citizens.

Nation Building, Stage II: The Crisis of Anti-Immigrant Sentiments in Germany

One of the effects of *ressentiment*, according to our thesis, is an increase in the (often negative) expressions of nationalism, as citizens attempt to reclaim the status they lost in the changing international order. Horrors such as ethnic cleansing in Bosnia are often cited as one grim consequence of these extreme forms of nationalism. Another commonly cited example is the anti-immigrant sentiment that often found violent expression in Germany following reunification. It follows from our thesis (based on the 1991 survey) that anti-immigrant attitudes in Germany should have a relationship with both *ressentiment* and national pride among citizens of both Eastern and Western regions, albeit for different reasons. This relationship should exist, even though the vast majority of Germans disapproved of the violent extremism associated with the anti-immigrant attacks.

As expected, a link exists between anti-immigrant sentiment and national pride, pointing to a protectionist nationalism existing in both sectors after reunification. Shortly afterward, citizens began to adapt attitudes (and take actions) aimed at addressing this deficit in national pride: many expressed anti-immigrant opinions to assert their rights to "German" identity. For this analysis, four questions were used to test the degree of anti-immigrant sentiment:

Question 1:   Do you feel disturbed by the foreigners in Germany? (Percentages indicate respondents answering affirmatively.)
Question 2:   Agree or disagree— "I have nothing against foreigners, but there are simply too many of them here." (Percentages indicate respondents agreeing with statement.)
Question 3:   Should German family background be considered in asylum decisions? (Percentages indicate respondents answering affirmatively.)
Question 4:   Should asylum laws be changed to make it more difficult to immigrate to Germany? (Percentages indicate respondents answering affirmatively.)

For each of the four questions, a higher percentage of positive responses indicates a higher level of anti-immigrant sentiment. When one breaks down responses on national pride for the former Eastern and Western sectors, the results indicate that for both regions, national pride correlates directly with anti-immigrant sentiment. The more proud individuals were to be German, the more likely they were to agree with anti-immigrant statements.

We observe here an apparent transfer of sentiments between the 1990 and 1991 surveys. In 1990, anomie correlated negatively with national pride. In 1991, anomie correlated with anti-immigrant sentiment, which, in turn, correlated positively with national pride. The change suggests a *process* by which feelings of powerlessness came to be associated with negative feelings about those considered "outsiders" in the nation. These feelings then become associated with a sense of national pride, as one begins to define one's country by the definition, exclusion, and rejection of other outsiders. Particularly for those in the former Eastern sector, anti-immigrant sentiment seemed to allow citizens to project their feelings of powerlessness (as outsiders) onto a different group in society, thereby regaining a sense—albeit a negative one—of identity and national pride.

The competing narratives of the instrumental performance of the former West and East German states raised the question of "Who is German?" relative to the laws, institutions, and very history of the people. It is not surprising that individuals would seek the more primordial aspects of nationhood to define their commonalities in a reunified Germany, since the instrumental aspects of their identities were so different. Of course, one cannot discount the effects of economic disruptions on national pride in the reunified state. In the East, citizens felt diminished esteem after moving from being on the right side of history to being the "poorer cousins" of Westerners who viewed them as victims of a failed system. In the West, citizens accustomed to being one of the great economic powers from the beginnings of their "economic miracle" in the 1950s, now found themselves combined into one nation with a burdensome, underperforming economic partner. It is therefore misleading to assume that threats to national identity and anti-immigrant attitudes were only limited to the former Eastern sector. The primordial aspects of national identity emerged in the West, where anti-immigrant views also took hold.

The feelings of powerlessness or anomie measured above also correlated with anti-immigrant sentiments. Individuals who agreed with the statement "I have nothing against foreigners, but there are just too many of them here" were also more likely to answer that:

1. Between elections there was no means by which one could influence government (by a margin of 59.8 to 44 percent).
2. Many times politics is so complicated, you cannot tell what is going on (57.6 to 47.9 percent).
3. People like me have no influence over government (59 to 40 percent); and less likely to answer that:
4. One can trust most people (45.5 percent to 33.8 percent).

The results were similar when individuals were asked "When there are few jobs, should positions be taken from foreigners?" Respondents who agreed were also more likely to agree on question 1 (by a margin of 58.3 to 50.3 percent), question 2 (57.8 to 48.2 percent), and question 3 (59.7 to 45.9 percent), and less likely to agree on question 4 (41 to 34 percent).

The combination of national pride and *ressentiment* proved a volatile mixture for certain elements in German society. It is not surprising that these attitudes should converge. In a period of status dislocation, national identity becomes a path to regaining a lost position and a sense of one's place in the world. It also raises the question of "Who is German?", particularly in the wake of reunification. The analysis indicates that this question is relevant in several of the forms discussed earlier. "Who is German?" can be interpreted in a primordial sense to mean, "Who should be allowed to claim a national identification with this particular country, its history, its culture, and the status that identification carries with it?" It can also be interpreted in an instrumental sense to mean, "Who should reap the economic benefits of citizenship?" Both sets of questions became relevant after reunification: both related to *ressentiment* and both promoted some degree of hostility toward foreigners in Germany.

Tragically, actions follow ideas; by 1992 anti-immigrant attitudes found violent expression in a series of attacks upon migrant workers, many of whom were Turkish. The oft-stated motive for such acts was that guest workers were taking away jobs that East Germans desired in a period of high employment. The reality, however, was that migrant workers in Germany as well as in other nations generally performed low-paying service tasks that the nation's citizens did not wish to do. The real issue for Easterners was how they could replace their accustomed narrative of being German with the new one without enduring the humiliations of defeat. The real issue for Westerners was how they could sustain their narrative of economic success while absorbing fellow Germans who should only have enhanced their position. For both sides, the challenges to their narratives found a scapegoat in foreign immigrants and guest workers. The irony was that the immigrants' cheap labor supported the instrumental performance of the German economy. Such considerations were pushed aside to assert the primordial aspects of German identity that both East and West supposedly shared.

The violence against immigrants in Germany might have continued relatively unabated along its tragic course had it not been for another factor affecting German national identity—its international image. Because of their experiences during the two world wars, Germans are particularly sensitive to how the world regards them. As such, Germans were aware that anti-immigrant violence recalled for the world their Nazi past (it did not help that many of the violent acts were committed by young neo-Nazi thugs). Other aspects of the model thereby came into play in creating national identity, as an increasingly negative global image threatened German national pride. While it was clear that this violence was neither supported nor condoned by a majority of Germans, it did precipitate a crisis that the reunified state needed to address: a crisis of identity, which had to be worked out according to the process of negotiation described above.

Nation Building, Stage III: National Consciousness, International Image, and the Construction of Identity

Whenever I have had foreign visitors, it is almost inevitable that when I introduce them to friends or relatives here, they are asked how they like the United States. In most cases the question is rhetorical, since we expect visitors to be polite and praise a country in which they are guests; in fact, usually the question arises just as a means of making polite conversation. In our travels through Germany, however, my family and I were often confronted with a different question, and a different situation. I recall an instance on a long train ride with my wife and then four-year-old son, where we began a conversation with another family with children of similar age. Instead of asking the question, "How do you like Germany?" they asked us, "How do you like Germans?" We were taken aback by that particular question, for there is a fundamental difference between asking how one likes a particular country and how one likes the people in that country. The former question covers geography, culture, food, popular entertainment, and, of course, the people; the latter question is quite specific, referencing the very character of the nation's people. It is virtually unthinkable for a citizen of the United States to ask of a foreign visitor, "How do you like Americans?" (if only because we generally assume that everyone who comes to the United States invariably finds us likable).

Given our experiences in Germany and the friends we had made, we of course recounted all of the positive relations we had formed with people in the FRG. However, when we were alone, we reflected on the unique nature of what we had been asked. The Germans' peculiar question is an artifact of their recent history and evidence of their self-consciousness regarding their national identity. For a long time, Germany was held as an example of the illiberal usages of national pride. As late as 1986, if a person wore the slogan "*Ich bin stolz, ein Deutscher zu sein*" ("I am proud to be a German") on their clothing, it was considered a sign of neo-Nazism. Because of the Holocaust and World War II, national pride was a topic approached delicately in the FRG, and their citizens are still generally self-conscious of how they are perceived in the world.

By 1992 these concerns seemed prescient; reunification had led to unrest and citizen concerns about Germany's status as a major nation in the world. Violence against immigrants exploded, often encouraged by neo-Nazi gangs. Not surprisingly, this violence tended to be concentrated in the former Eastern sector, although incidents occurred in the former Western sector as well. The former Eastern citizens, aware of their inferior economic position vis-à-vis the former West Germans, often reacted with violent expressions of their "rightful" German identity against foreigners.

The new citizens' status dislocations arose because of their new political status as members of German society, coupled with their inferior economic status vis-à-vis West Germans and certain immigrant groups. As a result, hopes about the future, which were closely linked to feelings about reunification, faded significantly among German citizens. Respondents saying they faced the coming year "with hopes" reached optimistic post–Cold War highs of 68, 56, and 56 percent in the years 1989, 1990, and 1991, respectively. These percentages dropped to only 37 percent and 41 percent in 1992 and 1993, respectively, partly owing to anti-immigrant violence (*Allensbach Surveys*, 1991, 1992, 1993). In this case, the assertion of Germany's national identity in reunification resulted in nightmarish reminders of the Third Reich.

Our analysis assumes that German citizens' sense of national consciousness and their perception of Germany's international image are linked. As such, the national crisis of anti-immigrant violence should have individual-level and macro-level effects on the manner in which Germans view and construct their national identities. We consider the individual-level effects first, by investigating whether a link exists between citizens' views of national consciousness (their *Selbstbild*) and their perception of Germany's international image (their *Fremdbild*). The evidence indicates just how much was at stake in citizens' negotiations of their national identity. Germans' perceptions of how other nations viewed their country were strongly related to how they felt about their nation and the tangible symbols of national consciousness.

In a survey conducted in the former Eastern sector from December 1990 to January 1991, just after reunification, the new citizens were asked a series of questions relating to national consciousness and their feelings about the newly constituted nation. One question directly addressed perceptions of Germany's international image, asking respondents whether they felt that Germans were "liked" or "disliked" by the rest of the world. While 49 percent felt that Germans were liked, and 27 percent felt that they were disliked, their opinions correlated consistently with other feelings about the country, as the following results indicate:

1. Of those who believed that Germans were liked, 79.6 percent were "very proud" or "somewhat proud" to be German; only 48.6 percent of those who felt that Germans were not liked were "very proud" or "somewhat proud" to be German.
2. Of those who felt that Germans were liked, 55.7 percent faced the coming year, the first of a reunified Germany, "with hopes"; only 33.5 percent of those who felt that Germans were not liked faced the year "with hopes."

3. Of those who felt that Germans were liked, 73.5 percent were happy to see the German flag; only 43.2 percent of those who felt that Germans were not liked were happy to see the flag.
4. Of those who believed that Germans were liked, 79.3 percent felt that "national consciousness" was a good thing; only 58.5 percent of those who believed that Germans were not liked felt that "national consciousness" was a good thing.
5. Of those who believed that Germans were liked, 56.5 percent felt that East and West Germans had the same national character; only 39.7 percent of those who believed that Germans were not liked felt that East and West Germans had the same national character.
6. Of those who believed that Germans were liked, 86.8 percent felt that a German could feel as proud of his or her country as an American, French, or English citizen; only 60.3 percent of those who believed that Germans were not liked felt the same;
7. Of those who believed that Germans were liked, 50.9 percent ascribed to the slogan of reunification, which proclaimed, "We are one people"; only 27.1 percent of those who believed that Germans were not liked felt the same.
8. Of those who believed that Germans were liked, 49.5 percent stated that they were "very happy" to be German; only 22.5 percent of those who believed that Germans were not liked stated they were "very happy" to be German.

These results constitute a response to perceived world opinion about Germany. Citizens from the former Eastern sector who believed that Germans had a negative international image were less likely to associate themselves with the idea of German national consciousness (questions 4, 5, and 7) or with the symbols of the nation (question 3). They were also less likely to have positive feelings about being German (question 8) and to express feelings of national pride, individually (question 1) or in relation to other nations in the world (question 6).

These findings illustrate a characteristic response to world opinion about a given nation: isolation. The idea of "isolation" in world opinion is generally evident when citizens or leaders express a desire to avoid association with the isolated nation. In the international arena, such opinions are expressed by such actions as closing embassies, recalling diplomats, canceling state visits, boycotting a nation's trade, or barring a country from international sporting events such as the Olympics. The above results reflect the *individual-level* effects of international isolation. The feeling that their country is disliked by other nations promotes a desire within citizens to dissociate themselves from the symbols, pride, and very notion of their national consciousness. Such feelings are especially salient in a nation such as Germany, whose sensitivity about its international image has been heightened owing to its Nazi past. Unless feelings of international isolation are resolved, the construction of national identity and the legitimacy of the nation remain in doubt.

Of course, the causal ordering might also go in the opposite direction, so that individuals who have negative feelings about their country and its symbols project their attitudes upon the rest of the world. We would argue, however, that in the German case, the causal relationship likely runs in both directions. Negative feelings about one's nation derive from somewhere, and one would be remiss in denying that Germany's image suffered from the historical judgment pronounced by other nations after World War II. As such, it seems likely that German citizens who perceive their country negatively tend to both project and absorb these negative attitudes as doubts about their national identity.

Such doubts are likely to intensify in a time of crisis—and 1992, following reunification, was a year of crisis marked by a sharp rise in anti-immigrant violence and xenophobia in Germany. In a survey conducted in March 1992, respondents were again asked if they regarded reunification with joy or worries. Individuals who viewed reunification "with joy" were more likely to believe that Germans were more liked than disliked by a margin of 50 to 40 percent; those who viewed reunification "with worries" were more likely to believe that Germans were more disliked than liked by a margin of 40 to 30 percent. Individuals who agreed there that was "too much anxiety in German society" were more likely to believe that Germans were more disliked than liked by a margin of 55 to 45 percent; those who disagreed were more likely to believe that Germans were more liked than disliked by a margin of 35 to 31 percent. Individuals who felt that the period after reunification was "happy" were more likely to believe Germans were more liked than disliked by a margin of 30 to 25 percent; individuals who believed that the period after reunification was difficult were more likely to believe that Germans were more disliked than liked by a margin of 59 to 50 percent. Finally, individuals who felt that reunification made life better were more likely to believe that Germans were more liked than disliked by a margin of 55 to 35 percent; individuals who believed that reunification made life worse were more likely to believe that Germans were more disliked than liked by a margin of 52 to 42 percent (*Allensbach Survey* 5062).

The findings indicate that when citizens perceived they had a negative image internationally, their feelings about reunification were also negative. Once again, a negative perception of *Fremdbild*, or Germany's image in world opinion, was associated with a negative perception of *Selbstbild*.

One may, of course, question whether a nation's citizens have an accurate perception of their country's international image. Certainly, Germans appear to have an inordinate sensitivity to their international image, even when other countries seem otherwise occupied. For instance, during the prewar Kuwaiti crisis between August 1, 1990, and January 15, 1991, the *Frankfurter Allgemeine Zeitung,* a German newspaper of record, contained almost as many references to world opinion on the upcoming German reunification as references to world opinion on the Iraqi invasion. By contrast, neither the *New York Times* nor the *Times of India* even mentioned German reunification in their references to world opinion during this period.[12] By 1992, reunification was a central aspect of German national consciousness, of how its citizens viewed their nation.

But the relationship between perceived international image and national consciousness is sufficient to indicate that at least on an individual level, citizens feel they must construct their sense of national identity from an internal negotiation between *Fremdbild* and *Selbstbild,* respectively. Of course, the correspondence between a nation's actual image in world opinion and its citizens' perceptions of their international image is difficult to establish, owing to the lack of time-series international survey data. However, some comparative studies do suggest that, at least within various countries, citizens have a relatively accurate view of how their fellow countrymen view another nation. A survey was conducted in 1989 to measure Germany's image in eight nations: France, Great Britain, Italy, Spain, the Netherlands, Sweden, the United States, and Japan. Respondents were asked two questions of relevance to this study: (1) "Do you like or dislike the Germans?" and (2) "Do most people in [your country] like or dislike the Germans?" The product moment correlation between the percentages of respondents who said, "I like Germans," and the percentages of respondents who said, "Most people in my country like Germans," was .8791, with a significance level less than .01. Similarly, the product moment correlation between the percentages who said, "I dislike Germans," and the percentages who said, "Most people in my country dislike Germans," was .9091, with a significance level less than .01.

In both cases, citizens' perceptions of Germany's image in each nation correlated very highly with the actual evaluation of this image on the national level. While these results represent only comparative opinions in different nations, they imply a strong association between perceived opinion about another country and the actual evaluation of that country within specific nations. As such, the results suggest that evaluations of world opinion regarding a given country are also generally known within nations, particularly in the nation in question (assuming it is an open society like Germany).

Crises of public confidence, which affect a nation's image in world opinion and citizens' national consciousness, interfere with the negotiation and construction of national identity. In Germany, the individual-level connections between national consciousness and international image were paralleled by macro-level negotiations in international forums and the media. One of the most fascinating examples of this was the swift reaction of German leaders and citizens to the challenges posed to their international image and, accordingly, to their national identity by the rise of anti-immigrant sentiments. Their responses targeted the rage that was tarnishing Germany's international image, as elites and non-elites struggled to distance themselves—and by association, their nation—from the criminal acts against immigrants. One possible alternative was to suppress one factor in the model of national pride (anti-immigrant sentiments) in order to elevate another factor in the model (their nation's international image). This will be discussed in the following section.

Macro-Level Efforts to Negotiate National Identity

For German intellectuals and citizens, the negotiation of their new identity became a matter of concern that involved all levels of society, not just the political leadership. In the wake of the anti-immigrant violence, German intellectuals began a highly publicized effort to redefine their nation abroad. This effort was directed toward domestic audiences and the international media primarily at the beginning of 1993.

On the elite level, intellectuals joined a campaign to counteract the negative images being broadcast in the media. Several German academics involved in international exchange programs submitted a letter to a German newspaper condemning the violence and stating that it was atypical of the nation's attitudes toward foreigners. Copies of this letter were circulated to academics in the United States who had participated in foreign exchange programs with German scholars. The clear intention here was to draw upon the goodwill these exchanges had generated to encourage their fellow intellectuals to defend their German colleagues. The effort, in and of itself, was neither insincere nor duplicitous; academic exchanges are, after all, as much about building friendships among nations as about sharing ideas. The only surprising aspect of this case was the *explicit* effort German intellectuals felt compelled to make on behalf of their nation.

Similarly, the Allensbach Institute, one of the most prestigious survey-and-research organizations in Germany, also saw fit to enter the discussion by publicizing a survey about citizens' negative attitudes toward the right-wing terrorists and their actions. Here again the purpose of the resulting report (which was available in English as well as German) was explicit. The report cites how "*pictures and news stories were transmitted to every corner of the globe*, creating the impression that a reunited Germany was on its way to becoming a hotbed of a new and dangerous right-wing extremism [emphases added]."[13] Included in the report was the rather interesting finding that respondents would rather live next door to a drug dealer than to a right-wing terrorist, emphasizing the isolation of the latter in German society. The report had a twofold message, aimed at both the nation's *Selbstbild* and *Fremdbild*, respectively. Its authors noted results that indicated the state of German national consciousness on the issue: "Rightwing rioters and hooligans, who until recently believed they were admired or at least tolerated by a silent majority of the German population, were operating under completely false assumptions."[14] They then followed up with their second intention to "curb the damage inflicted on *Germany's image abroad* [emphases added]"[15] with the survey results.

Elite efforts to burnish Germany's international image were complemented by nonelite mass action. German citizens also became involved in the effort to assert a more benevolent view of their national consciousness, both domestically and in the international media. In January 1993, candlelight vigils were held in dozens of major German cities to protest the anti-immigrant violence. Originally conceived by four individuals in Berlin as a means by which "the country's 'silent majority' [could] break its silence and show its repudiation of these attacks," the movement grew to involve over two million German citizens, or approximately one in every forty people in the country.[16] As with the publicity campaigns described above, this movement served two purposes. An organizer claimed that it addressed questions about German national consciousness, as "it [showed] that a majority of Germans are not secretly hostile to foreigners or sympathetic to fascism." As a result, he claimed, "the climate in Germany" had changed regarding citizens' public reactions to the attacks.[17] Beneath the surface, however, lingered the concern about the nation's *Fremdbild*. Another observer stated that these efforts were directed toward an international audience: "Some people go out and hold candles because they want to improve Germany's image in the world."[18]

German government officials were quick to use this publicity to establish a link between the efforts of citizens and opinion leaders and a drop in anti-immigrant violence in the early part of 1993. On March 17, 1993, Cornelia Schmalz-Jacobsen, the government's advisor on matters dealing with foreigners in Germany, announced:

> A year ago, even six months ago, it seemed that our society was paralyzed by violence . . . That has clearly changed. Our society and our political leaders have shown that this violence is something we do not want in our country.[19]

Schmalz-Jacobsen then attributed the "change in attitude" in part to the candlelight vigils and to "countless smaller initiatives by individuals and social groups." [20] *The Week in Germany*, a newsletter published by the German Information Center, echoed the statistics regarding the drop in attacks on foreigners in its March 19, 1993 edition.

All of these efforts illustrate a determined effort on the part of German citizens, intellectuals, and government officials to identify their national consciousness with antifascist and antixenophobic sentiments, and to protect Germany's international image after reunification. In part, because these individuals used their influence over media sources so effectively through careful public relations efforts, the negotiation appears to have been accomplished primarily in the nation's favor. Even as right-wing attacks increased again in the later months of 1993, analyses speculating about whether a resurgence of German nationalism was to blame did not reappear. Instead, these acts were interpreted as criminal behavior and they were treated as such by the international press.

This change in emphasis is reflected in the analysis of headlines in American newspapers regarding Germany's immigration issues for 1992 and 1993. In 1992, five major American newspapers carried thirty-one stories and editorials dealing with Germany's immigrant problems. [21] Of these, twenty-one, or 68 percent, had headlines concerning violence against immigrants, while ten, or 32 percent, dealt with the legal aspects of immigration policy in the FRG. In 1993, coverage of the immigration issue not only dropped in absolute terms, to twenty-one total stories or editorials, but the emphases changed dramatically as well. Violence against immigrants was represented in only three, or 14 percent, of the headlines, whereas the legal issues surrounding immigration occupied eighteen, or 86 percent, of the headlines.

The change in depictions of Germany in the foreign press paralleled changes in individual-level sentiments as well. The polls reflected increased optimism about the future among Germans after 1993. Among respondents in 1994, 58 percent said they faced the future with hope, up from 41 percent the previous year (*Allensbach Surveys*, 1993, 1994).

The image that Germans generally wished to project here is that in times of crisis, the competing narratives of German identity become melded into one, as citizens and leaders of the former Western and Eastern sectors seek to preserve their international image, and hence, their national pride. But this interpretation is too simplistic for a number of reasons. First, it falsely represents the negotiation of national identity as a process that has a defined beginning and end. The problems of negotiating identity within the context of two competing narratives about the fall of the Berlin Wall still exist for those in the West and the East. The process may have a definable beginning in reunification, but it continues as long as the reunited entity exists. Moreover, as one critic observed to me when I told this story, one does not wish to turn the process into a contest in which the "Bad Germans" are overcome through the goodwill and stringent efforts of the "Good Germans."

Second, simplifying the narrative obscures the actual conclusions one may draw from the events and the survey results. Recall that one of the individuals who organized the candlelight vigils declared that they showed that Germans were neither secretly hostile to foreigners nor sympathetic to fascism. Further, the survey findings and the government officials added that the vast majority of German citizens condemned anti-immigrant violence. But three separate issues are mixed here: (1) whether citizens generally held anti-immigrant attitudes; (2) whether citizens were open to fascist appeals; and (3) whether citizens condoned anti-immigrant violence. Even during the height of the attacks, evidence from the survey indicated the latter two attitudes did not exist. The *Allensbach Survey* referenced earlier showed that Germans generally considered right-wing hooligans to be undesirable in their society, and in September 1991, 75 percent of Germans felt that violence against foreigners should be severely punished.[22] However, the issue of foreigners and immigrants in Germany was not so easily dismissed. In December 1991, 65 percent of respondents agreed with the statement, "I have nothing against foreigners, but there are simply too many of them here"; similarly, in the same survey, 71 percent said they thought that most of the people in Germany "were against foreigners being employed" in their country.[23] Intolerance for fascist sympathizers and their violence does not translate into a tolerance for immigrants and foreigners, as many of the previous statements suggested.

This is not to say that the public demonstrations of German elites and citizens against antiforeigner violence were disingenuous. German citizens were clearly pained by the violence occurring in their country. I was told by an acquaintance who was visiting the United States at the time the anti-immigrant riots began that she literally wept when she saw these images of Germany on her television screen in America. But the root issue remains the preservation of national pride in the context of challenges due to changes in one's country's global status. Anti-immigrant attitudes are a means of bolstering the primordial aspects of national pride, and perhaps reconciling—at least for a time—competing narratives about what constitutes one nation. But those attitudes can cause harm to a nation's international image, and hence, to national pride, if they are expressed in a violent manner. The German people and their government appeared to have renegotiated their national identity by delicately balancing the underlying anti-immigrant attitudes common to the primordial aspects of *Selbstbild*, while acting against the overt violence that threatened their *Fremdbild*. In this instance, the society appears to have defused an instance of global rage that both followed from, and threatened, their national pride at this time. It remains to be seen whether this balance can be maintained under increasing pressures of immigration, particularly given Germany's membership in the European Union.

Conclusion

Global rage and reaction followed the steps outlined at the beginning of the chapter. In both regions of the formerly divided nation, there was clear evidence of *ressentiment*, or a status anxiety, resulting from the collapse of the Eastern bloc and related to national identity.. This sentiment was reflected in a resurgent nationalism associated with anomie and national identity, which exploded into rage among violent elements in the population. Because of this violence, we discovered a clear relationship between citizens' national consciousness (*Selbstbild*) and their perception of Germany's international image in world opinion (*Fremdbild*). Finally, in response to these challenges, the individual-level associations (and negotiations) of national identity were paralleled by macro-level negotiations carried out by political leaders, intellectual elites, and citizens, who directed their concerns toward a national and international audience by means of media and international scholarly contacts.

One may glean further from these events that the primordial aspects of identity tend to come to the fore in times of crisis. The question of who was "rightfully" German was not only an issue of economic rights and privileges, but also one of culture, identity, and history. Here, it is not surprising that anti-immigrant sentiment should arise, in part due to the competing narratives that existed in the former Eastern and Western sectors before and after the fall of the Berlin Wall and reunification. While the first group attributes the fall of the GDR to a failed regime, the second attributes it to a failed system of beliefs. It might be easier, in this context, to transfer the status anxieties that result to assertions of who is "not German"—for example, the immigrants from other nations. Such a transfer also avoids reconciling the different historical narratives about World War II and its aftermath on the two sides of the fallen Wall.

To what extent may one generalize these findings from Germany to other nations, though? Certainly, German reunification and the original reasons for its division might define a special set of circumstances and feelings of responsibility for their citizens. Perhaps there are regions where citizens are not as conscious or concerned about their international image in world opinion. Indeed, reactions to global rage are often neither as straightforward nor self-conscious as those that occurred in Germany. These questions raise the issue of the uniqueness of the German experience in the post–Cold War era. However, the processes of renegotiating national identity and its potential for upheaval are not limited to Germany alone. Other nations or groups created, and confronted, different threats to national pride and global security in the post–Cold War era.

4

China's Two Faces: The Contradiction of Chinese "Uniqueness"

•

Can states commit acts of rage? To this point, we have only dealt with cases of violence by non-state actors that actually threatened the state's authority, either indirectly (as in the case of al-Qaida) or directly (as in the case of anti-immigrant violence in Germany). However, our model of national identity includes increasing support for the institutions and laws of the country as a means of bolstering national pride. If leaders perceive that the state's authority is threatened, they may, in certain instances, use its coercive power not only to preserve the state or regime, but also to bolster their citizens' sense of pride. Wars based upon nationalistic sentiment, such as those in the Balkans and elsewhere, are post–Cold War examples of acts of rage committed by political leaders to assert their nations' identities. These actions may be counterproductive if they in turn hurt a country's international image. But in the post–Cold War era , the importance of reputation in world opinion is a lesson that some nations still need to learn.

The negotiation of a "usable" national identity often harks back to some defining historical moment in a country's past. The associated events may have preceded the end of the Cold War. In Germany, for instance, this moment was the Holocaust. For China, that moment occurred in Tiananmen Square in 1989. China had been a closed society from the 1948 revolution to the 1970s, allowing few, if any, Western visitors inside its borders. Richard Nixon visited China in 1972 in an attempt at rapprochement aimed at balancing Soviet power in the world. Chinese leaders then began a slow process of opening the country to more visitors in the following years. The events in Tiananmen Square occurred less than two decades later.

The details of this incident are etched upon the minds of observers and recorded in the film archives of major media outlets. What began as a series of postings on a government-sanctioned "democracy wall" in Beijing became the site of massive demonstrations by college students and others for greater democratization of China's system. As the crowds grew daily, the government ordered them to disperse. When they failed to do so, the army was called in to clear the students from the Square. But in an incredible act of defiance, the troops stationed in the city refused to march on young people from the same area. One vivid image captured by a photojournalist symbolized the young demonstrators' defiance, as a single student stood before a tank and halted its progress toward the demonstrations. The fear grew among Chinese leaders that the actions that had felled the government of Ferdinand Marcos in the Philippines in 1986 would be repeated in China.

The government was quick to respond to the threat. Troops were brought in from the provinces to break up the demonstrations. On television screens around the world, tanks and other military vehicles could be seen running over students and killing them in a massive attack upon the unarmed crowd. The state had reasserted its power and went about punishing the individuals deemed responsible for the demonstrations.

The extent to which the Chinese leadership was unaccustomed to the power of the global media was represented starkly in an interview with the officer in charge of the massacre. When he was accused of committing an atrocity, the officer did not defend his actions as necessary to restore order. Instead, he reacted as was the custom in a closed society—he denied it happened. The reporters asked more detailed questions, which were followed by more detailed denials. In each case, however, the officer's statements were undercut by footage of the troops' actions interspersed with the interview. The coverage followed this pattern: denial, brutal footage, more specific denial, and more brutal footage, until the credibility of the officer and the Chinese government was virtually destroyed.

Why would the official respond with such blatantly false denials? These denials were not merely a matter of individuals in a closed society trying unsuccessfully to respond to a new situation. Rather, it had to do with Chinese perceptions of the West and its media that had persisted for a long time prior to the massacre at Tiananmen Square. Wang Jisi notes how at that time, it was "still widely believed among China's political elites that the United States, joined by other hostile external forces, [was] intent on efforts to conquer, divide, destabilize, and demonize China."[1] If such a perception were not sufficient to justify actions against those who would destabilize the system with Western ideas, they were supplemented by a more generalized feeling of violation. As Zi Zhongyun notes, "The trauma of wounded national pride has become a recurrent mental pain for Chinese, in general, and social elite in particular."[2] In the presence of such feelings, expressions of violent rage by the government against the very representation of Western ideas become comprehensible. As Zhongyun notes:

> Rulers of successive Chinese governments tend to resist Western ideas of democracy and individual freedom, regarding them as a threat to their rule, and the imperialistic behavior of Western democratic powers inadvertently allows them to appeal to popular nationalistic feelings. Most liberal intellectuals also fear the loss of national cultural identity in the face of the strong impact of Western influence.[3]

However, these attitudes were antithetical to another desire among the Chinese leadership—"to integrate China into the international community."[4] The former narrative describes suspicion and feelings of *ressentiment* toward the outside world. The latter narrative describes a desire for recognition by the outside world. These opposing narratives provide the backdrop for the expressions of rage and reaction that affected Chinese national identity between 1995 and 1997.

China's Quest for International Status

China's attempts to take what it perceived as its rightful place in the international community were clearly hampered by the legacy of Tiananmen Square. In the 1990s, the Chinese government attempted to change its image by hosting the 1995 International Women's Conference (IWC) in Beijing. This conference, sponsored by the United Nations, was meeting to discuss women's issues for the fourth time since its inception. Chinese officials saw hosting it a means by which their international image could be enhanced. It did not turn out that way. It would be a few more years before China would have another opportunity to advance a positive international image, when the handover of Hong Kong to China took place in July 1997. The story of these two events and the different manner in which the Chinese government responded to them illustrates potential lessons learned in the negotiation of national identity.

But the story of this negotiation does not just involve China. The 1995 conference involved numerous negotiations regarding the national identities and international images of the participants that invite comparisons with the Chinese case. Past attempts to create agreements about what constituted universal rights of women had been thwarted by East–West and North–South conflicts that had overshadowed potential areas of consensus. Success was by no means assured even in the post–Cold War context; that agreement was in fact achieved showed that negotiations between national identity and global image were indeed possible. It is therefore useful to look at this successful negotiation before turning to China's failure in this regard in 1995.

This chapter will study the IWC in Beijing as an example of two clashes: the clash between nations, as women struggled to produce an international standard for women's rights amenable to their nations' norms; and the clash between the Chinese government and other nations, as China struggled to achieve the international status that it felt its standing as an emerging economic superpower warranted. The narrative content of the coverage suggests that this negotiation between identity and image was more successful in the first instance than in the second.

For evidence we examine the treatment of world opinion on the IWC in two newspapers: the *New York Times* (NYT) and the Chinese language *People's Daily* (PD). We assume that the manner in which press opinion treats identity issues is reflected in its coverage of world opinion. As such, this discussion raises the question of whether evidence of this process may be detected in the way in which the two newspapers construct world opinion. It is not assumed that either paper presents a complete or unbiased description of international public opinion, or that the two papers taken together can map the entire process. By explaining how the newspapers approach world opinion on issues relevant to national identity, the negotiation between their perspectives helps illustrate the process of identity formation on the national and international levels.

The analysis follows the four hypotheses delineated in Chapter 1. First, comparisons of media accounts are used to illustrate the feelings of *ressentiment* illustrated in the Chinese press. Second, we trace the reaction of the Chinese government to the perspective on world opinion offered in the American newspaper; not surprisingly, the government reacts with repressive tactics and anger when confronted with negative judgments in the *New York Times*. Third, we trace China's unsuccessful attempt to negotiate a national identity that enhances its status in the world to the contradictory narratives described in this chapter. These conflicting narratives help explain coverage of world opinion on the IWC in the *New York Times* and the *People's Daily*, especially as it relates to China's perspective on its nation's identity. Finally, we deal with the negotiation of identity in the handover of Hong Kong to China in 1997 and observe how the newspapers reflect a different perspective on China's global image; in this case, the two narratives are reconciled more successfully, without the expressions of rage that marked the negotiations of identity in 1995.

Before turning to China's negotiation of identity, though, it is useful to begin by considering similar processes that were carried out by other nations at the IWC. These negotiations illustrate that even the thorniest issues could be worked out, resulting in perhaps the most successful agreement on global women's rights that the conference had ever achieved. The first negotiation involves media coverage of world opinion on three related areas of conflict: (1) whether the United States should participate in the conference, in the light of its criticisms of China's human rights record; (2) whether the Vatican representative would be able to present the Vatican's perspective in a manner that would allow it to avoid international isolation; and (3) whether a consensus could be reached about the global rights of women that would have relevance across national boundaries. The media reports on the conference suggest that all of these negotiations appeared to enjoy some degree of success. I then attempt to explain media coverage of world opinion on these identity issues in the *New York Times* and the *People's Daily*. The resulting consensus emerges as a continuing story, in which newspaper coverage in the two dailies eventually converges to reflect an apparent agreement in their interpretations of world opinion.

The next negotiation involves media coverage of world opinion on China's behavior as host nation to the conference. The Chinese government wished the conference to be a public relations coup that would earn them international prestige and polish their global image. However, the analysis suggests that this negotiation between China's national consciousness and the international image it was striving to influence was less successful than the negotiations described earlier. The study shows significant differences in the two newspapers' perspectives on world opinion regarding China's behavior as host to the conference. These differences, and China's inability to negotiate a national identity that would garner it more international respect, are due in part to China's perspective on the process of world opinion. The process of world opinion did not go to completion in a manner satisfactory to the Chinese; this perspective is reflected in the *People's Daily*'s constructions of world opinion on the subject before and after the conference. Instead of repairing and enhancing China's damaged reputation in the world community, this negotiation became another example of global rage perpetrated by the Chinese government in its perceived defense of the state's authority. However, using respect for state authority as a means to bolster and protect national pride had ramifications for China's *Fremdbild* that did more damage to its sense of national identity and pride.

The Media, *Fremdbild*, and *Selbstbild*

This chapter studies all references[5] to world opinion in stories and editorials dealing with the IWC from the *New York Times* and the *People's Daily*, from August 6 to September 25, 1995. This subject was referenced twenty-two times in the American newspaper and forty-six times in the Chinese newspaper. A content analysis was performed on each of these stories using a predesigned survey instrument. References were initially classified as explicit or implicit. Explicit references used synonyms such as "world opinion," "international opinion," or "global-public opinion." Implicit references attributed some attitude or opinion to the world or the international community, in such phrases as the opinions of "international society," "world attention," or a "common voice from all over the world." Explicit references appeared in only two of the sixty-eight cases studied; all other references were implicit.

The survey also analyzed (1) the date of each reference, (2) the specific subject of each reference, and (3) the manner in which each reference used and combined the six key components of world opinion described earlier.[6]

The Agenda for World Opinion Regarding the IWC

As noted above, the issues dealing with world opinion during the IWC can be divided into two categories. The first concerns the negotiation of consensus regarding global women's issues and individual nations' national interests. These stories comprised 41.2 percent of all references: 7.4 percent dealt with the question of the United States' participation in the conference, 5.9 percent dealt with the potential isolation of the Vatican representative, and 27.9 percent dealt with the negotiation of a final consensus on global women's rights. The second concerns China's world reputation as a host for the conference. These stories comprised 58.9 percent of all references: 29.5 percent dealt with positive judgments on China, 16.2 percent dealt with negative judgments on China, and 13.2 percent dealt with neutral judgments on China. The timing and newspaper source of stories in these two categories reflect different degrees of consensus on world opinion between the American and Chinese newspapers on the two subjects.

The Search for Consensus I: Constructing a Global Document on Women's Rights

The search for consensus among delegates to the IWC began with a controversy over the conference's importance when compared with the United States' interest in isolating China for human rights abuses. Critics charged that the United States should boycott the conference. They argued that American interests in foreign policy and in protesting China's human rights policies were more important than any potential global consensus on women's rights. A United States boycott would have sent a message to China on these issues, but it would have also undermined the legitimacy of the conference. An American boycott could also have isolated the United States by making it appear more concerned with their conflicts with China than with creating an international consensus on women's rights.

The graph in figure 4.1 illustrates the references to this story in the *New York Times*; each line represents one story, by date. As the data indicate, the issue of American participation disappears as an issue in world opinion once the Chinese released Harry Wu, a U.S. citizen who was investigating human rights abuses in China. The release, along with Hillary Clinton's speech on women's rights as human rights, settled the issue of American participation. These compromises preserved American interests without undermining the legitimacy of the conference or the global consensus it hoped to reach on women's rights.

Figure 4.1 also shows the timing of stories regarding the potential isolation of the Vatican because of its strict stand on such issues as abortion and birth control. Prior to the conference, it was suspected that the Vatican would be the one holdout to a global consensus on these and other issues regarding women. However, the Vatican representative was successful in negotiating a face-saving compromise in which the Vatican endorsed the use of condoms for preventing disease (although not technically for birth control) and tacitly accepted other provisions on similar issues. Once

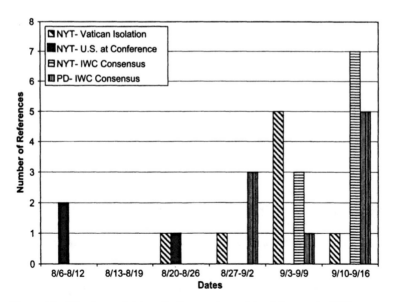

Figure 4.1 Number and dates of references to world opinion on the IWC consensus, by newspaper

again, the nation's representative successfully balanced national interest with international reputation to avoid isolation.

The results of these and other compromises are illustrated in the final coverage of world opinion on the IWC in the *New York Times* and the *People's Daily.* As one article in the American newspaper indicated, the conference could have represented a "clash of civilizations" as it struggled in vain to reach a global consensus on women's rights. However, the coverage of the conference in both newspapers concluded that an international consensus did emerge that delegates found compatible with their sense of national identities, albeit after extended negotiations. The pattern of stories on the conference's outcome by date suggests that both the American and the Chinese newspapers concluded that world opinion had recognized this consensus by September 16. On this date, both newspapers ran most of their stories or editorials noting how international public opinion reflected the consensus that had been reached.

The pattern of references thus reflects an apparent process in which potential issues of isolation (of China by the United States, and the United States and the Vatican by other countries) are resolved through compromise and an international consensus is reached. If the threat of isolation had not produced the desired results—if the Chinese had not responded to the American threat of a boycott of the conference, or the Vatican had not responded to the threat of isolation on women's issues—the consensus would have been jeopardized. The theory of negotiation of national identity helps explain the pattern of stories in the two newspapers. The data suggest that according to these two media outlets, world opinion recognized the agreements reached and the versions of national identity negotiated at the conference.

The Search for Consensus II: China's Quest for International Prestige

For the Chinese government, hosting the IWC was, in part, an exercise in global public relations. The Chinese leaders were anxious to enhance their reputation as a forward-looking nation dedicated to promoting women's rights and celebrating the achievements of their own female citizens. They were also motivated by a desire to be considered viable candidates to host the Summer Olympics and to enhance their worldwide reputation after the massacre in Tiananmen Square and subsequent accusations of human rights abuses. All of their efforts during the conference were therefore directed toward affecting world opinion regarding China's image. However, the Chinese leaders' actions met with mixed results. Demonstrators clashed with police on a number of occasions, and potentially dissident statements from inside the People's Republic were effectively silenced. Indeed, even Hillary Clinton's speech criticizing human rights abuses was moved to a venue away from the main conference and was not widely disseminated among the Chinese people. As an exercise in negotiating a national identity between *Selbstbild* and *Fremdbild,* these attempts were, for the most part, unsuccessful in achieving the image enhancement the Chinese leaders desired. Instead, the primary story became the violence and expressions of rage from the Chinese government.

This lack of success helps explain the patterns of newspaper coverage on world opinion regarding Chinese efforts to improve their international image by hosting the IWC. Figure 4.2 displays all of the stories and editorials that refer to China's image as host of the conference and whether world opinion on that image was positive, negative, or neutral, organized by date.

All of the references in the *New York Times* are negative. Negative reactions in world opinion are also noted in the *People's Daily* during an overlapping time period, although the Chinese newspaper often observed that the Western press and other sources unfriendly to China encouraged such criticisms. The neutral and positive references are confined only to the *People's Daily,* preceding and following the negative references. This pattern

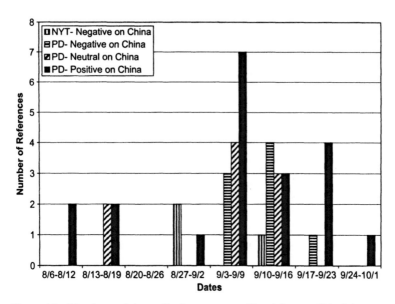

Figure 4.2   Number and dates of references to world opinion on China's image, by newspaper

indicates that while the Chinese newspaper acknowledged the negative reactions in other media sources (especially those from the United States), their writers acknowledged little movement toward a consensus or resolution of the two opposing views. The *People's Daily* pursued its government's agenda, asserting that the conference granted China an international prestige that it was due because of its emerging status as an economic superpower. The dates and content of references to world opinion show that the American and Chinese media sources held to different perspectives on world opinion. These perspectives reflect the failed process of negotiation between *Selbstbild* and *Fremdbild*, in contrast to both newspapers' perspectives of world opinion on the IWC's success.

The reasons for these different perspectives become evident when one examines the motivations and resources of the actors involved in the negotiation of national identity in these two cases. Regarding the success of the conference, the United States was a principal player with an interest in a global consensus on women's issues to justify its participation in the conference. All of its media resources were dedicated to covering the threats of isolation and the emerging consensus, thereby helping to move the process along. The Chinese media had another goal in mind: their nation's stature would be enhanced if they hosted a successful international conference on women's rights.

In the second case, the Chinese government was the principal player with an interest in seeing that its international image was enhanced. The *People's Daily* dedicated its resources to this end, constructing world opinion in a manner favorable to its nation. By contrast, the *New York Times,* reflecting the American perspective on world opinion, did not share these interests; indeed, the U.S. government wished, at once, to justify American participation in the conference, while not signaling a tolerance for what it perceived as Chinese human rights abuses. As such, the American newspaper did not share a similar interest in describing a successful negotiation on Chinese terms.

This conclusion begs the question of why differing perspectives on world opinion in this case turned out to be irreconcilable. After all, "negotiation" assumes that differing perspectives can be altered so that some consensus may be reached.[7] The difficulty in resolving these differences can be traced, in part, to the different notions of world opinion represented in the Chinese and Western newspapers. Further, the Chinese perspective on world opinion was one that, until then, had been particularly suited to the manner in which China previously constructed its national identity. However, in this case, the country's competing narratives created a contradiction that interfered with its quest for international recognition.

Comparative Structures of World Opinion in the
New York Times and the People's Daily

The analysis begins with the construction of a simple measure known as the Cumulative Index of World Opinion; this measure is used to indicate the depth of coverage on world opinion in a given newspaper.[8] It consists of a simple additive scale composed of the six components of world opinion described in Part 1 of this book; for each reference, the presence of a component is coded as 1, its absence is coded as 0, and the results are added to a score between 0 and 6. The greater the "depth" of a newspaper's use of world opinion, the higher the average score for references in that source.

The contrast between the American and Chinese newspapers on this index is striking. The *New York Times* had an average score of 4.57 while the *People's Daily* had an average score of 1.5; the Pearson's *r* value for this difference is .8775, with a significance of .0000. Moreover, there are clear patterns to the components that the Chinese newspaper tended to omit or emphasize relative to the American newspaper; not all components were more likely to appear in the latter newspaper.

The Chinese newspaper was slightly more likely to reference the nation's image than the American newspaper, by a margin of 56 to 36.4 percent; this difference is not significant. The Chinese newspaper was also more likely to reference the world as a unit than the American newspaper by a margin of 95.7 to 57.1 percent; this difference is significant ($r = .4822$; significance $= .0000$).

By contrast, all references in the American newspaper included the moral component of world opinion, as compared with only 6.5 percent of references in the Chinese newspaper ($r = .9070$; significance $= .0000$). The differences regarding the pragmatic component of world opinion were similarly skewed: 81.8 percent of the American references included it, while none of the Chinese references included it ($r = .8676$; significance $= .0000$). Finally, the American newspaper was more likely to reference the power of world opinion (90.9 percent of cases versus 4.3 percent of cases; $r = .8656$; significance $= .0000$) and the threat of isolation (63.6 percent of cases versus no cases; $r = .7363$; significance $= .0000$).

The analysis indicates an emphasis upon the world as a unit and the nation's image in the *People's Daily*. This finding is hardly surprising, given the interests of the Chinese government in hosting the conference. If a nation's leaders or citizens are interested in increasing their prestige internationally, their newspaper would be expected to focus upon questions of image and the world as a unit observing them in their perspectives on world opinion.

This finding is underscored when one compares the images upon which the two newspapers focus. The American newspaper was more likely to reference the image that a nation presented to the world, or its *Fremdbild*, by a margin of 68.8 to 20 percent; the Chinese newspaper was more likely to reference the image a nation has of itself, or its *Selbstbild*, by a margin of 55 to 0 percent. Since the newspapers were equally likely to reference both types of images together, the symmetric λ of .3333 indicates that the earlier margins were significant. This emphasis suggests that the Chinese government's concern with its international image, as reflected in the newspaper, was focused inward toward its own sense of image and national identity.

Equally relevant to the Chinese search for international prestige, how-ever, is what the *People's Daily* omitted in its references to world opinion. References to the moral and pragmatic components of world opinion, the power of world opinion, and the threat of international isolation are vir-tually absent. Combined with the previous results, these omissions suggest a concern with world opinion that is lacking in content and authority. The sense of world opinion in the Chinese newspaper appears inner-directed; the emphasis on the world as a unit and on its own self-image suggests a concern with what the Chinese government expects from the world, given its emerging position as an economic power. A quotation from the *People's Daily* clearly illustrates the Chinese government's intentions in hosting the conference:

> The Chinese Communist Party and government always support women's liberation. The founding of the New China put an end to Chinese women's thousands of years of suffering and oppression, and marked the beginning of a new age where Chinese women enjoy equal rights as men politically, economically, and socially, as well as in their family lives . . . Chinese women have made great contributions to maintaining world peace . . . By hosting this world conference on women, [the] Chinese government has made a great contribution to the international community . . . *It has also provided a good opportunity for China to know the world as well as for the world to know China.* (*People's Daily*, 1995a, p. 1; emphases added)

Certainly, the search for international prestige must include mutual scrutiny of a nation by the world, and vice versa. But one must acknow-ledge the power of world opinion (as expressed in the threat of isolation) and the content of world opinion (as expressed in the values and interests one shares with other nations) to understand how one's international image is forged.

Heeding the dictates of world opinion requires that one pay attention to the mores and interests of other nations and be concerned with the possible threat of isolation. A perspective on world opinion that focuses primarily on its effects within the nation does not allow for the crucial negotiations between national consciousness and international image that are necessary for the construction of a "usable" national identity—at least in the sense that "usable" suggests a national identity of which leaders and citizens can be proud because it carries status beyond the borders of the nation. To concentrate only on what one desires from world opinion without acknowledging or heeding its demands is to attempt to construct national identity from only one side of the negotiation. The necessary elements in the process of identity negotiation thus help explain why this process, as described in the *People's Daily*, was less successful than the negotiations in the media involving the delegates to the IWC.

In the case of the IWC, one was able to observe the threat of isolation and its resolution regarding the United States and the Vatican in the two newspapers' coverage of world opinion. Both nations yielded ground regarding the moral and pragmatic aspects of world opinion. The U.S. representatives' actions implied that the possibility of reaching a global consensus on women's issues temporarily overruled their disagreements with the Chinese over human rights and other issues. The Vatican representative's actions implied that this consensus temporarily overruled the Vatican's reservations about the morality of certain positions regarding the family and birth control. In both cases, the threat of isolation was extended, the actors responded, and the process of world opinion was able to go to completion.

The theory of negotiation thus appears to explain partially how the two newspapers cover world opinion, particularly as it relates to questions of national identity. But one must question the usefulness of these findings. For this conclusion begs the question of why analysts should be interested in the construction of a concept such as world opinion beyond the academic observation that press opinion on this subject, like so many others, seems to reflect the dominant governmental and private interests of the newspaper's nation of origin. We suggest that the usefulness of this approach is illustrated by addressing two further questions: (1) Why is the perspective on world opinion in the *People's Daily* so unsuited to the nation's desire to achieve some measure of international prestige, if media outlets tend to interpret world opinion in a manner congruent with their national interests? and (2) Do the differences between the perspectives on world opinion in the American and the Chinese newspaper make world opinion an ethnocentric concept leaning toward the West, and of little use or interest for understanding the creation of national identity in non-Western nations? While it is probably impossible to answer such broad questions on the basis of only two newspapers and a limited number of cases, we suggest that some useful insights might be drawn from the analysis for further research. These insights trace the construction of world opinion in the *People's Daily* in part to the strategies Chinese leaders have employed in the past to legitimize their rule and construct national identity within their borders.

The Cultural Context of the Construction of Identity

Once again, we reflect upon the effects of the collapse of the Soviet Union and the general repudiation of Marxist–Leninist models of development. As a nation that had contributed one version of the Communist state, China was especially vulnerable to feelings of *ressentiment,* or status anxiety, as it had formerly drawn its international position not only from its wealth and strength, but also from its position in the historical evolution to a Communist society. As Lucian W. Pye notes in an article appropriately titled "China's Quest for Respect":

> With the collapse of Communism in Eastern Europe, and the need to erase the memories of the ideological fanaticism of the Cultural Revolution and the Mao Zedong era, the leadership is confronted with a crisis of faith in Marxism and Leninism. Therefore it has had to look for a new basis of legitimacy, and it has sought to find it in nationalism.
>
> However, Beijing suddenly finds that the only version of nationalism available is a bankrupt one, barely better than an angry xenophobia, a crude "we" versus "them" view of the world ... Without the high culture nor the popular culture providing a coherent sense of Chinese nationalism, the country is left without a shared and inspiring vision of what the nation should stand for in the world of nation-states.[9]

The Chinese leadership had, in the past, thrived on existing within a closed society. As such, it was virtually impossible to threaten China with international isolation; their isolation was part of their national identity. This approach may be denounced as "crude" or "xenophobic," but it served the leadership's purposes while China remained a state representative of the Marxist–Leninist model.

Ironically, China was one of the nations poised to benefit when that model collapsed. As Pye notes, the economic reforms mounted by Deng should have made the Chinese "more self-confident and at ease with the outside world" particularly since "the Chinese take seriously the forecast that they will soon have the world's largest economy ... [Yet] Somehow all of their accomplishments over the past two decades have not produced as dramatic a change in their *international status* as they had expected to believe is their due [emphases added]."[10] As a result, *ressentiment* grew toward those whom Chinese leaders felt were depriving them of their due; it is not surprising that in this context, rage should follow upon criticism from the West.

Pye advocates a solution: the United States should assert "what it foresees as China's place in the world," and China should respond in such a way as to "start a debate as to alternative visions" in a negotiation that would "advance the quest for a new national identity." [11] This conflict was reflected in the alternative visions of world opinion in the *New York Times* and the *People's Daily* regarding China's image in hosting the IWC.

But therein lies the key conflict that prevents the sort of dialogue and negotiation that Pye advocates. First, the dialogue cannot be just with the United States alone (although given American influence in the international media that might be a good place to start); eventually, that dialogue must be between China and the international community, considered as a whole.[12] Second, this dialogue must take into consideration the values and interests of the international community. Chinese leaders have been reluctant to take this step in the past, precisely because they constructed national identity according to their differences with the mores and concerns of other nations and their embrace of their own international isolation. A great part of their identity to this point has been that their status was "special" and separate from other nations in the world. Culturally, the threat of isolation is something that has operated within Chinese society, not outside it, and certainly not against it. Further, this threat has protected the society from outsiders. In this way, the internal power of isolation has defined Chinese identity so that it has, as a matter of course, been isolated from the rest of the world. For the Chinese, there was no force of world opinion separate from their national consciousness, and there was no national consciousness separate from the state's authority. Defense of state authority and defense of national pride have thus become inextricable in the leaders' minds.

Hence, by definition, negative world opinion is, for the Chinese, attributed to Western (or American) manipulation of the international media, rather than to any "genuine" world opinion. As such, pronouncements on moral and pragmatic interests serving "all nations," (but not China, from their leaders' point of view), were less likely to be acceptable. From the Chinese perspective, who they thought they were defined who they were; *Fremdbild* was simply an extension of *Selbstbild*. But this assumption can only be maintained if a nation has minimal contact with the rest of the world. If other nations only enter the equation when a country wishes a degree of international recognition, there is little room for negotiation of a national identity acceptable to both sides. The Chinese perception of national identity has, to this point, truncated the perception of world opinion by denying its influence on China's image of itself. As Zhongyun notes, China is presently in

> the phase opened by Deng Xiaoping . . . in this period, great efforts are being made to integrate China into the international community and Mao's idea of "world revolution" is completely abandoned. Logically, this is the antithesis of "Chinese exceptionalism."[13]

The *People's Daily*, in the quotation cited earlier, seemed to acknowledge the necessity for "the world to know China and for China to know the world" in order for the nation to achieve the status they believed they deserved. However, when one examines the coverage of the IWC in the *New York Times*, and the critique of that coverage in the *People's Daily*, one discovers that the latter dismissed messages regarding world opinion that the Chinese government did not wish to hear. First, from the *New York Times* came the following critique of China's motives and actions:

> Chinese leaders remain determined to prevent discussion about individual rights and social and political change from seeping into their own tightly repressed society. *Coverage by the official Chinese media has been highly selective. But having sought the international prestige of playing host to this conference, Beijing is obliged to drop its attempts to censor the participants.* Instead it should let its own people benefit from the ideas and experiences discussed at the meetings . . .
> *At first China saw its role in the conference as a way to advertise its recent economic gains and its determination to take a more active place in international affairs* . . . But later Chinese leaders began to panic about what might happen as tens of thousands of experienced political activists and representatives from the *world's press* descended on Beijing. (*New York Times* 1995; emphases added)

In a response of sorts, the *People's Daily* reflected the angry perspective of its leaders:

> Certain Western media were blind and broke the rule of objectivity in news reports . . . [Their reports] deliberately distorted facts in order to attack China, which reflects the corruption of Western media and of press ethics . . . *These reports were filled with pride and prejudice of Western cultural imperialism . . . in an attempt to impose Western values on others.* (*People's Daily* 1995b; emphases added)

The Chinese case therefore presents elements that appear contradictory—on the one hand, their leaders express no fear of isolation, while on the other, they covet a higher level of status in the international community. Similarly, they want "the world to know China and China to know the world," but they accuse the Western media of cultural imperialism when it disapproves of China's actions. These contradictions are partially explained when one understands that the Chinese model their society upon the family: the parents (here, the government) guide the children (here, the citizens) in a hierarchical manner that allows limited opportunity for negotiation. There is little need for discussion, since it is assumed that the leaders know what is best for the people and for the good of the majority. As the official newspaper of the Chinese government, the *People's Daily* is a critical instrument for defining what national identity means for the Chinese people. It would be considered culturally inappropriate for Chinese citizens to question this interpretation, the equivalent of challenging one's parents or other caretakers who look after one's well-being. The state and its authority occupy this position in Chinese society not just because of traditions of autocratic rule, but also because they are viewed as a bulwark against invasion and internal chaos. In this sense, the primordial and instrumental aspects of identity become virtually inseparable, which creates a fundamental conflict with the United States specifically and the West generally. As Jisi notes:

> Chinese nationalism . . . emphasizes two things. The first is national pride, including the richness of Chinese civilization, its glorious ancient past, and the cohesiveness of a single, unified nation . . . The second is the national humiliation inflicted by Western imperialism in recent history . . .
>
> Chinese nationalism is clearly targeted at Western domination of the world. On the part of American nationalism, the conservatives and liberals alike find Chinese policies and practices alien to their principles. While the conservatives dislike China's centralized political system and see China's rising power as threatening to American national security, the liberals express antipathy toward what they describe as intolerance of diversity under the community leadership.[14]

As stated above, China also extends this vision of itself to the international community. Its leaders think of themselves as having an ethical and economic position that defines them as one of the "parent nations" to the world; they view the United States and other major powers in a similar manner. With such a view of one's place in the world, negotiation to establish one's identity becomes more difficult, as criticisms of one "parent" nation by another, to extend the metaphor, are considered inappropriate or rude. The challenge for the Chinese government, then, is to find a manner of conduct as a member of the international community that serves its purposes. This quandary helps to explain the particular pattern of references to world opinion in the Chinese newspaper.

One might argue, however, that to critique China's perspective on world opinion is to impose a Western vision of this concept upon it, as the second quotation from the *People's Daily* argues. Certainly, there is sufficient evidence that the United States exerts an inordinate influence over the international media, and one would expect it to use the media to serve its own interests. Hence, any critique of China's notion of world opinion could be interpreted as ethnocentrism at best, or a bald attempt to gain hegemony over China in the name of commonly held values in world opinion at worst. In either case, the newspapers' different perspectives call into question the usefulness of world opinion as a concept for the construction of national identity.

The problem with this conclusion is that it is not solely the beliefs or interests of the West that make an issue of China's national identity—it is also the desire of the Chinese leaders to achieve a level of international status that they feel they deserve and that they covet highly. The Chinese newspaper may legitimately argue over the *content* of world opinion; but the Chinese leaders' desire for international recognition and status recognizes the *existence* of world opinion. However, they will not obtain the prestige they seek if they do not permit negotiations between their national consciousness and their international image to take place—negotiations that must take into account the structure and demands of world opinion and that heed the opinions of other nations, even though the Chinese leadership need not accept them entirely. Hence, the vision of world opinion in the *People's Daily*, which omits its power, the fear of isolation, and its moral and pragmatic components, is necessarily unsuited for this negotiation. In this sense, the accusations of ethnocentrism or Western hegemony become less relevant; the critical consideration is that the insular view of national identity that served China so well in the past no longer suits the interests of its citizens and leaders. Wholesale repression is no longer an option in defending Chinese national identity on the world stage. Governmental acts of rage only tarnish the reputation and respect China's leaders have been trying to gain. Such judgments are not advanced as a partisan criticism of the Chinese leadership; rather, they argue that a strategy that worked under certain circumstances no longer serves its purposes.

Renegotiating Identity: The Handover of Hong Kong to China, 1997

Negotiating national identity and the pride associated with it remains an ongoing process. The Chinese leadership would have another chance to renegotiate its international image in July 1997 when the British lease on Hong Kong expired. The island was handed over to China and the whole world was watching. This transfer was unique in recent history for two reasons. First, it represented a change in sovereignty over a rich, semiautonomous area without the consent of its constituents or force of arms. Second, it ran counter to the trend often cited by Western analysts in the post–Cold War period, in which formerly incorporated areas such as the Eastern bloc nations were being granted autonomy.

The economic and political issues surrounding this change are a continuing source of discussion. But the transfer also raises critical issues for the formation of national identity: Would the former citizens of Hong Kong be perceived as Chinese citizens, or would they retain their identity and allegiance to the former island colony? How would the transfer of Hong Kong affect China's international image? Finally, how would the "infusion" of Hong Kong's citizens into Chinese society affect the way in which citizens of the People's Republic conceptualized their own national identity? These questions relate directly to issues of negotiating national identity and raise the possibility of expressions of global rage once again. As with the reunification of Germany, the integration of Hong Kong into the Chinese nation could prompt violence from either the citizens or the state. However, the Hong Kong case differs from the German one in two fundamental ways. Germany needed to integrate a poorer sector into a richer nation-state, whereas China needed to integrate a richer colony into a poorer nation-state. Further, Germany needed to integrate a formerly nondemocratic nation-state into a democratic one, whereas China needed to integrate a marginally democratic colony into a nondemocratic nation-state. Hence, whereas many of the primary adjustments that Germany faced fell on both the former Eastern and Western sectors (albeit for different reasons), in China, the former citizens of Hong Kong, rather than the Chinese, faced the primary adjustments.

This section will indeed address the challenges faced by former citizens of the semiautonomous colony as part of its approach to the negotiation of identity. However, the twin events of Tiananmen Square and China's response to the IWC raised challenges for China as well. Both events ensured that the international community—and in particular, the West—would be following the handover closely. The overriding question that China faced in this instance was how it would handle the integration of Hong Kong into its country. Would it openly attempt to repress any hints of democracy? Would it interfere with the market system operating in the former colony (given that Hong Kong was arguably one of the most capitalist entities in the world)? Finally, would China conditionalize citizenship for Hong Kong residents to the point where they would either flee to another country or refuse to identify with the Chinese nation-state? The last question is made more urgent by the fact that most

Hong Kong residents were, in fact, ethnic Chinese whose ancestors had emigrated from the mainland.

These questions guide the continuing inquiry into China's negotiation of its national identity, for they recall the conditions under which *ressentiment,* violence, and rage might be expressed. The potential for status anxiety among the colony's residents, who would now be absorbed into an overpowering entity, was significant. The potential was similarly great among Chinese citizens, who might resist or resent being compared with their rich and newly entitled citizens. Expressions of nationalism, and perhaps violence, could occur from either side, or from the Chinese state as it sought to assert its authority and control. In this case, the feared expressions of rage never materialized. Instead, owing to careful planning by the Chinese government, favorable circumstances, or both, China was able to renegotiate national identity successfully in the former colony and on the Chinese mainland.

The attention paid by other nations to China's actions and the potential effects upon its *Fremdbild* as a result, should not be underestimated. The transition is an obvious subject for world opinion, as nearly all nations had an interest in the outcome of this transfer. The United States watched for clues to the pattern of social change in China. Europeans had an interest in seeing the future of the former British colony. Asian nations observed China's actions for clues to the country's intentions as an emerging regional superpower. Finally, China watched the reactions of other nations, as it attempted to polish an international image that had been damaged in recent years by accusations of human rights abuses. The renegotiation of national identity for Hong Kong's and China's citizens will be studied as an interaction between the image they have of themselves and their international image in world opinion, as observed from the perspective of two nations with interests in the transfer.

Methodology

This section uses survey research data and newspaper content analyses to operationalize the main variables of *Selbstbild* and *Fremdbild,* respectively. For analyses of *Selbstbild* regarding the image citizens of Hong Kong have of themselves as the transfer draws near, we rely primarily upon survey data supplied through the Hong Kong Transition Project.[15] These data include the following information, collected as part of a longitudinal survey conducted over the past four years, although this study only makes use of data collected between February 1 and June 30, 1997:

- *Sovereignty:* citizens' preferences on the future status of Hong Kong (i.e. Independent, British colony, member of the British Commonwealth, or unification with China)

- *National identity:* citizens' identification of themselves as either Hong Kong Chinese, Chinese, Hong Kong citizen, Hong Kong British citizens, or other classification
- *Satisfaction with government:* citizens' feelings about the present Hong Kong government, the government of the People's Republic of China, and the performance of each government in dealing with the other
- *Concern about the future:* the extent to which citizens are worried about the future standard of living, personal freedoms, political stability in Hong Kong, and government efficiency after the transfer to China
- *Democratic values and political efficacy:* citizens' perceptions of their abilities to influence policy once the transfer occurs and their opinions regarding the influence of public opinion and elite rule on settling political issues
- *Factors affecting whether a citizen will stay or leave Hong Kong after the transfer:* these include changes in the standard of living, personal freedoms, family prospects, and prospect for economic and political stability in Hong Kong and
- *Expectations of the future government:* citizens' opinions on how the post-transfer government will perform compared with the present government in terms of corruption, crime, the state of the economy, education, and the environment

As in the German case, citizens' sense of identity and expectations of the future prove useful for measuring the *Selbstbild* of a nation, especially during times of political and social change.

For the analysis of *Fremdbild,* or the images of Hong Kong and China in world opinion, I follow the methodology of the previous section. World opinion on the transfer will be judged partially through content analyses of references to the concept in newspapers from the United States and China, nations with different interests in the transfer. From China, two editions of the *People's Daily* were analyzed: the mainland Chinese edition and the overseas edition; from the United States, the *New York Times* was analyzed. All stories and editorials referencing world opinion on the return of Hong Kong in these three newspapers were studied from January 1 through July 31, 1997; a total of 108 stories were analyzed. Of these, 53.7 percent (fifty-eight) were from the Chinese edition of the *People's Daily,* 22.2 percent (twenty-four) were from the overseas edition of the *People's Daily,* and 24.1 percent (twenty-six) were from the *New York Times.*

By comparing the manner in which the constructions of world opinion diverge or converge in these newspapers, one may determine how the differing perceptions of Hong Kong's international image might affect its citizens' construction of identity.

The study of newspaper references to world opinion is constructed around comparative analyses of dates of references, their content, and the stories' use of six components of world opinion as follows:

1. The content analyses will be examined to determine how the different newspapers' perspectives on world opinion enter into the renegotiation of China's international image.
2. The survey data will be examined to determine if citizens' conceptions of their national identity in Hong Kong alter as the transfer draws near.
3. The results will be used to map the negotiation of identity for Hong Kong citizens and Chinese alike, through the presentations of their personal images (*Selbstbild*), and the manner in which relevant nations' newspapers conceptualize their national identity (*Fremdbild*), over time.

The Chinese leadership faced a number of challenges in this negotiation, as the reciprocal negotiations of identity between Hong Kong and Chinese citizens would be carried out virtually in front of the entire world. However, China did have two advantages in this process. First, the handover was obligatory and represented a fulfillment of the British pact with China; international law and treaty obligations favored the Chinese side in this transfer. Second, the transfer of Hong Kong ended a symbol of colonial humiliation for China: the former colony was returned to its "rightful" owners. The mere handover, in and of itself, would bolster Chinese pride in a manner legitimized in world opinion, as wary as specific countries may have been about the change. The Chinese did not need to *earn* international respect in order to support national pride—they merely had to handle the transfer without running afoul of world opinion.

The Content of World Opinion on the Transfer

The transfer of Hong Kong to China was met by positive, negative, and neutral responses in the three newspapers studied. The positive references in world opinion generally cited China's inherent right to sovereignty over the island and how the peaceful return of Hong Kong occurred according to treaty and a recent process of negotiation. The negative references in world opinion generally criticized China's record on human rights and democratic freedoms and discussed the potential problems of integrating a capitalist entity into China's socialist autocratic system.[16] Finally, the neutral references in world opinion generally pointed to the international attention China was receiving as this transfer occurred; in many ways, these responses were among the most interesting, as the newspapers noted how the transfer also marked the recognition of China as a player on the world stage. The stories thereby suggested that China's actions and statements before, during, and after the return of Hong Kong would be a continuing subject for discussion in international opinion.

The content of these references reflects one expected result: the Chinese newspapers were more likely to reference world opinion on China in a positive light than the American newspaper. Positive references occurred in 91.4 percent of the stories in the domestic edition of the *People's Daily*, and 87.5 percent of the stories in the overseas edition; by contrast, only 20 percent of the references in the *New York Times* were positive. While there was a significant relationship between the newspaper and the direction of reporting,[17] the mode for reporting in the American newspaper (including 52 percent of the cases) occurred in the *neutral* category.

This result is significant because the American newspaper has usually been known for its critical analysis of Chinese behavior, particularly regarding pro-democracy movements and human rights. One need only compare the negative interpretation of world opinion during the IWC to the relative neutrality of references on the transfer. In this case, however, the *New York Times* appears to respond to the positive description of world opinion in the Chinese newspapers with the attitude that the international community was taking a "wait and see" attitude toward China on this issue.

The Agenda for World Opinion on the Transfer

When one examines the percentage of references to world opinion in each of the newspapers monthly, two patterns appear. First, the most commonly occurring date of reference to world opinion for all three newspapers, as shown in figure 4.3, was in June 1997; this result is not surprising, since the return of Hong Kong was to occur on July 1. Second, despite this similarity, there are significant differences among the dates on which other references occur in the three newspapers;[18] indeed, the patterns suggest that coverage in the *New York Times* and the domestic edition of the *People's Daily* begins to increase from April through June, and then declines in July. By contrast, the coverage in the overseas edition of the *People's Daily* varies in a narrower range from January until June, before dropping off in July.

A possible reason for these patterns is suggested when one examines the content of these references by newspaper and month. Figure 4.4 shows the number and content of references to world opinion on the transfer in the *New York Times*, sorted by month. Here, it is notable that the negative references peak in May and then decline slightly in June, whereas positive references occur only in June and July, and neutral references dominate,

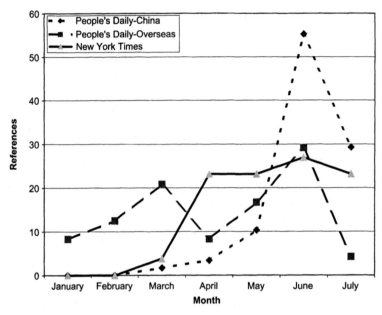

Figure 4.3   Percentage of references to world opinion, by newspaper and month

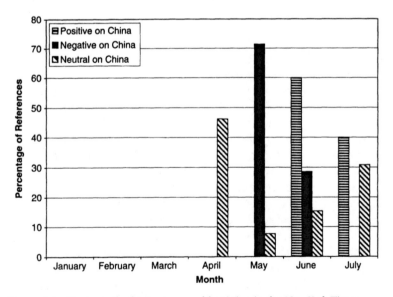

Figure 4.4   Content of references on world opinion in the *New York Times*, by month

occurring in April, May, June, and July. This pattern suggests that the American newspaper was more likely to describe world opinion as positive or neutral toward China on this issue, than it was to describe it as negative; more importantly, though, the tendency increases the closer one comes to the July 1 transfer date. Positive references outweigh negative ones in June, and only positive and neutral references appear in July; the American newspaper's evaluation of world opinion on the issue becomes more positive as the transfer date nears.

As expected, the content and number of references to world opinion in the overseas *People's Daily* are somewhat different, as shown in figure 4.5. The references are overwhelmingly positive, with negative references only occurring in February and March, and a neutral reference only occurring in May. In this case, the positive references still outnumber the negative references, and the tendency for coverage to become more positive as one approaches the July 1 transfer date is evident. Clearly, the overseas Chinese newspaper was consistently attempting to disseminate a vision of world opinion that displayed China in a positive light as the date neared. Finally, the mainland edition of the *People's Daily* also reflects the pattern of the overseas edition, as shown in figure 4.6. Here, too, positive references outweigh negative references, although the latter do appear briefly in June; more importantly, however, the references become more positive again as

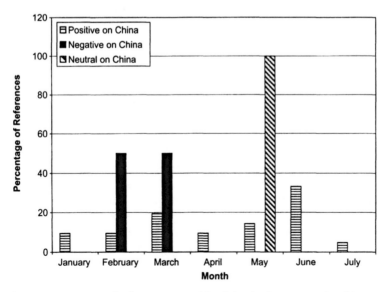

Figure 4.5 Content of references on world opinion in the overseas *People's Daily*, by month

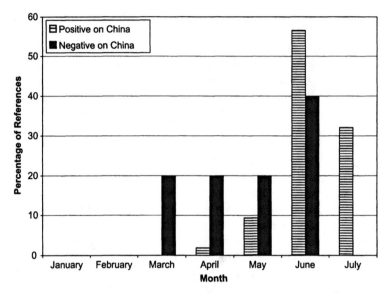

Figure 4.6   Content of references on world opinion in the mainland *People's Daily*, by month

one approaches the July 1 transfer date. Here again, the mainland edition of the Chinese newspaper consistently attempted to display China in a positive light as the date neared.

The pattern and content of these references suggest an attempt by the Chinese newspapers, especially the overseas edition, to disseminate a positive image of China in world opinion to its readers. The audience of the overseas edition, which comprises mainly Chinese students, scholars, opinion leaders, and businesspeople outside mainland China, suggests one reason why the overseas edition maintained a steady stream of stories on the transfer, building a positive momentum for world opinion through its interpretations of it. Another reason for this pattern is that China's claim of sovereignty over Hong Kong was recognized both within and beyond China.

What is more suggestive, though, is how the *New York Times* eventually echoes this perspective in June and July. While this parallel no doubt reflects the American newspaper's perception that the international community had generally accepted the transfer as inevitable, it still indicates a change in evaluation of international responses from the previous months. The mainland edition of the *People's Daily* amplifies this positive interpretation of global public opinion. These results suggest that the Chinese newspapers anticipated, to some extent, the task of presenting a positive image of themselves in world opinion to others; this possible explanation is supported when one examines how the different newspapers utilize the components of world opinion in discussing the transfer.

The Components of World Opinion: Comparative Analyses

The results indicate that of the six components of world opinion, four are significantly more likely to appear in the *New York Times* than in either edition of the *People's Daily:* the moral component, the pragmatic component, the power of world opinion, and the threat of isolation. Table 4.1 illustrates all the components, the percentage of references in which they appeared, and η values for each relationship.

However, references to the nation's image and the world referenced as a unit both appeared frequently in the Chinese newspaper, as indicated by the lower values for η on these relationships. The results suggest two conclusions. First, the Chinese newspaper stories reflect awareness that the international community was observing China and judging its actions. While the newspapers did not tend to admit publicly the moral or pragmatic judgments of world opinion, nor the power of world opinion to isolate them, they seemed to understand, and tacitly acknowledge, that their nation's image and prestige in the international community were at stake.

Indeed, the exclusion of these components suggests that the Chinese government was aware of the stakes in world opinion. Questions about the moral and pragmatic elements of world opinion and international isolation were sticking points in Chinese relations with other nations; Chinese leaders likely had no desire to enter into this discussion at such a critical time. Instead, questions of image and the world's acknowledgement of China's right to Hong Kong under international law were pushed to the forefront. By concentrating on the points where their argument was globally accepted, the two editions of the *People's Daily* could defend their positive interpretations of world opinion on the handover.

Table 4.1 Percentage of stories referencing the components of world opinion, by newspaper

Component	People's Daily (mainland edition)	People's Daily (overseas edition)	New York Times	η
Moral	0.0	16.7	84.6	.8122
Pragmatic	3.4	29.2	80.8	.7040
Power of world opinion	3.4	8.3	92.3	.8541
Isolation	0.0	0.0	46.2	.6279
Nation's image	53.4	45.8	84.6	.2970
World as a unit	75.9	87.5	65.4	.1759

These results are especially striking when compared with the previous results on the IWC. The defensiveness in the Chinese newspaper's coverage of world opinion was replaced by a confidence that China was acting within its rights while at the same time making right a perceived insult to its national pride by reclaiming Hong Kong.

The discussion of world opinion changes significantly in the *People's Daily* between 1995 and 1997. The defensiveness is gone when discussing international public opinion; while the newspaper still does not publicly admit the presence of several components of world opinion, its content appears directed to affecting the direction of this opinion. One may interpret this change in two ways. It is undeniable that the issue at hand was much different in 1997; the transfer of Hong Kong to China was viewed internationally as an event that was inevitable and generally acknowledged to be in accordance with treaty arrangements and generally accepted modes of international behavior. Yet, there also seems to be a more concerted effort on the part of the Chinese newspapers to attempt to present a favorable face to the world (even as far back as January in the overseas edition). The change from defensiveness to assertiveness suggests a possible change in attitude reflected in the newspapers (and perhaps in the Chinese leadership) toward world opinion. Indeed, the shift might explain why the emphasis was on the positive *content* of world opinion in the two newspapers, rather than upon the actual source of that opinion. The irony here is that when the Chinese newspapers pursued this strategy, their positive coverage eventually converged with (cautiously) positive coverage in the *New York Times* in the last two months of the study.

Our concern, though, remains the negotiation of national identity, not just among the Chinese but among Hong Kong citizens as well. Any signs of anger directed toward the outside world would no doubt affect the perceptions of the former residents of the colony. If the direction of world opinion tends to form one piece of the negotiation of national identity, how did these discussions in three newspapers with different audiences possibly affect the consciousness of Hong Kong citizens?

Linkages: National Consciousness in Hong Kong and the Construction of National Identity

The data for the analysis of national consciousness in Hong Kong during the six-month period prior to transfer was drawn from the Hong Kong Transition Project.[19] The results are drawn from two surveys, conducted during the period of our content analyses—the February 1997 survey and the June 1997 survey. Several measures did not change during this period; for instance, the level of optimism about Hong Kong's reunion with China, its economic performance, and its political performance generally remained the same between February and June. However, attitudes toward the reunion did change somewhat; those who stated they had no choice to accept the reality of the transfer, or that they were excited and hopeful because of it, increased from 35 to 49 percent, while those prepared to leave Hong Kong dropped from 29 to 22 percent over this period. This result parallels the results noted in the content analyses of world opinion, especially in the *New York Times:* a cautious optimism mixed with a sense that the change was recognized internationally as inevitable. It also suggests that Hong Kong residents grew less afraid about the prospective effects of unification with mainland China.

Another notable change that occurred in this period was in responses to the question of how China's leaders would affect Hong Kong. In February, 44 percent of respondents did not believe that China's leaders "would damage Hong Kong accidentally by interference" as compared with 41 percent who believed this would happen;[20] by June, the percentages had changed to 50 percent versus 38 percent, respectively. This shift suggests an increasing comfort level with the transfer, which matches the positive face put upon world reaction to it in the newspapers heading to July 1. If the Chinese leadership had displayed any of the rage shown in 1995, in either their interpretations of world opinion or their actions, it is unlikely the residents of Hong Kong would have become more comfortable with the transition.

Perhaps the most important question regarding identity, however, shows a potential problem China faced in integrating Hong Kong into the mainland. In February 1997, Hong Kong's citizens were more likely to consider themselves Chinese than as a "Hong Kong person" by a margin of 58 to 35 percent;[21] by June, this margin had fallen to 49 to 44 percent, respectively. This dramatic increase in the percentage identifying themselves as Hong Kong citizens suggests that these individuals, while accepting the transfer of the island to China, and becoming more optimistic about it, were more likely to hold onto a special identity to defend against potential integration into the mainland. By the same token, however, this change suggests a lack of fear among the residents of the former colony that their identity was likely to force a negative or angry reaction from their new rulers.

These results suggest a cautious, yet defensive, optimism in the renegotiation of national identity among Hong Kong citizens. While some positive evaluations tend to parallel the Chinese newspapers' presentation of world opinion on the issue, the increased tendency to hold onto the Hong Kong identity suggests the cautiousness reflected in the American newspaper. The citizens of Hong Kong appear to use this "added layer" of identity as a source of influence, as they negotiate the inevitable transformation of their national identity into Chinese citizens.

Conclusions

The results suggest that the negotiations described in the beginning of this section occurred with a minimum of upheaval in Hong Kong in 1997. One sees a rise in national consciousness (the stronger sense of *Selbstbild*, reflected in the citizens' greater likelihood to describe themselves as "Hong Kong persons") along with a concerted effort by the Chinese newspapers to portray world opinion as positive toward the transfer and eventual integration of Hong Kong into mainland China. The cautious optimism of the *New York Times* in evaluating this situation in world opinion reflects the idea that this negotiation will remain an ongoing, and at times, vigorous process:

> The decisions made here in Beijing on the fate of Hong Kong . . . may well affect the willingness of other countries to accommodate—or resist—China's rise as a world power. Hong Kong is the first test in a year of testing. China's leaders are going to be judged on how they manage the fragile enterprise of incorporating the free and vibrant society of Hong Kong into the much larger body politic of the Community mainland . . . If Mr. Jiang was forced to turn on the screws, the consequences could be disastrous *for his image and China's* [emphases added].[22]

Such a view is consistent with the greater tendency among Hong Kong citizens to embrace their separate identity as the transfer approached—and it will remain a significant issue as the Chinese government watches the mainland transform, and be transformed by, the island.

The analysis also suggests, however, that the Chinese leadership, at least as their views on world opinion are reflected in the *People's Daily*, is more likely to enter this negotiation by attempting to put a positive spin on its actions in world opinion. The evidence suggests that this strategy might have been somewhat successful, but that this process, too, will remain an ongoing one.

Indeed, when all is said and done, this transformation might have a significant effect upon the negotiation of identity among mainland Chinese. For if world opinion becomes important in the statement of sovereignty over Hong Kong, it suggests that the entire issue of Chinese identity might be opening more to negotiation with their formerly isolated *Selbstbild* and an increasingly influential *Fremdbild*. A caution here is that on this issue, the Chinese leaders correctly perceived world opinion to be generally on their side. Hence, they could claim sovereignty over Hong Kong as an *internal concern* that the *external world* supported. If, however, the perspective on world opinion reflected in the *People's Daily* acknowledges, even tacitly, an influence upon the negotiation of Chinese identity, that might turn out to be the most significant effect of the transfer of Hong Kong on China and its place in the international community.

Did the Chinese leadership learn a lesson after the disastrous effects of Tiananmen Square in 1989 and the IWC in 1995? The evidence is mixed. Certainly, the government has been generally more cautious in the image it projects to the world in keeping with its desire to be respected in its emerging status as a global economic and military power. In such a context, overt expressions of rage are less likely to occur. However, many of the underlying issues still remain. China must still negotiate a "usable" national identity beyond its traditional exceptionalism and isolation. Its leaders must find a way to protect the uniqueness that has been part of their national consciousness for so long, while making it compatible with the scrutiny of the global community. One should note that China will certainly have more leeway in this process than before as it continues its growth as an economic superpower. As mentioned before, China now is the second-largest holder of U.S. debt, and it regularly runs huge trade surpluses with the United States. Further, the linkage between the value of the Chinese currency and the U.S. dollar gives China additional leverage over the United States, formerly one of its harshest critics. It is no accident, therefore, that even recently, when China announced that it would use force to prevent Taiwan from asserting its independence, the United States' response was muted.

However, power alone does not guarantee a positive image in world opinion. A later chapter discussing the United States will illustrate this point. The negotiation of China's identity continues, and if heavy-handedness with Taiwan causes China's global image to deteriorate again, its newly developed economic strength may be insufficient to guard its national identity from the ill effects of a negative world image.

5

The Indian/Pakistani Nuclear Tests: Brinkmanship without a Cause

In 1998, Jaswant Singh, then Senior Adviser on Defense and Foreign Affairs in India, defended the nuclear tests his nation had conducted that May by stating that India existed in a "rough neighborhood."[1] Certainly, his claim was justified, given that India bordered on two traditional enemies, China and Pakistan. However, his defensive justification begins to fragment when one examines the circumstances more closely. While the Sino and Muslim civilizations represented by these antagonists had often clashed with the Hindu civilization, the strategic usefulness of exploding a nuclear device in response is questionable. China was unlikely to be intimidated by the Indian tests when the Chinese nuclear arsenal was far superior in number and sophistication. Pakistan responded soon after the Indian test by exploding its own nuclear device, effectively negating any strategic advantage India might have gained with its own potential threat.

Why, then, did India choose to reveal its nuclear capabilities at this time? The answer lies in India's desire to change its international image and promote national pride. In effect, its nuclear test was an act of rage prompted by what its leaders perceived as global indifference to India's rightful position in the world. One must acknowledge that even in the context of this book, this is an unusual argument to make; nuclear weapons capabilities are nearly always discussed in the context of strategic calculation, not national pride or rage. However, a close examination of Singh's argument reveals an underlying "civilizational" justification for his nation's actions, along the lines described by Samuel Huntington. Huntington's argument allows Singh to offer both a civilizational defense and a nationalistic one, owing to the particular classification of India in the theory. Huntington describes India as the single representative of Hindu civilization. Hence, Hindu civilization is India and India is Hindu civilization. As a consequence, any advancement of India's civilizational identity is also a justification for the advancement of India's national identity.

Singh begins by arguing that while the end of the Cold War made Europe and the Western nations safer; "it did little to ameliorate India's security concerns."[2] He then asserts:

> The great thaw that began in the late 1980s only melted down the ancient
> animosities of Europe. We have not entered a unipolar order . . . It would be
> a great error to assume that simply advocating the new mantras of global-
> ization and the market makes national security subservient to global trade.[3]

In claiming that the end of the Cold War has not ushered in "a unipolar order," Singh appears to be echoing Huntington's thesis: "The argument that a universal culture or civilization is now emerging takes various forms, none of which withstands even passing scrutiny."[4]

Singh's assertion that the end of the Cold War had little effect upon India's place in the world is somewhat disingenuous. For even though he declares that in the aftermath of Indian independence in 1947 and the beginning of the nuclear age and the Cold War, "India rejected the Cold War paradigm and chose the more difficult path of nonalignment,"[5] he later acknowledges the close relationship India enjoyed with the Soviet Union. But this relationship does not figure into India's calculations as heavily as before, because "the Soviet Union's successor, Russia, *has consid-erably less international prestige. Inevitably, the previously existing alliance between India and the former U.S.S.R. has eroded* [emphases added]."[6] This assertion implies that India's association with the Soviet Union was as much about international prestige as it was about strategic concerns; hence, in the aftermath of the Cold War's end and the disruption of previ-ous paths to global status, India's position changed dramatically. The nation needed to redefine its place in the new global configuration, in keeping with hypothesis 1 in Chapter 1.

Singh also dismisses the notion that world opinion may somehow reward Indian restraint in nuclear arms with a positive international rep-utation. Instead, he argues that world opinion is a ploy used to maintain the "unequal division between nuclear haves and have-nots."[7] He explicitly rejects the moral and pragmatic arguments in world opinion for nonpro-liferation:

> The current disharmony . . . between India and the rest of the globe is that
> India has moved from being totally moralistic to being a little more realistic,
> while the rest of the nuclear world has arrived at all its nuclear conclusions
> entirely realistically. With a surplus of nuclear weapons and the technology
> for fourth-generation weapons, the other nuclear powers are now beginning

to move toward a moralistic position. Here is the cradle of the lack of understanding of the Indian stand.[8]

Singh's rejection of world opinion echoes another important point in Huntington's critique: that global culture inevitably means Western liberalism, and that the phrase "global community" is merely a euphemism for the interests of Western nations.[9] The basis for the Indian argument is parity with the rest of the world regarding nuclear issues. Singh states that it is hypocritical for nuclear states to lecture the nuclear have-nots on proliferation and to preach the virtues of deterrence in the West while they expand their own nuclear arsenals.[10] Indeed, the very manner in which he phrases this charge carries a tone of civilizational anger at the implication that only Western nations have the necessary restraint to make deterrence operable. For even though Western nations are not the only ones in possession of nuclear weapons or the only ones calling for nonproliferation among other specific nations, Singh directs his criticisms at the West. By painting the conflict as one of the "West versus the Rest," he implicitly invokes one of Huntington's main theses.[11]

Two other features stand out in Singh's article—an underlying tone of anger at the manner in which India has been regarded in the post–Cold War era and a sense of national pride at the international status that the nuclear tests conferred upon his country. Consider the tone of the following statements:

Nuclear weapons powers continue to have, but preach to the have-nots to have even less.[12]

The first 50 years of Indian independence reveal that the country's moralistic nuclear policy and restraint paid no measurable dividends, *except resentment that India was discriminated against* [emphases added].[13]

Restraint . . . has to arise from strength. It cannot be based upon indecision or hesitancy. Restraint is valid only when it removes doubts, which is precisely what India's tests did.[14]

It is worth noting that Singh's accusations and his subsequent anger were not unjustified. Nuclear nonproliferation policy had been unevenly applied, even during the Cold War era. Strobe Talbott notes that a number of nations, including Iran, Iraq, Libya, and North Korea, while joining the Nuclear Non-Proliferation Treaty (NPT), still pursued their own nuclear weapons programs. Further, it was generally acknowledged that Israel's program was already operable. As Talbott puts it, "For many Indian politicians, government officials, defense experts, and commentators, the NPT embodied 'the three D's' of U.S. nuclear policy—dominance, discrimination, and double standards."[15] It is no wonder that a post–Cold War India, which had lost its international status as a (marginally) nonaligned nation, should react with rage at such a policy.

Also contained in Singh's essay are assertions of the pride of Indian people at the achievement of their new status as members of the nuclear club:

> These five tests, ranging from the sub-kiloton and fission variety to a thermonuclear device, *amply demonstrated Indian's scientific, technical, and organizational abilities,* which until then had only been vaguely suspected . . . Suddenly the strategic equipoise of the post-Cold War world was rattled [emphases added].[16]

> The tests of May 11 and 13 . . . were intended to reassure the people of India about their own security. Confidence-building is a continuous process to which India remains committed.[17]

> India is now a nuclear weapons state . . . That reality can neither be denied nor wished away. This category of "nuclear weapons state" is not, in actuality, a conferment. Nor is it a status for others to grant.[18]

Singh's claims about the security concerns behind the Indian nuclear tests mix curiously with three themes visited frequently so far in this book: international status, national pride, and a potentially angry confrontation with the international community. These themes are consistent with hypothesis 2 in Chapter 1. The special emphasis on India's own capabilities as defining its new global status is especially important here; accordingly, it is unnecessary to await the judgment of world opinion about the nation's place in the new global configuration. By its own actions, India (and in turn, Pakistan) has redefined that global configuration. While Singh speaks continually in his essay of the patience and deference India has displayed toward the international community on the nuclear issue, his final statement challenges world opinion with the new reality.

Talbott notes how these themes were palpable in the days leading up to the nuclear tests and in the negotiations shortly thereafter. The rage and frustration regarding India's international status was evident among "many in the nation's political, scientific, and military elite, who believed [since the 1970s] that India could not attain . . . *the full respect of the world* unless it had . . . a nuclear weapons program [emphases added]."[19] Indeed, several of the Indian supporters of nuclear weapons development still "fulminated" against a twenty-year-old law that required sanctions against India by the United States for proliferation "as though it had been enacted two weeks, rather than two decades, earlier [emphases added]."[20] The Bharatiya Janata Party (BJP), which would ultimately gain power and conduct the nuclear tests, was generally characterized as a Hindu nationalist party. Although the BJP objected that its form of nationalism was cultural rather than religious, there was one issue that united its followers: "No matter what the differences within the BJP on other issues, there was near-unanimity within its ranks and among its supporters in other parties on the importance of nuclear weaponry as a guarantee of India's safety and strength and *an enhancement of international prestige.*"[21] Rage, national pride, and the quest for global status once again interconnect, as a nation whose position in the world was transformed by the end of the Cold War struggles to reassert its national identity and gain status in world opinion.

The strategic considerations prompted by Singh's implied "clash of civilizations" argument therefore conflict with Talbott's interpretation that the Indian nuclear tests were meant to bolster national pride. As with other acts of rage discussed thus far, however, the final arbiter would be the international community, which, through its reactions to the tests, would determine whether these actions did indeed bolster India's global status and enhance its national pride. As such, this issue provides an excellent opportunity to analyze whether the conflicts that led to the nuclear test were civilizational, or whether they were based upon India's desire to assert its national identity and project an international image that would command the world's respect. The "clash of civilizations" argument should provide ample cover for India's actions, given the fact that India's relations with its neighbors have been defined along the civilizational fault lines that Huntington predicted, as noted earlier. But this argument would only hold true if the rest of the world accepted it and if India's actions were consistent with it. This chapter argues that Indian leaders went ahead with the test, not out of strategic considerations about threats from other civilizations, but out of a rage born of global indifference in the post–Cold War era and a desire to gain international status as part of the "nuclear club."

Methodology

This chapter examines this premise by focusing upon the nuclear tests by India and Pakistan in 1998 and analyzing the discourse conventions of world opinion on this subject. The study utilizes five newspapers representing three of the civilizations Huntington describes: the *New York Times,* the *London Times,* and the *Irish Times* (Western civilization); the *China Daily* (Sinic civilization); and the *Hindustan Times* (Hindu civilization). It studies all references to world opinion on the Indian and Pakistani nuclear tests from May 12 through June 14, 1998. Between these dates, 138 references occurred in the five newspapers; of these, 17.4 percent (twenty-four) were in the *New York Times,* 13 percent (eighteen) were in the *London Times,* 16.7 percent (twenty-three) were in the *Irish Times,* 32.6

percent (forty-five) were in the *Hindustan Times,* and 20.3 percent (twenty-eight) were in the *China Daily.*[22]

While a newspaper's national origin does not *determine* its discourse, it does provide clues to how certain issues are discussed and how certain terminologies are framed. .Past studies have shown how the discourse on *world opinion* varies with nation, region, and historical context, but that one may detect an international consensus forming when the meaning and agenda for world opinion converge across several nations' newspapers.[23]

This chapter analyzes whether discussions of the nuclear issue follow the pattern defined by global opinion theory or by the "clash of civilizations" theory, by studying the construction, agenda, and content of world opinion in the newspaper stories. If these factors tend to vary more *across* civilization boundaries, the global opinion theory is supported; if these factors vary more *within* these boundaries, the "clash of civilizations" theory is supported. Further, the study analyzes whether it is possible to map a *process* of opinion formation and consensus that isolates errant nations, as predicted by global opinion theory.

The Content of World Opinion on the Nuclear Tests

The first step in the analysis compares the content of world opinion on the nuclear tests across the various newspapers. Each reference to world opinion was coded in two of eight categories: first, if world opinion was positive, negative, or neutral on India, or if India was not mentioned;[24] and second, if world opinion was positive, negative or neutral on Pakistan, or if Pakistan was not mentioned.[25] The results indicate that India was much more likely to be the subject for world opinion during this period than Pakistan. India was discussed in references to world opinion in 93.5 percent of the newspaper stories, as compared with Pakistan, which was mentioned in 58.7 percent of the newspaper stories. This difference probably reflects the former nation's initiative in the nuclear tests and the general expectation that Pakistan would soon follow India's example.

The analysis also showed that the direction of world opinion did not vary according to civilizational categories. When the newspapers were divided into the three civilizations they represented, there was no discernible relationship between the content of world opinion on India or Pakistan and the newspapers' nation of origin.[26] The direction of world opinion also did not vary according to global opinion categories. When the newspapers were divided into two groups, representing the Indian paper and the rest of the world's newspapers, there was no relationship between the content of world opinion on India or Pakistan and the newspaper in which the stories were published.[27] These results would appear to support the global opinion thesis, despite the lack of variance among the latter categories, since the results suggest a universal awareness of the direction of world opinion regardless of the newspapers' nations of origin. However, the following results suggest that the newspapers did not acknowledge this awareness simultaneously.

The Agenda for World Opinion on the Nuclear Tests

The second step in the analysis compares the dates upon which references to world opinion on the Indian and Pakistani nuclear tests occurred in the various newspapers. Figure 5.1 divides the period under study into three-day segments and compares the percentage of references per time segment in the *Hindustan Times* with the combined percentages of references in the other four newspapers.[28] The results indicate that the Indian newspaper was behind the other newspapers in referencing world reactions to the tests.

The Pearson's *r* for this relationship is .166, with a significance level of .052; further, a multiple range analysis reveals no differences among the dates of references for the other newspapers.

This relationship is elaborated further in figure 5.2, which compares the percentage of references to *negative* expressions of world opinion on India. Here, the *Hindustan Times* again lags behind the other newspapers in the

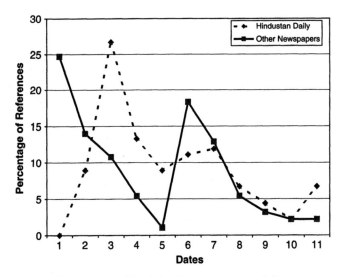

Figure 5.1   References to world opinion, by newspapers and dates

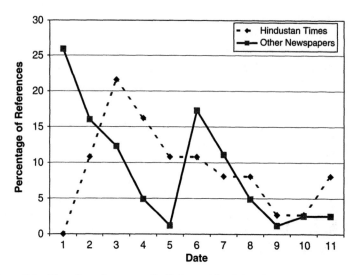

Figure 5.2   Negative references to India in world opinion, by newspaper and date

timing of references; the Pearson's r for this relationship is .208, with a significance level of .026, and the multiple range analysis also reveals no differences in the timing of references among the other newspapers. These differences suggest that the newspapers from other areas of the world were quicker to recognize that the Indian nuclear tests were a subject for world opinion than the *Hindustan Times.* Such a finding is not surprising, since the Indian newspaper would be more likely to take a perspective that attempted to ignore world condemnation of the tests.

However, one might hypothesize an alternative explanation: the *Hindustan Times* simply might have been slower to reference world opinion during this period than the other newspapers. But this explanation is refuted in figure 5.3. Here, negative references to world opinion on Pakistan are mapped for the Indian newspaper and the four others combined. The results show no significant differences between the dates of references on this subject[29] among the newspapers. The results therefore suggest that the particular *issue* in question—nuclear testing—made the Indian newspaper slower to recognize negative world opinion (at least as it was reflected in these other newspapers).

The Components of World Opinion: Comparative Analyses

When one examines the references to the six components of world opinion across these newspapers, the *Hindustan Times* differed from all other

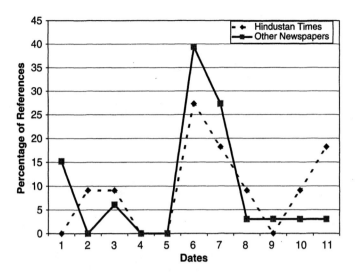

Figure 5.3   Negative references in world opinion to Pakistan, by newspaper and date

newspapers in two respects. It was less likely to reference the *moral component* of world opinion, by a margin of 55.6 to 78.5 percent (η = .237); and it was less likely to reference the *world as a unit*, by a margin of 8.9 to 40.9 percent (η = .326). These differences signify a tendency for the Indian newspaper to minimize moral considerations, and the unity of the world, in its condemnation of the tests.

A possible explanation for this might be that the Indian newspaper was reluctant to acknowledge moral issues and world condemnation because it was the primary subject for world opinion, as shown above. If this were true, the Indian newspaper would be as likely to reference these components in reference to Pakistan as the other newspapers. However, the *Hindustan Times* was less likely to include the moral component in stories that referenced a negative world opinion toward either nation;[30] a similar pattern existed for stories including the world as a unit.[31] These findings suggest a possibly broader outlook guiding the Indian newspaper during this crisis.

Alternatively, these results might instead reflect the *Hindustan Times'* embrace of the "clash of civilizations" paradigm. First, if, like Huntington, one considers a value consensus in world opinion as reflective of "a universal culture or civilization" whose existence does not "withstand . . . even passing scrutiny,"[32] one is less likely to reference a moral component in using the concept. Similarly, if one considers the term "international community" as only a "euphemistic collective noun" designed to represent the interests of the West, one is less likely to reference the world as a unit (as an "international community" or some other entity). What is suggestive here is that the *Hindustan Times* references the components of world opinion in a manner consistent with the "clash of civilizations" theory. What is perhaps even more suggestive, though, is that the other newspapers sampled do not share this perspective, despite their origins in two different "civilizations."

An editorial in the *Hindustan Times* reflects the "clash of civilizations" perspective as a defense against world condemnation, especially by China. It is significant how the author of this quotation evokes the historical and primordial ties upon which Huntington's thesis relies:

> We didn't go into a tantrum when China went nuclear; China does not have to go into a tantrum because India has gone nuclear.
> *The two great countries have to think in civilizational terms.* They have to recover from two centuries of foreign exploitation . . . They have to try to understand each other's points of view . . .
> When Buddha heard of Ajatshatru of Magadha attacking the Licchavi confederacy led by Vaishali, he was dismayed that his disciples . . . should have attacked his Sakya kinsmen. He sighed and said that perfect peace would never come until all the nations of the earth were equally mighty. Let India, China—and the US—all heed the sage counsel of the enlightened one and not think and act petty.[33]

Several of the elements of the "clash of civilizations" thesis are brought to bear here. The paradigm for approaching the nuclear issue, according to the author, is to think in "civilizational terms," which entails recognizing the common bond India and China have against outside exploitation. Also significant is the reference to ancient rivalries that led to war during Buddha's time; here, the author attempts to evoke historical precedents for the separateness and sovereignty of different civilizations, represented by India, China, and the United States.

The *China Daily* did not share this perspective.. In an editorial published on the same day, the Chinese newspaper stated that "New Delhi defied *international opinion*" by conducting the nuclear tests, and that "India's right-wing Hindu nationalists, who head a coalition government . . . increased defense spending in a bid to raise the country's *international standing*" (*China Daily*, June 30, 1998). A nation described as acting to increase its international prestige (despite the initial reactions of world opinion) is not thinking in civilizational terms. Indeed, a letter to the editor of the *China Daily*, titled "India Disturbs Asian Stability," described how India's actions interfered with any attempts at Asian unity, however described:

> The recent Indian nuclear tests have sparked worldwide concern . . . India should really give up its nuclear option in the interests of maintaining world peace and stability and promoting international co-operation and development . . . For economic prosperity the whole of Europe is uniting. Why cannot Asia do so, whose natural and human resources are much richer than those of Europe?[34]

Disaggregating the Concept of "World Opinion": A Conflict of Paradigms

The parallels between the *Hindustan Times'* perspective on world opinion and the "clash of civilizations" perspective are also evident in the manner in which the different newspapers construct world opinion from its component parts. A factor analysis was conducted including all six components of world opinion, in two ways. In the first, the sample was divided along civilizational lines; in the second, the sample was divided along lines suggested by the global opinion thesis. The results, presented in table 5.1, indicate that there is little difference in the structure of factors of the "Western" and "Sino" civilization newspapers; the number and construction of factors, and the factor loadings, are similar for the three Western newspapers and the *China Daily*. The only deviation occurs in the factors from the *Hindustan Times*.

Given the similarities between the Western and the Chinese newspapers, we may characterize the factors in the following manner:

- The *opinion consensus* factor consists of the moral and pragmatic components, both with a positive factor loading. This factor indicates that the international judgment of the value and interest issues for all nations is clearly linked in world opinion for the nations involved.
- The *communitarian power* factor consists of the threat of isolation, the nation's image, the power of world opinion, and the world referenced as a unit. This factor indicates an integrated approach to the influence of world opinion. The international community (or some other global entity) exercises its power by threatening a nation with isolation, thereby affecting its image internally and externally among other nations.

These factors are evident in many of the stories and editorials contained in the Western and Chinese newspapers. The *China Daily* published the

Table 5.1   Factor analyses of components of world opinion

	Factor 1	Loading	Factor 2	Loading	Factor 3	Loading
Western civilization (United States, Great Britain, Ireland)	Moral component	.88286	World as a unit	.55739		
	Pragmatic component	.85875	Nation's image	.73211		
			Isolation	.61066		
			Power of world opinion	.65596		
Sino civilization (China)	Moral component	.78593	World as a unit	.78023		
	Pragmatic component	.88352	Nation's image	.58566		
			Isolation	.63756		
			Power of world opinion	.71496		
Hindu civilization (India)	Moral component	.82774	Power of world opinion	.69369	World as a unit	.74725
	Pragmatic component	.82332	Isolation	.77936	Nation's image	−.67236

following editorial on May 15, 1998, displaying all of the components described in the two factors:

> India conducted two more nuclear tests on Wednesday, turning a deaf ear to the *international community's* indignation over its three tests on Monday . . . it is only natural that *concern and indignation* are aroused from peace-loving people around the world . . . With rising condemnation and serious economic as well as political sanctions from the outside world, India faces *unprecedented isolation* . . . It should now be clear that the trick of achieving popularity through a series of nuclear tests by the incumbent Indian government is a *big risk for the interest of the Indian people.*[35]

Similar commentaries appeared in the Western newspapers:

> Now that the damage has been done, the international community must do all it can to minimize it . . . *The international community will be at one in sharing this aim* . . . The United States, to its credit, was quick to suggest it will impose sanctions on India . . . It is possible that India intends to go no further, that the tests were no more than a feel-good exercise . . . But the tests were an irresponsible exercise that could rapidly get out of control . . . India

must be persuaded, in the broadest terms, that there must be no more tests, and that *the only way to repair the damage* it has done is to sign the test ban treaty without reservations.[36]

A government as oblivious to *international norms and sensitivities* as the current one [in India] is unlikely to respond well to outside intermediaries, which have historically been important in various crises. Under the circumstances, the BJP government has served notice that it is an *inappropriate recipient* of the military co-operation India has enjoyed.[37]

The nuclear tests have forced India to reset its political as well as its philosophical compass. *They brought worldwide condemnation to a country that had long preached the gospel of peace*, with Prime Minister Atal Bihari Vajpayee proclaiming India to be the possessor of "the capacity for a big bomb" that had given it a new measure of international power. But as the test series ended, many Indians concluded that *the repercussions abroad*, including severe economic sanctions imposed by the United States, could be matched by similarly far-reaching political effects at home.[38]

Clearly, the effects of India's isolation and the power of world opinion are shown in its transformation from a nation that was known for "preach[ing] a gospel of peace" to one receiving "worldwide condemnation" According to the Western and Chinese newspapers, the Indian nuclear tests represented an attempt to gain international prestige and respect as a nuclear power. The construction of world opinion in these newspapers and the content of their stories suggest that the attempt backfired upon the Indian government.

The factors that emerged from the analysis of the *Hindustan Times* suggest that this newspaper responded to the worldwide condemnation of the tests in a fundamentally different manner:

- The *opinion consensus* factor mimics a similar factor among the other newspapers; it consists of the moral and pragmatic components, both with a positive factor loading. This factor indicates that the international judgment of the value and interest issues for all nations is clearly linked in world opinion for the nations involved.
- The *power factor* differs in a fundamental manner from the previous newspapers' factors, however. It consists of the power of world opinion and the threat of isolation, both with positive factor loadings. But it disaggregates this power from the nation's image and the world referenced as a unit, which appear in the next factor. As such, the Indian newspaper acknowledges the power of other nations to isolate it, but it keeps these considerations separate from any consideration of the world as a unit or its nation's image.
- The *image threat* factor contains the world considered as a unit with a positive factor loading, and the nation's image with a negative factor

loading. This configuration indicates that when the world was referenced as a unit, India's image tended not to be mentioned. Clearly,
there is an effort here to disaggregate India's image from any acknowledgement of an international community or other global entity that
would pass judgment on it.

Why the *Hindustan Times'* stories did not acknowledge the existence of
any international entity when mentioning India's national or international
image becomes clear when one examines some examples. In an editorial in
the *Hindustan Times*, K. R. Malkani debunked Chinese statements that
India had flouted the "common will of the international community":

> With Russia, Britain, and France opposing sanctions, and non-aligned
> nations and Arabs welcoming the Indian explosion, what is the "interna-
> tional community" that they are talking of? . . . As a *great civilization*, China
> needs to think coolly and maturely, and not position itself on the wrong side
> of India, another *great civili*zation.[39]

This theme is continued in other articles in the Indian newspaper:

> Condemnation by the *Western world* notwithstanding, the series of nuclear
> tests conducted by India have drawn an overwhelmingly positive response
> from the *Arab world*. (*Hindustan Times*, 1998).
>
> [India's] present decision and future actions will continue to reflect a com-
> mitment to sensibilities and obligations of an *ancient civilization*, and sense
> of responsibility and restraint. (*Hindustan Times*, 1998a)
>
> Mr. Ashok Singhal once said that "Mr. Clinton knows that a Hindu India
> will be the friend of the US in the next world war between the pan-Islamic
> forces and the US."[40]

Two themes dominate these quotations. First, the existence of an "international community" condemning India is denied; while condemnation
comes from China and the "Western world," other peoples, such as the
Arabs, applaud India's actions. Second, the stories urge the reader to think
in terms of civilizations—whether it be the ancient civilizations of India or
China, or the "clash of civilizations" that might occur in a coming war
between the United States and the "pan-Islamic forces." These direct and
indirect references to the "clash of civilizations" thesis are made explicit in
the following quotation, where the author even suggests that Pakistan
might be an ally against the Muslim civilizations in West Asia:

> It would seem that, with all our antipathies, we recognize, in the inmost
> reaches of our mind that, after all we are One People. The Pakistanis are

closer to the Indians than they are to Arabs, Iranians, and Turks. *In the global context—in the language of Prof. Huntington of "Clash of Civilizations" fame*—Pakistan is only a fault-line between "Hindu" India and "Muslim" West Asia.[41]

The clear implication is that the Indian newspaper defines the "global context," not in terms of international public opinion, but in terms of Huntington's thesis. In this, it draws a page directly from Huntington, who stated that the "common interests [of India and the United States] in containing China are likely to bring India and the United States closer together. The expansion of Indian power in Southeast Asia cannot harm US interests and could even serve them."[42] The Indian newspaper's embrace of Huntington's thesis explains why it acknowledged world opinion more slowly in its stories than the other newspapers, why it is less likely to mention the moral component of world opinion and the world as a unit than the other newspapers, and why its construction of world opinion tends to avoid discussion of its image and any entity such as an "international community" together. The *Hindustan Times* thus uses the civilizational interpretation as a defense against the negative judgment of world opinion. The image of India it wishes to project is that of one civilization among many in a world defined by civilizations. The irony, however, is that this "global context" is belied by the agenda, content, and structure of world opinion in the newspapers from other "civilizations" studied here.

Conclusion

This study shows how the conflict between the "clash of civilizations" and "global opinion" paradigms plays itself out in the references to world opinion. The *Hindustan Times* references the "clash of civilizations" thesis explicitly, but always in a specific context—as a defense against the global condemnation of India's nuclear tests. The newspaper at once acknowledges the negative responses to its nation's actions, but classifies them as representing the diverse reactions of specific "civilizations," not as a unified reaction of some global community expressing a "world opinion." By deemphasizing the moral component and the world as a unit in its references to world opinion, the *Hindustan Times* advances the "clash of civilizations" thesis as a *defense* against the effects of international opinion, apparently to protect its image, which its stories tend not to discuss in conjunction with any global entity.

As stated earlier, it is natural for the Indian newspaper to invoke the civilizational argument, since that thesis also serves to advance Indian national identity. For India, like China, is both a civilization (in theory) and a nation-state (in practice). According to Talbott, Singh's opinions about Islam further strengthen the civilizational argument:

> I also found troublesome the way Islam fit into Jaswant's worldview—or, more to the point, the way it seemed to be inherently at odds *with his concept of Hindu civilization* . . . For example, in his paean to Hinduism, Jaswant noted how this most polytheistic of the world's great religions included a dizzying array of female goddesses, thus proving itself egalitarian, in contrast to Muslim society, with its proclivity for male chauvinism and misogyny. Hinduism, over the millennia, had proved itself absorptive and hospitable, while Islam was all about conquest and conversion by the sword . . .
> What concerned me, in hearing it from Jaswant, was what it implied about the BJP's ideology and therefore about the party's approach to governance. If someone as sophisticated as Jaswant saw Islam this way, it meant that there were surely many who held more primitive and virulent forms of this view.[43]

Huntington's argument therefore provides a twofold cover for the BJP's nationalism. It states their agenda in terms of civilizations rather than nationalism, and it allows them to attack Islam, a civilization not represented by just one nation-state, as Hinduism is. These results are consistent with hypotheses 3 and 4 in Chapter 1.

But this narrative was apparently not successful in boosting India's international image. The rhetorical defense is belied by the agenda, content, and structure of world opinion reflected in the other newspapers. Despite the Indian newspaper's appeal to China on civilizational grounds, the Chinese newspaper reflected the patterns on world opinion displayed by the Western newspapers. The articles in the *Hindustan Times* embrace a "clash of civilizations" narrative, but the structure of discussions about the nuclear tests in the other newspapers conforms to global opinion theory. The Indian newspaper's arguments describe a narrative that is contradicted by the analysis of the Chinese and Western newspapers. The civilizational narrative fails when confronted with the international judgments and isolation of world opinion in the Western and Chinese newspapers.

The remaining question is whether the BJP's narrative remained successful on the national level in India. Anecdotal evidence suggests that the nuclear tests did indeed create an upsurge in national pride. However, they did little to bolster the party's electoral fortunes. Instead, pocketbook issues took over and contributed to huge setbacks in state elections, despite the BJP's attempts to change the subject:

> On the hustings, BJP leaders kept trying to focus on national security, but to little avail. At a preelection rally in Jodhpur, in Rajasthan, when Vajpayee

boasted that the nuclear tests had heightened India's prestige, angry voices in the crowd shouted complaints about the sevenfold increase in the cost of onions.[44]

While the global reaction to India's act of nationalistic rage did not necessarily precipitate the decline in the BJP's fortunes, the nuclear tests ultimately did not help the party, despite the upsurge in national pride. This conclusion does more that support the nationalistic narrative; it also suggests that the alternative narrative is often used as a means of defense against world opinion and as a tool to fragment international consensus along arbitrary lines. Certainly, the *Hindustan Times* attempted such a strategy, calling upon Chinese, Arab, and even Pakistani examples to buttress its claims. It is possible, then, that the "clash of civilizations" thesis attains credibility, not through the inherent sense of the groupings it describes, but rather through its ability to disrupt global opinion processes. Such a strategy is likely to be of questionable usefulness so long as world opinion affects international status, and international status affects national pride.

6

The War at Home: Identity Versus Values

In the fall of 2003, I corresponded with a colleague in the United Kingdom about how the war with Iraq had hurt the United States' image throughout the world. We discussed the dangers of isolating a superpower, and I paraphrased Bernard Lewis, saying that the world could ill afford an "American rage" brought about by threats to its citizens' safety and identity. My friend's response chilled me: "Aren't we seeing that right now?" he asked.

At first, it seems almost heretical to imply that Americans' reactions to the horrors of September 11, 2001 were an example of global rage. That U.S. citizens would respond to the events of that day with a mixture of shock and fury is not only understandable, but also thoroughly justified. But it is the nature of the emotional narrative constructed by the Bush administration to direct this anger that makes the aftermath of 9/11 a fit case for this study. This narrative began with the attacks upon America and was to end with the defeat of Saddam Hussein in Iraq. How and why that narrative was constructed, how a horrific act by non-state actors became the justification for a war against a state that had not attacked the United States, is the primary story here. The war against Iraq came to be framed as part of a civilizational quest by the Bush administration in response to the attacks. The narrative was also designed to focus American anger in a specific manner, in a way that bolstered a national pride damaged by the ongoing fear of terrorist attacks.

The strategy failed. The narrative did little to justify the war against Iraq to the rest of the world, instead hurting the United States' international standing and ultimately affecting how Americans viewed their nation. More importantly, the Bush administration's actions exacerbated the very conditions that promoted terrorism. The narrative was a dual failure—it failed to move world opinion toward the United States' view of the situation, and it failed to explain the actual motivations behind the administration's targeting of Iraq, motivations that had more to do with national identity than any "clash of civilizations."

The first section below traces the failure of the United States to convince the world that it had ample justification for attacking Iraq. The second section traces why the narrative of a "clash of civilizations," which the Bush administration implicitly endorsed in its doctrine and discourse, failed as a narrative in the United States. Instead, it encountered the inherent contradictions between the professed conflict between the values of the West and Islam, and the actual values embraced by American conservatives and the citizens of Muslim countries.

The 2003 war with Iraq marked the first time world public opinion had been strongly arrayed against the United States on a major issue in the post–Cold War era.[1] The world has disagreed with America in the past on specific issues such as the banning of landmines during the Clinton administration and the imposition of sanctions against South Africa due to apartheid during the Reagan administration. But these past disagreements never prompted mass demonstrations and world leaders allying themselves against the United States, as occurred with the 2003 Iraq war. These new circumstances were evident when the United States could not even muster a simple majority in the United Nations Security Council for its decision in March 2003 to go to war.

These circumstances are even more acute when one considers that the United States enjoyed a tremendous wave of global sympathy after the terrorist attacks of 9/11,[2] and that many of the allies who oppose the United States now, such as France and Germany, aided the campaign against terror in Afghanistan in 2001–2002. Further, a Pew Research Center poll released in 2002 indicated that the image of the United States had deteriorated in an extraordinary number of nations around the world in the previous two years.

The primary questions, then, are: Did the Iraq war change the image of the United States over the past two years? How may we trace world opinion and analyze it to answer this question, and what are the ramifications for present and future U.S. policy? How does the present American isolation from the international community affect its ability, and the ability of other nations, to promote cooperative global ventures and ensure a peaceful and safe international environment? Finally, how will this isolation impede the effectiveness of such bodies as the United Nations and the Security Council in humanitarian and peacekeeping endeavors?

These questions assume, of course, that the United States is perceived in a negative light in world opinion. The process of world opinion assesses certain sanctions for violating the judgments of the international community. However, it is difficult to even discuss sanctions when dealing with the United States. Because America is the sole remaining superpower, actions such as boycotts of goods or the deportation of ambassadors are not viable options. The international community must rely more upon indirect, or "soft," sanctions, such as criticizing the image of the United States abroad, questioning the nation's reputation, and other more abstract strategies. The status of the United States as a superpower, therefore, makes the study of the potential effects of a negative image in world opinion more difficult. In this chapter, I address this problem by studying perceptions of world opinion in newspapers of record from two nations that do not have "major nation" status: the Dominican Republic and Iran. While the two nations have dissimilar histories and geographic locations, both share some critical characteristics that make them useful subjects for analysis. Both countries were subjects of U.S. intervention—in the dispatch of Marines to Santo Domingo in the 1960s and in the intervention to reinstall the Shah of Iran in the 1950s, respectively. Both countries also had potentially tenuous positions vis-à-vis the United States at the beginning of the Iraq war, albeit in different ways. The Dominican Republic had reason to fear U.S. economic retaliation if it criticized the intervention in Iraq. Iran had reason to fear U.S. military intervention since the war with Iraq was fought on its border.[3] As such, both nations provide case studies of how world opinion is conceptualized in nations under the "shadow" of the United States.

However, there is one critical difference in the official policies of these two nations. While Iran is no friend to Iraq, it opposed the U.S. intervention there; by contrast, the Dominican Republic was part of the "coalition of the willing," sending 302 troops, or approximately 12 percent of its armed forces, to help the U.S. effort there. This difference in policy actually allows for some striking conclusions, given that the newspapers' perspectives on world opinion regarding the United States contained some critical similarities.

What follows proceeds in four steps. The approach and methodology is described and applied to newspapers from these two nations, showing the relative timing and content of their references to world opinion. Next, the components of world opinion are analyzed and compared between the two nations. Finally, the construction of world opinion is linked to the relative positions and concerns of the two countries regarding the impending war with Iraq. The section concludes by discussing the extent to which peripheral nations such as these two might participate in the process of world opinion, given the constraints on their actions due to their position vis-à-vis a superpower such as the United States.

Methodology

This chapter studies media perspectives on world opinion regarding the 2003 U.S. war against Iraq. The study utilizes two newspapers from the nations under study: the *Listin Diario* from the Dominican Republic and the *Tehran Times* from Iran. It studies all references to world opinion on the Iraq war from March 1 through May 5, 2003, using a predesigned and pretested instrument. Between these dates, forty-four references occurred in the two newspapers; of these, twenty-seven (61.4 percent) were from the Dominican newspaper and seventeen (38.6 percent) were from the Iranian newspaper. The *Listin Diario* was analyzed in the original Spanish version, while the *Tehran Times* was analyzed in English translation. Further, it is important to note that the Dominican newspaper is independent of government control, whereas the Iranian newspaper is not.[4]

The approach used here has been applied in several other cases throughout this book. However, analyzing the potential isolation of a superpower could prove qualitatively different from analyzing the isolation of less-powerful nations. The United States is the proverbial "900-pound gorilla" in foreign affairs. How, if at all, might the perceptions of world opinion in countries such as the Dominican Republic or Iran affect its status?

The Timing and Content of World Opinion in the Two Newspapers

The timing of references to world opinion on the war with Iraq is somewhat different between the two newspapers, as shown in figure 6.1 (for these portions of the analysis, the dates of the study were coded into

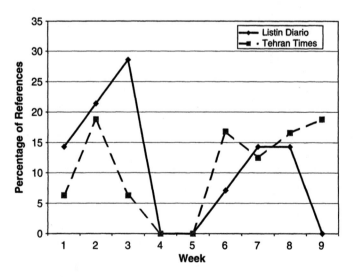

Figure 6.1   References to world opinion, by week and newspaper

weeks). Indeed, the dates of the references in the *Tehran Times* are significantly behind those of the references in the *Listin Diario* ($r = .369$, $p =$
.042). There is, however, a specific pattern evident in the time lag between
the two newspapers. Figure 6.2 shows the timing of the references to world
opinion in the two newspapers again, with one change—the results for the
Dominican newspaper are graphed against the *next week's* results for the
Iranian newspaper. Hence, the percentage of references in the *Tehran
Times* is compared with the percentage of references from the previous
week in the *Listin Diario*. The resulting chart shows an amazingly similar
pattern, as if the Iranian newspaper were "following the lead" of the
Dominican newspaper by a lag of approximately one week.

A similar pattern can be observed when one analyzes the content of
world opinion regarding Iraq and the United States. The *Tehran Times* was
significantly more positive in its perception of world opinion on Iraq than
the *Listin Diario*. In the Iranian newspaper, 82.4 percent of the references to
world opinion on Iraq were positive, as compared with none of the references in the Dominican newspaper, where most of the references (70.4 percent) were neutral (Spearman correlation = .689, $p = .000$). This finding
is suggestive, since Iran and Iraq had generally poor relations stemming
from a long war in the 1980s in which over a million soldiers were killed on
both sides. More predictably, the perception of world opinion on the
United States was significantly more negative in the *Tehran Times* than in
the *Listin Diario;* indeed, 100 percent of the references to the United States

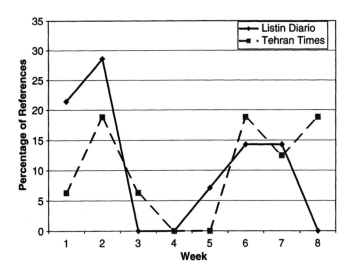

Figure 6.2 References to world opinion, by lagged week date and newspaper

were negative in the former newspaper, as compared with 58.4 percent of the references in the latter newspaper (Spearman correlation $= -.489, p = .001$). The only surprising result here is that in the Dominican newspaper, there were more negative references to the United States than to Iraq.

When the negative references to world opinion on the United States are examined weekly, a pattern similar to the overall pattern for world opinion emerges. Figure 6.3 shows these results graphed by week; the *Listin Diario* tends to cite these negative references before Iraq by a significant margin ($r = .323, p = .082$). However, when the results are graphed with the one-week lag for the Dominican newspaper in figure 6.4, as in figure 6.2, the pattern of references is strikingly similar. Once again, it appears as if the Iranian newspaper were "following the lead" of the Dominican newspaper by a lag of approximately one week.[5]

These findings beg the question of why the *Listin Diario* appeared to be "leading" the *Tehran Times* by approximately one week, both in the percentage of references to world opinion generally and in the negative evaluations of the United States in world opinion specifically. The manner in which both newspapers construct world opinion, as well as their relative positions in the world, suggests some answers.

The Components of World Opinion on the War with Iraq

The two newspapers differed significantly in only two of the six components of world opinion. The Iranian newspaper was more likely to reference

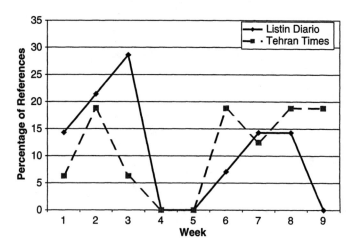

Figure 6.3   Percentage of negative references to world opinion on the United States, by week and newspaper

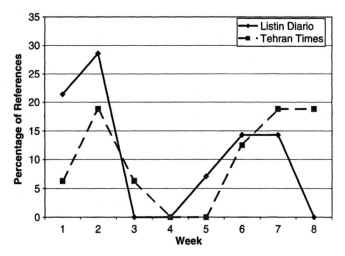

Figure 6.4 Percentage of negative references to world opinion on United States, by lagged week date and newspaper

the moral component ($r = .521, p = .000$) and the power of world opinion ($r = .379, p = .020$) than the Dominican newspaper. The only other notable finding in this regard was that both newspapers tended overwhelmingly to reference the world as a unit, even though there was no significant difference between them in the frequency of these occurrences (59.3 percent of cases in the *Listin Diario* and 76.5 percent of cases in the *Tehran Times*). When one examines the position of Iran in this crisis, its newspaper's reliance on the moral power of world opinion is not surprising. It is a given that Iran would have little recourse if the United States decided to expand the war with Iraq into Iran. A strategy to avoid this circumstance could have been to rally world opinion against the United States on the moral grounds that it would be doubly damned if it invaded a second sovereign nation that had made no overt threats in recent years. While this strategy obviously did not prevent the U.S. incursion into Iraq, the additional opprobrium that would accompany another incursion might be a sufficient deterrent.

The Dominican Republic had more to fear from economic, rather than military, reprisals from the United States. This country depends a great deal on tourism from the United States and could not afford to be characterized as challenging the moral authority of that nation as a means of gaining influence in world opinion. For the Dominican Republic to suffer the fate of France, where Americans were boycotting the nation and its products, would entail too great an economic blow. Further, the moral issues in world opinion were more complex for the Dominican newspaper than for the Iranian newspaper. The *Listin Diario* condemned both Iraq and the United States; the *Tehran Times* overwhelmingly condemned the United States but was more positive on Iraq. The former newspaper perceived world opinion as ambivalent toward the moral propriety of supporting either the United States or Iraq.

Of these two threats, military and economic, to the nations involved, however, the military threat was clearly more imminent and direct. This circumstance suggests a reason why the *Tehran Times* lagged approximately one week behind the *Listin Diario* in echoing a general condemnation of the United States in world opinion. Given the prominent place the issue had in several nations' agendas, the Iranian newspaper apparently took a "safety in numbers" strategy in adding its voice to world opinion that had already been expressed by other nations regarding the U.S. incursion into Iraq.

This strategy is reflected in the manner in which the two newspapers construct world opinion. Following the previous methodology, I used a factor analysis to study these relationships. All six components of world opinion were analyzed for the two newspapers. For the *Listin Diario*, the six components were reduced to four, represented in three factors, as shown in table 6.1, which includes the components and their factor loadings:

- The first factor, which we shall designate the *image effect factor*, combines the threat of international isolation with the nation's image—in this case, the image of the United States.
- The second factor, which we shall designate the *power factor*, combines with the image criticism of the former factor to provide an indirect means by which the Dominican Republic can challenge the authority of the United States.
- The third factor, which we shall designate as the *shared interest factor*, combines with the other two to emphasize that the newspaper's criticism of the United States is based upon shared interests with other nations in the world.

The history and circumstances of the Dominican Republic suggest reasons why its newspaper interpreted world opinion in this manner. Criticizing a nation's image, which is an indirect means of condemnation, can have serious ramifications. The *Listin Diario*'s interpretation of world opinion suggests an indirect challenge to the United States' reputation in the world, rather than other forms of isolation that might involve sanctions, or explicit snubs that would invite retaliation. This tactic might seem of questionable effectiveness with a monolithic power such as the United

Table 6.1   Factor analyses of components of world opinion

	Listin Diario
Factor 1: *Image effect factor*	
Threat of isolation	.746
Nation's image	.785
Factor 2: *Power factor*	
Power of world opinion	.818
Factor 3: *Shared interest factor*	
Pragmatic component	.908
	Tehran Times
Factor 1: *Exclusion factor*	
Power of world opinion	.760
Threat of isolation	.792
Pragmatic component	.779
Factor 2: *Moral community factor*	
Nation's image	.625
Moral component	.861
World as a unit	.780

States. But other studies have shown that a decline in a nation's international reputation can precipitate a parallel decline in its citizens' evaluation of their country and a diminished national pride, even for a superpower.[6]

Voicing criticism in this manner also provides a means for a small nation to wield some power as a counter to U.S. influence, if only in the eyes of its own citizens. If enough other nations joined in on this criticism, America would abdicate part of what Joseph Nye calls "soft power," or influence over world opinion, necessary to pursue its global aims.[7] It is not surprising that the *Listin Diario* describes potential limitations on the United States' power to intervene in other nations' affairs as in the shared interests of all nations, as shown in the third factor. Indeed, support for the incursion into Iraq was generally low among the countries of South and Central America because of the history of U.S. interventions in those places. The above analysis also indicates that condemnation of the United States for violating a nation's borders is not considered equivalent to support for Iraq in world opinion here, and so, the moral component is omitted. Instead, the Dominican newspaper suggests that damage to the United States' international reputation is appropriate punishment for its actions.

The Dominican newspaper describes the extent to which the United States was isolated in its impending war with Iraq, noting the mass demonstrations all over the world against the incursion:

A total of more than 100 million people demonstrated yesterday in various European, Asian, and U.S. cities against the imminent war with Iraq ...

Moreover, 53 percent of approximately 1000 German respondents said they were in favor of *political or economic sanctions against the United States* if the administration initiates a military action against Saddam Hussein's regime without a corresponding UN resolution ... [In Pakistan] they carried signs that said "We want peace, no war," "The Iraqis want food not bombs," and *"A friend of the United States is a traitor."* (*Listin Diario*, March 9, 2003)

While the *Listin Diario* might have been reluctant to advocate specific sanctions against the United States, it showed that other nations' citizens were not similarly inhibited. In another article, the newspaper noted how demonstrators in Rio de Janeiro called for an economic boycott of U.S. goods. This threat of isolation was accompanied by damage to the United States' image abroad in places such as Pakistan, where even association with the United States was sufficient to brand one a "traitor." Finally, the manner in which the United States behaved toward the United Nations projected an image of an arrogant bully: "By weakening the process of the United Nations Security Council, [the U.S.] has offended the dignity of nations ... the superpower went over the UN's head and offended all the nations of the world with its arrogance" (*Listin Diario*, March 14, 2003).

The *Listin Diario* also explicitly compares world opinion on the U.S. invasion of Iraq and the U.S. occupation of the Dominican Republic in 1965:

War against Iraq recalls the occupation of the Dominican Republic by the United States ... The 1965 intervention of the United States *provoked indignation and protests all over the world.* (*Listin Diario*, April 28, 2003)

But there are other threats for all nations to consider: "*Humanity sees that after the invasion of allied troops in Iraq, without the approval of the United Nations, this agency will be short-lived*" (*Listin Diario*, March 26, 2003). These two statements suggest that the threat of U.S. military intervention—one that the Dominican Republic faced equally with Iraq and other nations in the world—was made more dangerous by the potential loss of the United Nations as an arbiter.

The construction of world opinion in the *Tehran Times* reflects a different strategy for participating in the process of world opinion. The two factors derived describe a definition of a moral international community based upon a nation's maintenance of a positive global image (the *moral community factor*) and the shared interest that all nations have in exerting their influence against those who violate this community's strictures (the *exclusion factor*):

- The first factor, which we shall designate as the *exclusion factor*, suggests that the power of world opinion is properly wielded by isolating errant nations who violate the common interests of all nations.

- The second factor, which we shall designate as the *moral community factor*, suggests that membership in a world community (the world as a unit) requires maintaining an international reputation in concordance with the moral imperatives accepted by other nations.

Iran is a nation that has been internationally isolated for many years. Its newspaper's construction of world opinion reflects an awareness of this status, even as it attempts to participate in the formation of world opinion. As with the Dominican newspaper, it associates the isolation of the United States with pragmatic interests all nations share—in this case, preventing military incursions into sovereign nations without clear justification. The Iranian newspaper, like the Dominican newspaper, perceives the power of world opinion as one means by which the U.S. incursion into Iraq may be limited to just that nation.

At the same time, the Iranian newspaper appears to perceive that an international community bound by certain moral judgments does exist and that it can be used to affect the United States' image in the world. But the *Tehran Times* displays a reluctance to combine morality with isolation. Because Iran violated the customary protection for diplomats during the hostage crisis of 1979–1980, and supported terrorism in other areas of the world, it has been isolated internationally on moral grounds for some time. As such, its newspaper links a negative moral judgment of the United States to the United States' image in the world. This interpretation of world opinion is partially a defensive measure and partially a means of claiming some moral equivalency between its own actions and those of a chief antagonist. Since the Bush administration labeled Iran as part of the "axis of evil" with Iraq and North Korea, Iran's leaders might be understandably anxious to apply similarly negative labels to the United States.

Although states are justified in using their power to isolate Iraq, respect for a nation's sovereignty (in this case, Iraq's) is in the common interests of all nations, as is argued in this quotation from the *Tehran Times*:

"The Islamic Republic as a victim of one of the wars of aggression, the major victim of terrorism and only victim of weapons of mass destruction [from Iraq], certainly understands the international community's frustration ... But it also knows that another war in the region should never be decided easily or hurriedly ..."

Zarif said that *neither the Iraqi people nor the international community could accept any encroachment on the sovereignty and independence of a UN member state* "no matter how short some may claim it to be at the outset ..."

"The stakes have gone far beyond Iraq. *The rush to war placed the current functioning international system on the line* ... It is quite irresponsible to rejoice over the fantasy of '*the post-UN world*' as a hawkish columnist did yesterday." (*Tehran Times*, March 15, 2003; emphases added)

One recognizes here the issues at stake for the "international community," which, though it is frustrated, also realizes the common interests of not violating the sovereignty of a "UN member state." As a result, it is the United States that is implicitly threatened with international isolation for disrupting the "current functioning international system." (Contemplating a "post-UN world" here suggests the separation of the United States from the international community and its institutional instruments such as the United Nations—a move that could only have negative consequences for world security and peace.)

The Iranian newspaper also perceives world opinion as morally condemning the United States for rushing to war with Iraq, implying that the war has hurt the United States' image in the world community:

Leader of the Islamic Revolution Ayatollah Seyed Ali Khamanei … said the U.S. leaders are currently pursuing the ambitions of colonial powers of the eighteenth century, and stated that the White House policymakers were wrong to think their dreams to occupy Iraq for a long time would ever be materialized given the prevailing world conditions … The Leader of the Islamic Revolution further said … that *the image of the U.S. had already been distorted before the world public opinion.* "The U.S. leaders want to deter other nations from resisting their plans … However, *the resistance of nations will eventually frustrate their efforts to achieve sinister goals.*" (*Tehran Times*, March 17, 2003; emphases added)

The damage to the United States' image "before world opinion" is linked here to the world responding as a unit to frustrate the United States' actions (or "sinister goals"), which are perceived to be immoral. In this instance, the moral condemnation by the international community both follows from, and implicitly causes, damage to the United States' international reputation.

The preceding analyses and statements illustrate that both the Dominican Republic and Iran participate in judging world opinion about the United States' war with Iraq. It remains to evaluate the significance of these findings in light of the relative positions both nations hold in the international community.

What We Can Learn from Peripheral Nations about World Opinion on the United States

It might appear incidental that these two nations' newspapers reflected a similar condemnation of the U.S. invasion of Iraq. Certainly, their stories' perspectives were affected by the countries' places in the world. The position of the Dominican Republic as a small, underdeveloped nation that fears the ramifications of preemptive U.S. military intervention, but is economically dependent in many ways on the United States, is commensurate with its newspaper's construction of world opinion. The *Listin Diario* interprets world opinion as praising neither Iraq nor the United States in the impending war. Rather, Iraq is to be condemned for creating a situation that provides a justification for the "preemptive war" threatened by the Bush administration, while the administration is to be condemned for opening the door to such interventions in other nations.

The position of Iran as an underdeveloped, yet oil-rich nation that is internationally isolated is also commensurate with its newspaper's construction of world opinion. The *Tehran Times* suggests that the United States has lost the moral battle for world opinion to Iraq, despite Iran's history of victimization at Iraq's hands. It suggests that the power of world opinion will isolate the United States for violating a principle of national sovereignty that protects all nations—the obvious subtext being that the United States, if it moves into Iraq, must not be allowed to violate Iran's borders as well. This stance also allows Iran to seize the moral high ground against the United States, which has damaged its international image by threatening the unity and institutions of the global community. Given that Iran has had a negative image in world opinion since the hostage crisis in 1979, its newspaper rather predictably condemns the United States in the same terms.

These two newspapers arrive at a similar conclusion, despite their nations' differences: the impending war with Iraq did harm the United States' image in world opinion. Both newspapers also suggest the ramifications of the United States' move toward war with Iraq; these ramifications run from damage to the United States' image internationally to the potential destruction of the international system. Included in these warnings is the possibility of rendering the United Nations and its Security Council irrelevant to any future cooperative global ventures, thereby weakening the potential for a peaceful, secure international environment. Absent the leadership of the United States, either through implicit or explicit abdication or due to its damaged reputation, humanitarian and peacekeeping efforts might suffer irrevocable consequences.

Research on world opinion must move beyond media content analyses. Studying newspapers gives some general guidance about elite perceptions of world opinion and demonstrates how these perceptions change as global events occur. Since these are influential publications, the shifts they record can be interpreted as both *reflecting* and *affecting* world opinion to some extent. However, the problem with this approach is that it is difficult to describe precisely what one is measuring. References to world opinion in the media may reflect the economic and political origin of the nation in question, but studying them, while interesting, cannot reasonably answer all the questions posed above.

Another approach is to use the many global public opinion polls that have been fielded on the war on Iraq. These surveys yield important information about citizens' perceptions about the war on terrorism and related topics, most notably the international image and foreign policy of the United States. Further, the frequency of these polls allows one to trace trend data for many of these issues. Here, the results reflect a similar view of the United States. Indeed, the polls taken between 1999 and 2003 reflect a steady decline in positive evaluations of America across a variety of nations. Figure 6.5 illustrates these results for a number of different countries, including allies (France, Germany, and Turkey) and members of the "coalition of the willing" (Britain, Italy, Spain,[8] and Poland). There is little doubt that these findings are linked to the United States' handling of the situation in Iraq.

The question facing Americans, then, is, What went wrong? How did a world sympathetic to the United States after the attacks of 9/11 turn so hostile, and what effects did this hostility have on American identity and national pride? The answer lies in part in the failure of the Bush administration's emotional narrative linking the attacks to the war against Iraq.

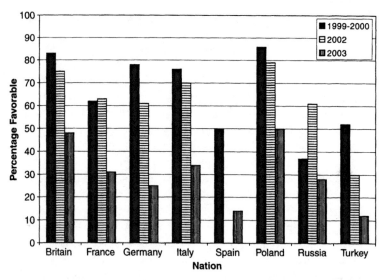

Figure 6.5   Percentage favorable views of the United States, by nation and year, 1999–2003

The Clash of Values

It is a given in George W. Bush's view of the world that the issue of terror-ism is primarily a conflict over values. In a speech he gave shortly after the September 11 attacks, Bush, explaining the terrorists' motives, said that they were trying to "remake the world so they could impose their beliefs on others."[9] Bush also offered an answer to the critical question on Americans' minds:

> Americans are asking: "Why do they hate us?"
> They hate what they see right here in this chamber, a democratically elected government. Their leaders are self-appointed. They hate our free-doms: our freedom of religion, our freedom of speech, our freedom to vote and assemble and disagree with each other ...
> This is not, however, just America's fight ... This is the world's fight. This is civilization's fight ...
> Freedom and fear, justice and cruelty, have always been at war, and we know that God is not neutral between them.[10]

Is the reference to a clash of values and the invocation of God in Bush's speech equivalent, however, to a "call to arms" in a civilizational clash with the Islamic world? The Bush administration can legitimately claim that its *overt* statements belie such an interpretation. The president has always been careful to quote Islamic clerics when he wishes to state that Islam and terrorism are not equivalent and that radical Islam has little or nothing to do with the Muslim religion. However, the references to values, God, and those that "hate our freedoms" send an *implied* message fine-tuned to a Judeo-Christian, Western narrative. As Benjamin R. Barber notes, "There is ... something unsettling in the parity of rhetoric that has al-Qaeda portraying America as an infidel nation doing the work of the Devil and America deploying analogous Old Testament language to condemn al-Qaeda as driven by evil ones (even if they *are* evil)."[11]
One encounters a similar tone in Bush's 2004 address to the United Nations:

> We've witnessed the rise of democratic governments in predominantly Hindu and Muslim, Jewish and Christian cultures ... When it comes to the desire for liberty and justice, *there is no clash of civilizations*. People every-where are capable of freedom, and worthy of freedom.[12]

But the mere mention of the "clash of civilizations" sends a dual signal to the domestic and international communities, especially since Bush then goes on to speak about the development of American democracy. Even when he rejects the notion that there is not "only one form of democracy" and states that "democracies, by definition, take on the unique character of the peoples that create them,"[13] the ambiguity of such phrases such as "liberty," "freedom," and "justice" implies that the definition of such terms will likely be cultural when one comes down to specifics. On the specific level, there are indications that from the world's point of view, this administration and its domestic allies may speak of universals, but they have in mind a Judeo-Christian definition of these terms.

In a tense world, political actors are often characterized by the most extreme of their supporters, particularly when the actors do not specifically denounce the extreme statements. Hence, the following statements, made by supporters or members of the Bush administration, resonated around the world as reflective of the administration's sentiments:

> "Just turn [the sheriff] loose and have him arrest every Muslim that crosses the state line."—Representative C. Saxby Chambliss, Republican, Georgia.[14]

> "Islam is a religion where God requires you to send your son to die for him. Christianity is a faith where God sent his Son to die for you."—Attorney General John Ashcroft.[15]

> "[Islam] is a very evil and wicked religion—wicked, violent and not of the same God (as Christianity)."—The Reverend Franklin Graham, head of the Billy Graham Evangelistic Association.[16]

> "I knew my God was bigger than his," Lieutenant General William G. Boykin said of his Muslim opponent. "I knew that my God was a real God, and his was an idol."[17]

The president need not directly say these things; if he fails to denounce these words, they come to represent U.S. policy to the Muslim world. As Samer Shehata, Professor at the Center for Contemporary Arab Studies at Georgetown University, notes:

> This isn't partisan politics. This is about U.S. national security: what kind of cooperation are we going to get from countries in the Muslim world; how are populations going to react to the United States as a result of Lt. Gen. William my-god-is-bigger-than-your-god Boykin, as it were? And the idea that ... Secretary Rumsfeld agreed to the idea that an investigation would be held, as it were, and that this gentleman, Mr. Boykin, hasn't been kicked out of government immediately, is very, very troubling to me. It's troubling because what message does it send to the Arab and Muslim world?
>
> We've seen a pattern here with people like Jerry Falwell and Franklin Graham, close to the administration, saying things like Mohammed is a terrorist; Islam is an evil religion. I was in Egypt when the Jerry Falwell thing

happened. There were reports all over the place. I was on BBC trying to talk about this. *The image was all over.* People are seeing this and they're saying ... what's going on here? Is it really a war against Islam as opposed to a war against terrorism? So it's a U.S. national security issue. *We cannot have this kind of image abroad* [emphases added].[18]

There has always been a close relationship between the Bush administration and certain Christian fundamentalists, a relationship made stronger by claims that the Christian Right provided Bush with his margin of victory in 2004. It is therefore not surprising that the Bush administration would be reluctant to break publicly with such groups, especially on the president's signature issue, national security. It is also not surprising, then, that individuals around the world, particularly those in Muslim countries, would feel that the administration's war on terror was a war on Islam, and that the administration embraced the "clash-of-civilizations" thesis. Indeed, if one observes the *actions*, and not just the *rhetoric*, of the administration, its members seem to embrace Huntington's approach.

In the introduction to this book, I noted that both the Arab and Israeli newspapers rejected the "clash-of-civilizations" thesis as a justification for the attacks of 9/11. Generally, other nations have greeted this interpretation coolly, explaining in part why the Bush administration's appeals often fell on deaf ears, for instance, in many parts of Europe. Indeed, the very fact that many nations in Europe (which Huntington characterized as part of "the West") refused to join the U.S. effort in Iraq suggests that there are critical fissures in the "natural alliances" he describes.

There is a second, more fundamental reason why the "clash-of-civilizations" thesis cannot justify the Bush administration's actions: the fundamental clash of values that the president often claims underlies the conflict between the United States and terrorism.

The Clash of Values: The Real Fault Lines

I have noted how the Bush administration's rhetoric has often preached about universally shared values such as "democracy," "freedom," and "justice." Bush cites these values positively as the goals of U.S. foreign policy and negatively when he describes the terrorists as individuals who attacked the United States because they hated these values. If one were to accept this argument in the context of a "clash of civilizations," one would assume that there was a significant gap in support for these values in Muslim nations as compared with the West. However, several analyses suggest that this gap does not exist.

Pippa Norris and Ronald Inglehart explore this issue in detail in a survey titled "Public Opinion among Muslims and the West."[19] Using the World Values Study, they divided nations into Western and Muslim, according to Huntington's classifications. They then compared support for four different aspects of democracy: approval of democratic performance, approval of democratic ideals, disapproval of religious leaders in politics, and disapproval of strong leaders. In three out of the four cases, support for democratic political values was equal among Western and Islamic nations. The two only differed on disapproval of religious leaders in politics, with Islamic nations less likely to hold this position than the Western, Christian nations.[20]

Other studies have produced similar results, even when the Islamic nations surveyed varied, or when the researchers surveyed only the Muslim populations of certain nations. In a 2003 survey, the Pew Global Attitudes Project studied Muslims in Kuwait, Nigeria, Jordan, Lebanon, Morocco, Pakistan, the Palestinian Authority, Turkey, and Indonesia. With the exception of Indonesia, Muslim citizens in these countries agreed with the statement "democracy can work here" as opposed to the statement "democracy is a Western way." Similar results were obtained in a 2002 survey of Muslims in Senegal, Uzbekistan, Ghana, the Ivory Coast, Uganda, Mali, Tanzania, and Bangladesh.[21] The results were less consistent, but still similar when the project surveyed predominantly Muslim nations on the questions of whether it was "very important" that "people can openly criticize the government," that "there are honest two-party elections," and "the media can report without censorship." Here, majorities supported these positions in Mali, Turkey, Bangladesh, Senegal, and Lebanon. In Pakistan and Indonesia, majorities supported the first position but not the latter two, and in Uzbekistan and Jordan, minorities supported all three positions.[22] The general results are therefore consistent with the findings of the Norris and Inglehart study, except on one point. When asked whether "religion is a private matter and should be kept separate from government," respondents in many countries with Muslim pluralities agreed. Indeed, the percentages agreeing in several of these nations, notably Turkey (73 percent), Lebanon (56 percent), Uzbekistan (55 percent), and Bangladesh (53 percent) either equaled or exceeded the percentage agreeing in the United States (55 percent); Indonesia (42 percent), Pakistan (33 percent), and Jordan (24 percent) had the lowest levels of agreement.[23] The separation between religion and state may not be unique to the American version of Western democracy, as Norris and Inglehart's study shows.

At the same time, there *are* important differences in values between the Western and Muslim nations, but as Norris and Inglehart state, these differences are more about eros than they are about demos; that is, the two groups of nations differ with respect to their views about gender roles and the rights of women. Predominantly Muslim societies were significantly less likely than Western societies to approve of homosexuality, abortion, divorce, and overall gender equality.[24]

But is the "clash of civilizations" distinction regarding democracy actually disproved by these results? After all, one may argue that a society that does not protect the rights of women and does not practice tolerance toward alternative lifestyles can hardly be called "democratic." Indeed, Laura Bush chastised the Taliban regime in November 2001 for its oppressive treatment of its female citizens, noting that their harsh measures were one more indicator of the repressive nature of that government.[25] Democracies, it is implied, do not attack their women any more than they attack each other. Democracies tolerate diversity, even when it extends to sexual preference, as a basic human right. One may validly argue, then, that the "clash of civilizations" between Western and Islamic nations is not a conflict over democratic procedures, but a conflict over democratic values. In effect, eros becomes demos when one considers the fundamental human rights that underlie democracies.

The civilizational conflict alluded to by the Bush administration and explicitly stated by several of its supporters and members, then, could still justify this administration's aims to further "democracy," "freedom," and "justice" in the world. One need only accept that a democracy that represses individual rights on the basis of gender or sexual preference is no democracy at all. However, problems arise with this interpretation when one examines how the issues that divide Islamic and Western nations in the Norris and Inglehart study play out in the American political context.

For the following analysis, I utilized the classification of nations from Norris and Inglehart; I then added two other groups for comparison— self-described liberals and conservatives in the United States. Each of the issues examined in the previous study were reexamined according to these four classifications. The resulting means are presented in figures 6.6–6.9.

The results indicate a similar pattern in all four instances. In each case, the mean liberal attitudes were closer to the mean attitudes of the Western nations than the mean conservative attitudes. Conversely, the mean conservative attitudes were closer to the mean attitudes of the Muslim nations than the mean liberal attitudes were. In the case of abortion, the mean conservative attitudes were actually *lower* than those of the Muslim nations.[26] These findings are underscored by the results of an ANOVA analysis. Hochberg's measure of categorical comparisons indicates no significant differences between the Western nations' attitudes and the U.S. liberals' attitudes on the four issues.[27] However, both the Western nations' and U.S. liberals' attitudes are significantly different from both the U.S. conservatives' and the Muslim nations' attitudes at the .000 level. Also,

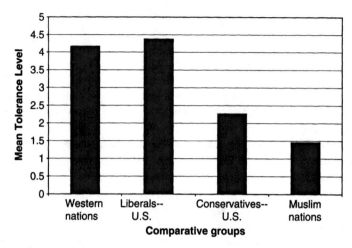

Figure 6.6   Comparative tolerance toward homosexuality (means)

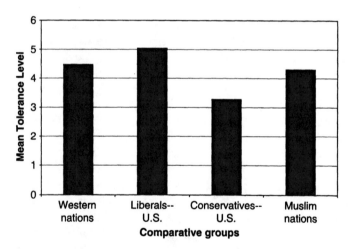

Figure 6.7   Comparative tolerance toward abortion (means)

while the attitudes of U.S. conservatives' are significantly different from the Muslim nations' attitudes at the .000 levels, they are still closer to the scores of the Muslim nations than they are to the scores of the Western nations. As Garry Wills notes regarding many of Bush's fundamentalist supporters: "Where else do we find fundamentalist zeal, a rage at secularity, religious intolerance, fear of an hatred for modernity? Not in France or Britain or Germany or Italy or Spain. We find it in the Muslim world, in

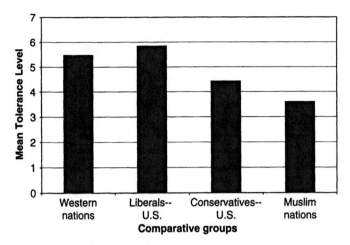

Figure 6.8   Comparative tolerance toward divorce (means)

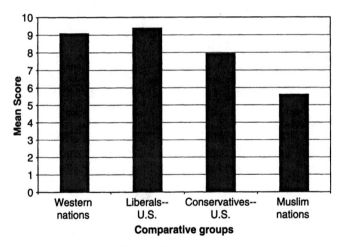

Figure 6.9   Comparative gender equality scores

Al-Qaeda, in Saddam Hussein's Sunni loyalists."[28] Emulating our enemies while claiming that they hate us for what we are will not stem the tide of global rage.

These results support the previous argument that despite the statements of many of the Bush administration's supporters and members, there is no "clash of civilizations" between Muslims and the West, at least from their conservative point of view. In fact, the fault lines between the "civilizations" reflect the fault lines in American society. In this conflict, conservatives in the United States are closer to the Muslim view of the world than that of the Western nations or American liberals. As such, American conservatives who argue that there is a "clash of civilizations" between Islam and the West are, quite literally, their own worst enemies.

The Real Clash

If there is no genuine "clash of civilizations" between Muslims and the United States, though, what is the substance of the conflict in the conservative worldview that dominates the Bush administration? If Muslim nations desire democracy, often have as much of a wall separating religion and state as America, and are closer to U.S. conservatives than they are to the Western nations on gender issues, where is the fight, especially if the United States is willing to expend American lives and resources to spread democracy? Put another way, how did the United States' justifiable anger after 9/11 lead to its becoming another case of global rage in the eyes of the world with the Iraq war?

We should realize that the damage to our international image is directly related to our own citizens' perceptions of the progress of the Iraq war. Figure 6.10 presents results over time from ABC surveys about the war and the United States' position in the world.[29] For this chart, I subtracted the percentage of those who felt that the war was wrong from the percentage of those who felt that the war was right; I graphed these results against a similar measure, composed of the percentage of those who thought that the war made the United States stronger in the world minus the percentage of those who felt that the war made the United States weaker in the world. The correlation between these results over time is clearly evident: as relative support for the war declined, Americans' perceptions of the strength of their nation's position in the world declined accordingly. The latter measure is as close as we tend to come to a perception of our *Fremdbild*, or the manner in which other nations view us. For Americans, positive world opinion had declined with the declines in their perceptions of the wisdom of the Iraq war. Given our previous analysis, it is not unreasonable to assume that our national pride would also be affected by these perceptions. These results strongly suggest that hypotheses 3 and 4 from Chapter 1 apply to the American case as well. We observe a potential link between our citizens' image of our place in the world and our actions amidst the Bush administration's unsuccessful attempts to convince the rest of the world of its motives.

The administration's general response has been to divide world opinion as a means of denying it. Hence, we distinguish "New Europe" from "Old

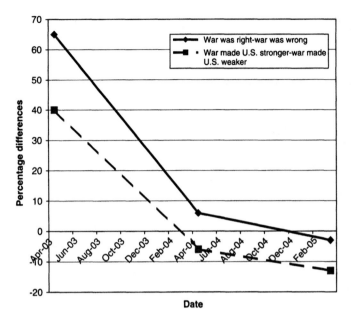

Figure 6.10   Differences between U.S. responses on Iraq war and whether the war made the United States stronger in the world

Europe," and the "coalition of the willing" from the unwilling (who apparently do not form a coalition). This categorization is as expedient as it is useless. If there are South American nations that did not support the invasion of Iraq, do we then distinguish the "New New World" from the "Old New World"? More importantly, when we say that a nation "supports" us, we are talking about their leaders, not necessarily their people. In many nations classified as part of the "coalition of the willing," a majority of citizens disagreed with their leaders' involvement in the Iraq war—an ironic circumstance in the supposed pursuit of democracy.

But it is the innocent pursuit of democracy that we believe motivates us and differentiates the United States from the rest of the world. Barber notes that while many other nations have proclaimed their uniqueness throughout history, "No nation ... has been so committed to its exceptionalist myths in its policies and practices as the United States, and none have made exceptionalism so central to their national life and their international politics. Among the exceptionalist myths that fire the American imagination, the myth of innocence is perhaps paramount—buttressed by the ideology of independence."[30] As such, George W. Bush can state that the goal of American foreign policy is to spread democracy and thereby attribute altruistic motives to the United States. After all, we are willing to spend our political capital, our resources, even perhaps the lives of our military personnel in bringing the benefits of freedom to the rest of the world. All we ask for in return is the natural security that follows from democratic reform; since (it is argued) democracies do not attack other democracies, all nations, including the United States, would be safer if all nations adopted democratic practices and procedures. Despite the accusations that others may level at us, we have no imperialistic designs on other countries.

This defense assumes, of course, that we believe that other nations are not only capable of creating and maintaining democracies, but also in defining what constitutes a democracy—and it is here that the Bush administration projects a quasi-imperial hubris. For Americans are too easily convinced that they not only invented democracy and perfected it, but that they are also its most perfect representation on Earth. We maintain this myth with an appropriate nod to Great Britain, which did, after all, produce John Locke, to provide the inspiration for the Declaration of Independence. Yet, we still maintain that the British form of government, with its inherited monarchy and traditions, is inferior to our more perfect union.

American traditions support this belief: citizens of the United States associate their system of government with what it means to be American. It is no accident that in the original study of The Civic Culture (1965), while other countries were proudest of certain characteristics that their citizens associated with their ethnicity (i.e., Italy with its artistic traditions, Germany with its technological achievements), U.S. citizens were proudest of "our system of government[31]"—and this result held steady, even while other measures of confidence in the government and its institutions declined through the 1980s and beyond. The reason for this result is that our system of government, or democracy, is an integral part of our national identity. Although Americans may be skeptical of institutions on the specific level, we do not allow institutional mistrust to challenge a pride in the system in a way that would threaten our very identities. For this reason, the original measure of national pride outlined in Chapter 2 has a special resonance in the United States. That measure included such factors as how proud citizens were about their country regarding the way democracy works, its political influence in the world, its armed forces, and its fair and equal treatment of all groups in society. Our belief in our democracy and our fair treatment of all groups in our society becomes the measure of our political influence in the world, as enforced (when necessary) by our military. As such, when an American president advocates "advancing democracy" as a goal, it translates into advancing American national identity throughout the world. The basic measure of pride used in the study becomes self-reflexive when applied to the American case—we project our identity and express our global rage under the guise of "advancing democracy." We fulfill the first and second hypotheses from Chapter 1, where our anxieties result in the projection of an idea of democracy that we do not even recognize as the key element of our identity.

But advancing democracy as a means of projecting American identity serves neither purpose. As a strategy, it undermines democracy by robbing individuals in the nations where we intervene of the fundamental pride of self-determination that is instrumental to a successful nation. It undermines our identity by pitting us against the rest of the world, thereby hurting our national pride by harming our international image. The roots of terrorism lie in a *ressentiment* and the assaults on national and individual pride resulting from a changing global environment. Projecting American identity as the one true solution to this surfeit of pride only exacerbates the humiliation. In the name of democracy, we become part of the problem.

Part III

Conclusion

7

Addressing the Real Problem: Draining the Swamps of Despair

In the film *Control Room,* a commentator from the Arab network Al-Jazeera watches as American forces tear down the statues of Saddam Hussein shortly after the beginning of the Iraq war. She shakes her head in disbelief at the apparent quick defeat of the Iraqi forces. "Where is the Republican guard?" she asks in a voice filled with humiliation, even though she did not support Saddam Hussein.

Defeat in war, including conquest and occupation by a foreign power, is a humiliating experience, not only for those who lose but also for those who identify with them. Historically, the shame of Germany's loss in World War I was a strong contributing factor to World War II. More recently, the Israelis' quick victory in the aptly named Six-Day War in 1967 precipitated the Yom Kippur War in 1973, as Arab nations wished to erase the humiliation of their swift loss to a nation they outnumbered. No doubt, one of the forces fueling the present insurgency in Iraq is the desire of many soldiers and citizens to prove that the United States' victory was neither as quick nor as limited in losses as the tumbling statues of Saddam Hussein suggested. As Antony Beevor noted about the Iraqis just after these events in 2003, "Few countries love their liberators once the cheering dies away. This is especially true when they feel humiliated."[1] It is for this reason also that one of the most dangerous countries in the world today is Russia, which, owing to its loss of the Soviet Union, its defeat in the Cold War, and its devastated economy, provides fertile ground for demagogic appeals to restore the glory of the Russian empire.

But the problem of global rage is not merely felt in those countries that were defeated in the Cold War. Even the supposed "victors," or others who were nonaligned, may feel the effects of global status deficiencies that could lead to violent expressions of identity. Global rage presents a special problem because its effects are not related to a specific nation's defeat in a war, but rather to the collapse of a value system that provided an alternative to the capitalist, developmental model. Nations seeking international status feel the grinding effects of these status deficiencies every day in subtle ways, even when the most powerful and rich nations are not flaunting their superiority. In that sense, the humiliation that leads to global rage is different in kind from the humiliation a nation suffers after a defeat in war. A victor gracious in victory and generous in rebuilding the conquered areas may ease the latter type of humiliation. Examples such as the Marshall Plan, which was enacted after World War II, come to mind. But the seeds of *ressentiment* are sown by just the everyday activities of the major powers, especially the United States, which inadvertently and often innocently export their cultures for profit. Moreover, as we have seen, even the major powers are capable of global rage, especially in reaction to relative shocks to their global standing, such as the horrors of 9/11. Economic aid, as in the Marshall Plan, cannot solve a problem that is potentially endemic to all nations.

What, then, are the prospects for restraining global rage by state and non-state actors? It is perhaps best to begin with strategies that will not work, even though they are presently being practiced.

Fire with Fire, Rage with Rage

The natural inclination, especially for the most powerful nations, is to fight rage with rage. One answers unjustifiable acts such as the attacks of 9/11 or the bombing of embassies or civilian targets with swift, decisive, and overwhelming force. The problem with this solution is that it is both ineffective and self-defeating unless a state is responsible for these acts. Otherwise, one cannot respond swiftly to an enemy that "hides in plain sight," disappearing among civilians in another country. One cannot be decisive when one cannot identify who should be held responsible for these acts. And one cannot use overwhelming force when the targets are either single individuals or small groups hiding among innocents in the population.

This strategy becomes self-defeating when targets are chosen arbitrarily, out of a need to express global rage at a person or group considered to be an antagonist. Simply put, it was for this reason that the international community generally supported the United States' attacks on the Taliban in Afghanistan but condemned the U.S. war with Iraq. The former targeted an unrecognized government that was harboring terrorists; the latter was never seen as the "imminent threat" described by President Bush.[2] It is no accident that the U.S. invasion of Iraq was viewed by many individuals in the Middle East and beyond as a means of humiliating Islam in a quasi-civilizational war of values. Even Bush's stated commitments to democracy in the region, as sincere as they may be, have come to be understood as part of the Western "white man's burden" to bring a democratic civic religion to the heathens.

One cannot characterize one's enemies as the embodiment of evil and then invade their nation with a combination of "shock and awe" that one claims is aimed only at the evildoers, as such actions cause extensive civilian casualties as well. The torture of prisoners at Abu Ghraib served to reinforce the feeling that the true purpose of the United States was to humiliate the Muslim captives, many of whom were so shamed by the acts forced upon them that they preferred to die rather than return to their villages and families upon release. It is an inviolable rule of human nature that once one personifies the enemy as pure evil, one becomes sorely tempted to adopt his tactics. Crushing cities under enormous military power, or crushing individual dignity under torture, further serves to diminish an individual in the eyes of the world, even if the world sympathizes with them. Such a strategy adds fuel to the fires of global rage and robs individuals of the civic pride a participatory society requires. For democracy demands ongoing, empowered citizenship; elections may be a necessary part of the system, but they are not sufficient if individuals do not remain engaged in civic participation between elections. Global rage can occur even in democratic countries, and the humiliation that lies beneath it, if sustained, will ultimately destroy any attempts at a democratic system.

A related and more frightening problem is what will occur as these strategies fail. The theory of liberal nationalism prescribes a healthy national pride as the solution to feelings of *ressentiment*. As nation-states fail to provide such pride owing to the nature of the global system and its related status hierarchy, they will fail in spectacular ways. Into the vacuum will move such non-state actors as al-Qaida and other shadowy groups that are often impossible to hold accountable because they do not have an "address" where they can be located. One need only measure recent events in the context of our analysis to see how far along we are on the path to this frightening scenario.

The failure of states to provide pride was based upon two major deficits in the post–Cold War world—a deficit of power that made former actors on the world stage (Western, Communist, or nonaligned) often irrelevant to the new order; and a deficit of identity that proved that these actors were not on the right side of history and that their basic values were lacking. Al-Qaida, with its attacks on September 11, 2001, was able to become a world actor by altering the foreign and domestic policy direction of the United States. In foreign policy, the United States embraced questionable leaders such as Putin in Russia[3] and Musharraf in Pakistan as allies in the war on terror, despite their undemocratic tendencies. In domestic policy, it altered many of its basic assumptions about its citizens' civil liberties and rights.

To take another example, the bomb attack on the Madrid train station led to a Socialist victory in Spain and the subsequent withdrawal of troops and support from the U.S. war in Iraq. The Madrid bombing was not a direct case of cause-and-effect, since the Conservative government lost the election largely because it mishandled the aftermath of the attack by first trying to blame it on Basque separatists. But al-Qaida could still claim that their actions had made them significant actors on the world stage.

Adherents of non-state groups such as al-Qaida can claim a pride in advancing a conflict between civilizations that many of the world's leaders resisted. In the "Introduction," I noted how prominent newspapers in Israel and Saudi Arabia denied that the attacks of September 11 were a harbinger of a "clash of civilizations." Since then, Huntington's thesis has gained currency among many foreign policy thinkers and has become an implicit theme in much of the Bush administration's rhetoric. As the Israeli *Ha'aretz* noted, "Thanks to these bin Laden notched up a major triumph: a terrorist gang that does nothing to help the population in the name of which it purportedly murders was transformed by the West and anointed the representative of a billion people" (October 4, 2001). Restructuring or reinforcing the interpretation of Islam among the world's leaders is a heady achievement—one that no doubt stimulates pride in al-Qaida members and supporters. Such successes lend credence to the nightmarish scenario in which non-state actors fulfill the needs of place and identity for their followers; in an international system so organized, global rage and chaos would likely be the norm.

World Opinion as a Solution

In the conclusion of his book, *Fear's Empire*, Benjamin R. Barber argues that "the emerging voice of global public opinion" can speak "to issues that go far beyond their neighborhoods—suggesting that interdependence makes the idea of a global neighborhood less of an oxymoron than it used to be."[4] But the preceding analyses show that the process of world opinion still operates in the reality of a world of nations. World opinion may be a likely basis for a form of transnational identity. But its power to affect national identities is more important at this point in history. While it may promise to undergird an international order sometime in the future, it now serves primarily to confer the global status that is a necessary ingredient for national pride. The failure of world opinion to restrain the evil angels of our existence has more to do with the structural bases of global status than with any deficiency in its reach or power. If anything, global rage traces its roots to the global status hierarchy, thereby illustrating the influence of world opinion on our lives.

One must also understand that terrorism is only one symptom of the general disease of global rage. Too often, the two are seen to belong to entirely different categories. It is generally argued that terrorism is the weapon of the weak or disenfranchised groups such as al-Qaida or the PLO. Yet, even the most powerful of states can commit acts of global rage. Unless one sees terrorism as one symptom of this general disease, one cannot hope to eradicate it.

Leaders such as Osama bin Laden or terrorist organizations such as al-Qaida do not cause terrorism; they commit terrorist acts. Terrorism will outlive their demise or disruption. It is a tragic lesson of history that no society has lacked individuals willing to commit the most heinous crimes for a cause. But it is others who are willing to follow such leaders—who are willing to fly planes into buildings or serve as suicide bombers in Palestine—who make these individuals such a threat. Cutting off the heads of these organizations without eliminating their ability to recruit adherents is as useless in this case as it was in the fight against the mythical Hydra. If we continue to deceive ourselves that Palestinian suicide bombers committed their acts because Saddam Hussein paid their families $25,000, for example, we will also believe incorrectly that unseating him will solve the problem. Unless one drains the swamps of despair, they will continue to breed disease and pestilence, led by new leaders that surface from their depths.

This does not mean that world opinion has no role to play in the battle against despair and *ressentiment*. On the contrary, it is the major weapon against global rage, and, in turn, against terrorism. But wielding this weapon requires a major effort backed by creative leadership.

As a first step, one must return to the root causes of global status deficiencies—an international environment in which there now exists a single hierarchy joining wealth, power, and global rank in world opinion. As long as there are inequalities of power and wealth, this hierarchy will remain; further, while one may wish for those nations on the top to share their resources to reduce such inequalities, it is unrealistic to assume this will occur anytime in the near future. If anything, the trend seems to be running in the other direction in the United States, where the emphasis is on guns for defense, not butter for foreign aid. Even if the richest nations shared resources, they would not be willing to redistribute their wealth sufficiently to erase the differences among nations.

The only way to erase global status deficiencies, then, is to make the present hierarchy of nations less relevant. Other more benevolent alternatives than injured nationalism or political fundamentalism must be created to foster national status and pride. New hierarchies that reorder the global ranking of nations must be created—hierarchies that serve the purpose of promoting values other than power or wealth for judging a nation's worth. Some writers have suggested that such alternatives to the existing developmental hierarchy might be based upon the principles of feminism or multiculturalism.[5] Other writers, notably James Kurth[6] and Francis Fukuyama,[7] have argued the opposite—that so long as our enemies practice a decidedly "male" violence, we must meet their challenge with hegemonic masculinity. As such, the only women qualified for leadership are those who, like Margaret Thatcher, take on a masculine role.

The latter arguments are consistent with the findings in Chapter 6 about conservative and Muslim attitudes toward the role of women. Fukuyama especially argues that the conflict for status is natural, unavoidable, and inherently violent. Feminist theorists, among others, are correct in noting that the hierarchy of values that prompts global rage is a social construction, not a "natural" feature of human existence. Where the feminist and multicultural theorists fall short is in describing an alternative hierarchy of values that is sufficient to confer status globally on citizens of various nations. Faced with this problem, they often argue that the world would be a better place if we abandoned such structural hierarchies altogether. While that may be true, the dismantling of hierarchy, like the redistribution of resources, is unlikely to occur anytime soon. Other feminist and multicultural theorists have suggested that different hierarchies of values might prove a source of pride that serves as an alternative to the present developmental model. But one generally finds that the alternatives they propose are basically a set of assurances that new values should and will emerge when the dominant paradigm is overcome.

Terrorism is often described as the weapon of the weak. Such an assertion necessarily absolves the major powers from being accused of practicing "terrorism." Instead, such nations are assumed to have sufficient resources to project power by other means, providing them with an ethical high ground in international affairs. This assumption necessarily limits the tools major powers can bring to bear upon the plague of international terrorism. An indiscriminant and reckless display of power by nations such as the United States and its allies will only underscore the relative weakness of the other nations in conventional terms. In turn, this will invite an unconventional response, one that is likely to be directed against civilians, the most vulnerable targets in an open society.

The arrogant use of power sends a message to the world that one knows that the intended target is weak and cannot strike back; it directly attacks the global status of the nation or peoples in question. Individuals subjected

to that form of attack, be it military, cultural, or economic, real or imagined, seek to find other means to increase their status in the world and to
protect their identities. Their justifications may be nationalism or religious
fundamentalism—any ideology that explains their present weakness and
offers an alternative view of history and development that promises the
future will be different. Such perceptions provide fertile ground for the
growth of terrorism.

It is of little interest, when all is said and done, to ponder the psychological motivations of a leader like Osama bin Laden or others of his type.
It is of profound importance, however, to understand how such individuals find recruits for their actions. As long as international status has basically one standard with a few nations clustered near the top, and those
nations can only respond to attacks after the fact by means that reinforce
the weakness of other countries, the swamp of despair from which terrorism springs will remain.

The only solution is to reconceptualize global leadership, particularly
from an American point of view. Some theorists have envisioned that
international public opinion might restrain extreme nationalism or religious fundamentalism, and the atrocities that so often accompany them.
The reality is more sobering. World opinion actually plays a complex role
in the resurgence of nationalism or religious fundamentalism and the rage
that often accompanies it. International public opinion supplies the global
status that resentment-prone individuals seek in their construction of
identity. The "social value" of citizenship—whether it be in a nation or a
defined group—is measured by its capacity to grant status to individuals
internationally. The examples studied here, coupled with the rise of terrorism as a truly global phenomenon, indicate that the stakes in this effort
could not be much higher than they are now.

The problem will not be solved by a crude multiculturalism that
declares all cultures "equally valid." Amin Malouf, in his book *In the
Name of Identity: Violence and the Need to Belong*, advocates extending a
multicultural model that has worked within nations to the entire world.[8]
There are two problems with this formulation. First, how well the multicultural experiment works in nations is still an open question; the United
States, with its mix of cultures, is often cited as a successful example, but
critics often charge that this mixture undermines the nation's unity.
Second, the idea of an international multiculturalism suggests that a
global pluralism can exist while the capitalist model still predominates,
granting international status only to those nations on the uppermost
rungs. It is unlikely that this situation will alter itself without direct intervention by the major powers.

Another major problem with a simplified notion of globalized multiculturalism is that it opens itself to the type of caricature that Allan Bloom
practices in *The Closing of the American Mind:*

> The study of history and of culture teaches that all the world was mad in the
> past; men always thought they were right, and that led to wars, persecutions,
> slavery, xenophobia, racism, and chauvinism. The point is not to correct the
> mistakes and really be right; rather it is not to think you are right at all. The
> students, of course, cannot defend their opinion. It is something with which
> they have been indoctrinated. The best they can do is point out all the opin-
> ions and cultures there are and have been. What right, they ask, do I or any-
> one else have to say one is better than the others? If I pose the routine ques-
> tions designed to confuse them and make them think, such as, "If you had
> been a British administrator in India, would you have let the natives under
> your governance burn the widow at the funeral of a man who had just
> died?" they either remain silent or reply the British should never have been
> there in the first place ... The purpose of their education is not to make
> them scholars but to provide them with a moral virtue—openness.[9]

Condemning a culture on the basis of specific practices reduces that culture to a mere set of ideas; but a culture is more than ideas—it is a set of
relationships that can, in fact, outlive the failure of ideas. Otherwise, a society and its moral system would never survive the complications of social
life. As James Baldwin notes, "The betrayal of belief is not the same thing
as ceasing to believe. If this were not so there would be no moral standards
in the world at all."[10] We must begin by acknowledging that there is a link
between the manner in which we think about ideas and the manner in
which we approach history. If we view our present world configuration as
the result of a clash of ideas—or "civilizations"—with one eventual victor,
we may come to view the interactions between cultures in the same way,
historically. Hence, we could easily justify dominance by assuming that we
are more evolved, historically, than the cultures we come to dominate.
Such a conclusion not only justifies abominable behavior, it also encounters serious intellectual problems. It fails to acknowledge that the evolution
of our "thought" and the evolutionary model of history are somehow
linked, making conflict and the fight for a "dominant" culture a foregone
conclusion.

An alternative solution lies in rethinking our notions of history and
"development" within a globalized context.In trying to imagine what this
would imply, I would suggest an alternative model to the "clash of civilizations" theory—and the resulting clash of visions of history—that
Huntington advances. I propose that we begin by acknowledging that once
contact is established in a globalized world, "their" story and "our" story

become one history. The challenge is to imagine what this new history—as narrative and idea—would look like. To fail to do so is to indulge in denial by assuming that there is, and should be, one true dominant culture and that then everything will be fine. The reality of global rage does not allow us such innocence.

We require a way of thinking about the interaction of cultures as a process without winners or losers—as a story that unifies two histories, each affecting the other. Instead of conceptualizing the interaction of cultures as a clash of ideas, we must engage in a dialogue aimed at finding universals; this project would focus upon symbiosis, rather than domination, of ideas or cultures. For if we continue to see cultural contact in terms of a clash of ideas, we are always reduced to questions of power—and any society whose basic ideas are justified only by power will find that in an increasingly multicultural world, "their center cannot hold"; for us, things can, and will, fall apart.

In an interconnected world, however, there are alternatives; one merely has to discover them and bring them forward. The real promise of technologies such as the Internet is that they allow for the transmission of information and ideas without the burden of producing something that must be consumed. Put another way, one can disseminate things that others find of value without forcing them to serve the profit motivations that underlie the present developmental hierarchy. The challenge is to ensure that these alternative paths to global and individual status do not carry with them the potential for violence. Further, they must be tied to the tangible, not the metaphysical, if they are to be accepted universally. Emulating our enemies while claiming they hate us for what we are will not stem the tide of global rage. Our creative powers, which can remake so much, must be turned toward generating values that can sustain the dignity of a multiplicity of peoples.

Such an intervention must involve discovering aspects of specific cultures that distinguish them from others *and form the basis for international status beyond a capitalist model of development.* One cannot merely say that one will accept all cultures—whether Western capitalist, fundamentalist (of whatever type), or postmodern—in their entirety. That would entail accepting contradictory doctrines while ignoring the harmful aspects of many traditions. Rather, the major powers must take the lead in emphasizing that there are aspects of cultures within nations or regions that are deserving of international recognition and respect and act to promote this perception globally. Only then can any of the major powers claim that a truly pluralistic view exists regarding status and cultures on a global level. The second strategy follows upon the first. We must integrate the positive aspects of other cultures—the points upon which we can agree—into a unified notion of history and development. This will not be an easy task, as it will involve disrupting the current hierarchy of values, potentially jeopardizing the positions of all nations, including our own. In principle, it should be possible for world opinion—guided by imaginative leadership and given the right circumstances—to elevate nations to international status on the basis of their identities without involving virulent forms of nationalism or political or religious fundamentalism. We must understand that in the present global configuration, such a task is not based on idealistic or altruistic motives. It is instead a matter of survival.

Notes

Part I

Introduction: World Opinion on September 11, 2001—If the World Doesn't Hate Us, Why Would Someone Do This?

1. John Vinocour, "The New World Order Is a Clash of Civilizations," *International Herald Tribune*, September 13, 2001: 1.
2. Samuel P. Huntington, *The Clash of Civilizations and the Remaking of World Order* (New York: Simon and Schuster, 1996), p. 39.
3. Huntington, "The Clash of Civilizations?" *Foreign Affairs* 72, no. 3 (1993): 191.
4. See, for instance, Frank Louis Rusciano, *World Opinion and the Emerging International Order* (Westport, CT: Praeger, 1998) and Hedley Bull and Adam Watson, *The Expansion of International Society* (Oxford: Clarendon Press, 1984).
5. James Mayall, *Nationalism and International Society* (New York: Cambridge University Press), p. 19.
6. Rusciano, *World Opinion*, p. 164.
7. Mayall, *Nationalism and International Society*, p. 7.
8. Rusciano, *World Opinion*, p. 24.
9. Ibid., p. 156.
10. Joseph Nye describes a more productive use of a nation's influence over world opinion as "soft power" in his book *The Paradox of American Power*. He notes how propagating our values can be a positive force, so long as we pursue it through persuasion, rather than through some combination of superior military or economic force (Nye, 2002, pp. 1–40).
11. Owing to archival problems, the first week after September 11, 2001 was unfortunately not included in the analysis of the *Arab News*. All subsequent analysis thus does not include this newspaper's results for the first week.
12. The Nigerian *Guardian*, for instance, is published in a nation with a predominantly Muslim population. It is not included within the "Islamic civilization" newspapers, though, for two reasons. First, Nigeria is placed within "African civilization" in Huntington's typology; second, the *Guardian* was chosen specifically because it is a secular newspaper from Nigeria. Certainly, there are newspapers in that nation written from the Islamic perspective, but they were

not chosen for that reason and because they are not generally newspapers of record like the *Guardian*.

13. Edward S. Herman and Noam Chomsky, *Manufacturing Consent: The Political Economy of Mass Media* (New York: Random House, 1988).

14. In order to assure inter-coder reliability on these items, all results were reviewed, first in the research group, and then by the principal investigator, for consistency of interpretation.

15. The remaining 50 percent of the references were neutral. Only those stories that evaluated the United States were included in this portion of the analysis, for a total of 213.

16. The η value for these results was .410.

17. See Frank Louis Rusciano and Roberta Fiske-Rusciano, "Towards a Notion of 'World Opinion,' " *International Journal of Public Opinion Research* 2 (1990): 305–322.

18. See Frank Louis Rusciano and Bosah Ebo, "National Consciousness, International Image, and the Construction of Identity," in Rusciano, *World Opinion*, ch. 3.

19. Frank Louis Rusciano and Roberta Fiske-Rusciano, "Towards a Notion," in Rusciano, *World Opinion*, ch. 1.

20. See, for instance, Rusciano and Fiske-Rusciano, "Towards a Notion," 305–322.

21. Due to archival problems, the first week after September 11, 2001 was unfortunately not included in the analysis of the *Arab News*. All subsequent analyses thus do not include this newspaper's results for the first week.

22. See Frank Louis Rusciano, "Media Perspectives on 'World Opinion' During the Kuwaiti Crisis," in *Media and the Persian Gulf War*, ed. Robert E. Denton (Westport, CT: Praeger, 1993): 71–87.

23. Unfortunately, it is impossible to test whether the dates of references to world opinion converge on the attacks in the first week, since that week is missing from the archival data for the *Arab News*. Anecdotal evidence suggests it is likely they did converge for the Western civilization's and other civilizations' newspapers; it is more difficult to predict the results for the *Arab News*. The important point here is the divergence that occurs between the Muslim newspapers and the others following September 19, 2001.

24. Tukey's post-hoc test was used in the ANOVA (analysis of variance) analysis for these comparisons. When one examined the differences among the individuals "civilizations" in the "other" category, the results were remarkably the same. The Western newspapers differed significantly in evaluating world opinion on the United States only from the *Arab News* and *Pravda*. By contrast, the *Arab News*, besides differing significantly from the Western newspapers, also differed significantly from the Indian, Chinese, and Argentinean newspapers; only the Nigerian *Guardian* and *Pravda* did not show significant differences there.

25. The analysis excludes the first week of the study, where archival problems interfered with results from the *Arab News*; also, cases were weighted by the total number of cases per week for the three groups.

26. Michael Doran, "The Pragmatic Fanaticism of al Qaeda: An Anatomy of Extremism in Middle Eastern Politics," *Political Science Quarterly* 117, no. 2 (2002): 185.

27. Ibid., 186.

28. Ibid., 190.

29. The one exception was Eastern Europe, where equal percentages of respondents (40 percent) thought the conflict was a clash of civilizations between Islam and the West as though it was merely a battle between the United States and al-Qaida.

30. Huntington, "The Clash of Civilizations: A Debate," in *A Foreign Affairs Reader* (New York: Council on Foreign Relations, 1993).

31. Bernard Lewis, "The Roots of Muslim Rage," *The Atlantic,* September 1990, p. 53.

32. Ibid.

Chapter 1 The Cold War World Turned Upside Down

1. Robert L. Bartley, "The Case for Optimism: The West Should Believe It Itself," *Foreign Affairs* (September–October 1993): 15.

2. Shlomo Avinieri, *Proceedings of the Conference on Europe in the New World Order* (Georgetown University: Washington, DC, 1991), p. 25.

3. Liah Greenfeld, "Nationalism and Class Struggle: Two Forces or One?" *Survey* 29 (1985): 153–174.

4. There is some controversy over which nations should be included in the second- and third-world categories. For instance, nations such as Vietnam or Albania could have been classified in either group, depending upon the analyst's purposes and orientation.

5. Paul J. Best, Kul B. Rai, and David F. Walsh, *Politics in Three Worlds: An Introduction to Political Science* (New York: John Wiley and Sons, 1986).

6. J. L. Talmon, *The Origins of Totalitarian Democracy* (New York: Praeger, 1960), pp. 1–2.

7. Eugene Rostow, *The Stages of Economic Growth: A Non-Communist Manifesto* (London: Cambridge University Press, 1971). Rostow self-consciously proclaims his book, *The Stages of Economic Growth,* to be a "non-Communist manifesto" in its subtitle. Similarly, Daniel Bell's thesis on the emergence of postindustrial society necessarily includes an extended critique of the shortcomings of the Marxist theory of development; see Bell, *The Coming of Postindustrial Society: A Venture in Social Forecasting* (New York: Basic Books, 1973), pp. 99–112.

8. Some authors, notably Mowlana and Wilson (1990) and Rogers (1978) have argued that the major paradigms of development are of little use in analyzing nations in certain comparative contexts, and should be abandoned. However, they fail to outline a convincing alternative that has gained wide acceptance

among social scientists and opinion leaders. Hamid Mowlana and Laurie J. Wilson, *The Passing of Modernity: Communication and the Transformation of Society* (New York: Longman, 1990); Everett M. Rogers, "The Rise and Fall of the Dominant Paradigm," *Journal of Communication* 28 (1978): 64–69. See also Bosah Ebo, "Africa and the West in the New World Information Order" (paper presented at the Northwestern University Conference on Communication and Development. Chicago, IL, 1983) for a more detailed discussion.

9. Of course, the Communist nations also promised a higher standard of living to nonaligned third-world countries. However, this appeal was based upon an interpretation of development that argued that the third world was subject to a permanently lower standard of living owing to its economic arrangements with Western nations, which included the acceptance of Western theories of development.

10. Yael Tamir, "The Right to National Self-Determination," *Social Research* 58 (1991): 587.

11. Liah Greenfeld, *Nationalism: Five Roads to Modernity* (Cambridge, MA: Harvard University Press, 1992), p. 487.

12. Greenfeld, "Nationalism and Class Struggle, 15–16.

13. O. Obasanjo, *Proceedings of the Conference on Europe in the New World Order* (Georgetown University: Washington, DC, 1991), p. 94.

14. Zbigniew Brzezinski, "Power and Morality," *World Monitor* (March 1993): 24.

15. Fred Hirsch, *The Social Limits to Growth* (Cambridge, MA: Harvard University Press, 1976).

16. Robert B. Reich, "What Is a Nation?" *Political Science Quarterly* 106 (1991): 193–209.

17. A. A. Mazrui, *The Africans: A Triple Heritage* (Boston, MA: Little, Brown, Inc., 1986). In this manner, this chapter uses Mazrui's commentary on the "social construction" of reality regarding Africa as just one critical resource from the third-world literature that is relevant to the discussion of nationalist phenomena.

18. Gyorgy Csepeli, "Competing Patterns of National Identity in Post-Communist Hungary," *Media, Culture, and Society* 13 (1991): 325–339.

19. Ibid., 327.

20. Harry Pross, "On German Identity," *Media, Culture, and Society* 13 (1991): 342.

21. K. J. Gergen, "Social Construction in Question," *Human Systems: The Journal of Systematic Consultation and Management* 3 (1992): 171.

22. Eric Waddel, "Language, Community and National Identity: Some Reflections on French–English Relations in Canada," in *Canadian Politics: An Introduction to the Discipline*, ed. Alain-G. Gagnon and James P. Bickerton (Lewiston, NY: Broadview Press, 1990), p. 61.

23. C. Gilligan, *In a Different Voice* (Cambridge, MA: Harvard University Press, 1992), p. 160.

24. Frank Louis Rusciano, *Isolation and Paradox: Defining "the Public" in Modern Political Analysis* (Westport, CT: Greenwood Press, 1989), pp. 79–110.

25. On the "two notions of world opinion," see Christopher J. Hill, "World Opinion and the Empire of Circumstance," *International Affairs* 72 (January 1996): 109–131.

26. Carlos Fuentes, interview in *A World of Ideas*, ed. Bill Moyers, p. 307 (New York: Doubleday, 1989).

27. Bernard Lewis, *What Went Wrong: Western Impact and Middle Eastern Response* (New York: Oxford University Press), pp. 26–28.

28. Jack A. Goldstone, "States, Terrorists, and the Clash of Civilizations," in *Understanding September 11*, ed. Craig Calhoun, Paul Price, and Ashley Timmer (New York: New Press, 2002), p. 142.

29. Lewis, *What Went Wrong*, p. 62.

30. Ibid.

31. Goldstone, "States, Terrorists," p. 143.

32. Ibid., p. 144.

33. Ibid., p. 143.

34. Timur Kuran, "The Religious Undertow of Muslim Economic Grievances," in *Understanding September 11*, ed. Craig Calhoun, Paul Price, and Ashley Timmer (New York: New Press, 2002), p. 68.

35. Ibid., pp. 68–69.

36. Mark Juergensmeyer, "Religious Terror and Global War," in *Understanding September 11*, ed. Craig Calhoun, Paul Price, and Ashley Timmer (New York: New Press, 2002), p. 36.

37. Kuran, "Religious Undertow," p. 69.

38. Juergensmeyer, "Religious Terror," p. 36.

39. Data compiled from surveys gathered from the Interuniversity Consortium of Social Sciences.

40. Pippa Norris and Ronald Inglehardt, "Muslims and the West: Testing the 'Clash of Civilizations' Thesis," in *Proceedings of "The Restless Searchlight: Media and Terrorism"* (The Kennedy School, Harvard University, Cambridge, MA, September 1, 2002), p. 12.

41. The Western nations include Australia, Austria, Belgium, France, Ireland, Italy, Malta, Portugal, Spain, Switzerland, Britain, Canada, Denmark, Finland, Iceland, New Zealand, the Netherlands, Northern Ireland, Norway, Sweden, the United States, and West Germany. The Muslim nations include Albania, Azerbaijan, Bangladesh, Egypt, Iran, Jordan, Morocco, Pakistan, and Turkey. The rest of the nations include Belarus, Bosnia, Bulgaria, Georgia, Greece, Macedonia, Moldova, Montenegro, Romania, Russia, Serbia, the Ukraine, Croatia, the Czech Republic, East Germany, Estonia, Hungary, Latvia, Lithuania, Poland, Slovakia, Slovenia, Argentina, Brazil, Chile, Colombia, the Dominican Republic, El Salvador, Mexico, Peru, Uruguay, Venezuela, South Korea, Taiwan, Vietnam, China, Nigeria, South Africa, Tanzania, Uganda, and Zimbabwe.

42. A Hochberg test was used to measure the significance of the differences among the means.

43. The Hochberg test indicated significant differences between the mean values for the Islamic nations and the Western and Other nations.

44. See Tom W. Smith, "An Experimental Comparison of Clustered and Scattered Scale Items," *Social Psychology Quarterly* 46 (1983): 163–168; and J. A. Davis and Tom W. Smith, *General Social Surveys: 1972–1982* (Chicago, IL: National Opinion Research Center, 1982).

44. The Gamma values for "least-liked group holding office" were .052 for Western nations and .033 for Other nations. The Gamma values for "least-liked group teaching" were .060 for Western nations and .049 for Other nations. The Gamma values for "least-liked group participating in a demonstration" were .074 for Western nations and .112 for Other nations.

46. The Gamma values for "least-liked group holding office," "least-liked group teaching," and "least-liked group participating in a demonstration" were .200, .185, and .233 for Islamic nations, respectively.

47. The Gamma values for "least-liked group holding office" were .039 for Western nations and .078 for Other nations. The Gamma values for "least-liked group teaching" were .153 for Western nations and .055 for Other nations. The Gamma values for "least-liked group participating in a demonstration" were .057 for Western nations and .016 for Other nations.

48. The Gamma values for "least-liked group holding office," "least-liked group teaching," and "least-liked group participating in a demonstration" were .636, .434, and .608 for Islamic nations, respectively.

49. Lewis, *What Went Wrong*, p. 159.

50. James Baldwin, "Stranger in the Village," *The Price of the Ticket: Collected Nonfiction, 1948–1985* (New York: St. Martin's Press, 1985).

Chapter 2   How We Come to Be Who We Are: Constructing Identity around the World

1. See Sidney Verba and Gabriel Almond, *The Civic Culture: Political Attitudes and Democracy in Five Nations* (Boston, MA: Little, Brown, 1965), p. 13.

2. Liah Greenfeld, *Nationalism: Five Roads to Modernity* (Cambridge, MA: Harvard University Press, 1992), p. 487.

3. Jeff Spinner-Halev and Elizabeth Theiss-Morse, "National Identity and Self-esteem," *Perspectives on Politics* 1, no. 3 (September 2003): 515–532.

4. Ibid., 517.

5. Ibid.

6. Ibid., 517–518.

7. Ibid., 518.

8. Viera Bacova, "The Construction of National Identity—On Primordialism and Instrumentalism," *Human Affairs* 8, no. 1 (1998): 32–33.

9. Ibid., 41.

10. Richard Kiely, Frank Bechhofer, Robert Stewart, and David McCrone, "The Markers and Rules of Scottish National Identity," *Sociological Review* (2001): 33.

11. M. Lane Bruner, "Rhetorics of the State: The Public Negotiation of Political Character in Germany, Russia, and Quebec," *National Identities* 2, no. 2 (2000): 159.

12. Spinner-Halev and Theiss-Morse, *Perspectives on Politics* 1 (2003): 519.

13. The nations included in this study included Austria, Bulgaria, Canada, the Czech Republic, East Germany, West Germany (although reunified, these were studied separately), Great Britain, Hungary, Italy, Ireland, Japan, Latvia, Norway, the Netherlands, New Zealand, Poland, the Philippines, Russia, Slovakia, Slovenia, Sweden, Spain, and the United States. Data compiled from surveys gathered from the Interuniversity Consortium of Social Sciences.

14. All of the nations in the sample are representative democracies of one form or another.

15. Although it is notable that the relationship is positive and significant for all nations in the sample.

16. The factor loadings for each of the variables were democracy (.743), political influence (.769), social security system (.726), armed forces (.554), and fair treatment (.721). The factor loadings for each of the variables was things ashamed of (.553) and desire to take part in international actions (.880).

17. Indeed, if one accepts the model of "core" and "peripheral" nations, in which the former's exploitation of the latter kept countries' relative economic positions static, this hierarchy would not change at all over time as a general rule.

Part II

Introduction: National Identity as a Personal and Global Concept

1. Peter L. Berger and Thomas Luckman, *The Social Construction of Reality* (Garden City, NY: Doubleday, 1966), p. 160.

2. Samuel Huntington, "The Clash of Civilizations?" *Foreign Affairs* 72 (Summer 1993): 24.

3. John R. Zaller, *The Nature and Origins of Mass Opinion* (New York: Cambridge University Press, 1992).

4. Karl Deutsch, *Nationalism and Social Communication* (Cambridge, MA: MIT Press, 1966).

5. Elisabeth Noelle-Neumann, *The Spiral of Silence: Public Opinion—Our Social Skin* (Chicago: University of Chicago Press, 1992).

6. Vincent Price and Hayg Oshagan, "Social-Psychological Perspectives on Public Opinion Research," in *Public Opinion and the Communication of Consent,* ed. Thomas L. Glasser and Charles T. Salmon (New York: Guilford Press, 1995), p. 178.

7. W. James, *The Principles of Psychology* (New York: H. Holt, 1890).

8. J. M. Baldwin, *The Elements of Psychology* (New York: H. Holt, 1893).

9. George H. Mead, *Mind, Self, and Society* (Chicago: University of Chicago Press, 1934).

10. Price and Oshagan, "Social-Psychological Perspectives," p. 178.

11. James R. Beniger and Jodi A. Gusek, "The Cognitive Revolution in Public Opinion and Communication Research," in *Public Opinion*, p. 258.

12. Frank Louis Rusciano and Roberta Fiske-Rusciano, "Towards a Notion of 'World Opinion,'" *International Journal of Public Opinion Research* 2, no. 4 (1990): 320.

13. See Rusciano and Fiske-Rusciano, "Towards a Notion" and Rusciano, "Media Perspectives on World Opinion during the Kuwaiti Crisis," in *Media and the Persian Gulf War*, ed. Robert E. Denton (Westport, CT: Praeger, 1993).

14. See the example of India during the Persian Gulf Crisis in Rusciano, "Media Perspectives," pp. 79–80.

15. See Elisabeth Noelle-Neumann, *The Spiral of Silence: Public Opinion—Our Social Skin* (Chicago: University of Chicago Press, 1984) and Price and Oshagan, "Social-Psychological Perspectives," p. 203.

16. Price and Oshagan, "Social-Psychological Perspectives," p. 205.

17. Damarys Canache, "Looking out My Back Door: The Neighborhood Context and Perceptions of Relative Deprivation," Paper presented at the annual conference of the American Association for Public Opinion Research, Fort Lauderdale, FL, May 18–21, 1995.

18. See D. Garth Taylor, "Pluralistic Ignorance and the Spiral of Silence: A Formal Model," *Public Opinion Quarterly* 46, no. 2 (1983): 311–335, and others on "pluralistic ignorance."

19. Solomon Asch, "Group Forces in the Modification and Distortion of Judgments," in *Social Psychology*, ed. Solomon Asch (London: Routledge and Kegan Paul, 1952).

20. Noelle-Neumann, *Spiral of Silence.*

21. Zaller, *Nature and Origins*, p. 75.

22. Ibid., p. 78.

23. See Liisa Malkki, "Citizens of Humanity: Internationalism and the Imagined Community of Nations," *Diaspora* 3, no. 1 (1994): 41–68.

Chapter 3   Fences Make Good Neighbors: Who Is "German" without the Wall?

1. It is notable, though, that Germany had previous experience with terrorist acts, notably by such groups as the Beider-Meinhof gang during the Cold War. However, these incidents were associated with Cold War conflicts and were generally halted following reunification.

2. C. Maier, *The Unmasterable Past: History, Holocaust, and German National Identity* (Cambridge, MA: Harvard University Press, 1988), pp. 49–50.

3. The Allensbach surveys consist of a stratified sample of 1500 respondents in the FRG ages 16 and above.

4. See Tom W. Smith, "An Experimental Comparison of Clustered and Scattered Scale Items," *Social Psychology Quarterly* 46 (1983): 163–168.

5. M. Lane Bruner, "Rhetorics of the State: The Public Negotiation of Political Character in Germany, Russia, and Quebec," *National Identities* 2, no. 2 (2000): 161.

6. Harry Pross, "On German Identity," *Media, Culture, and Society* 13 (1991): 346.

7. Konrad H. Jarausch, *The Rush to German Unity* (New York: Oxford University Press, 1994), p. 204.

8. Jurek Becker, "My Father, the Germans and Me," *German American Cultural Review* (Winter 1994): 6.

9. Elisabeth Noelle-Neumann and Renate Koecher, *Allensbacher Jahrbuch der Demoskopie 1984–1992* (Munchen: K. G. Saur, 1993), p. 554.

10. Bruner, "Rhetorics of the State," 163.

11. Ibid.

12. See Frank Louis Rusciano, "Media Perspectives on 'World Opinion' during the Kuwaiti Crisis," in *Media and the Persian Gulf War*, ed. Robert E. Denton (Westport, CT: Praeger, 1993), pp. 71–87.

13. Institut für Demoskopie Allensbach, "Germans Shun Extremists," p. 1.

14. Ibid., pp. 5–6.

15. Ibid.

16. Stephen Kinzer, "Germany Ablaze: It's Candlelight, Not Firebombs," *New York Times*, January 13, 1993, A4.

17. Ibid.

18. Kinzer, "Stepson of German Politics: Is Fatherland Proud?" *New York Times*, February 22, 1993, A4.

19. Kinzer, "As Strife Recedes, Germans Breathe Easier," *New York Times*, March 18, 1993.

20. Ibid.

21. The newspapers surveyed included the *New York Times*, the *Los Angeles Times*, the *Washington Post*, the *Wall Street Journal*, and the *Christian Science Monitor*.

22. Noelle-Neumann and Koecher, *Allensbacher Jahrbuch*, p. 531.

23. Ibid.

Chapter 4   China's Two Faces: The Contradiction of Chinese "Uniqueness"

1. Wang Jisi, "China–U.S. Relations at a Crossroads," in *China–United States Sustained Dialogue: 1986–2001*, ed. Zhao Mei and Maxine Thomas (Dayton, OH: Kettering Foundation, 2001), p. 54.

2. Zi Zhongyun, "Chinese Exceptionalism: Past and Present," in *China–United States*, p. 42.

3. Ibid., p. 43.

4. Ibid., p. 45.

5. Each story or editorial that uses the concept of world opinion is counted as a single case for this analysis, regardless of the number of times the item invokes the concept. As such, the term "references" is used interchangeably with "stories and/or editorials" in this book. The case basis of sixty-eight references therefore translates into sixty-eight stories or editorials that used the concept of world opinion regarding the IWC. Regarding intercoder reliability, all content analyses were performed and scrutinized by all three authors; any disagreements over coding of the data were worked out by mutual agreement.

6. These components were originally derived from newspaper content analyses, and have proven useful in disaggregating references to world opinion in such newspapers as the *New York Times*, the *Frankfurter Allgemeine Zeitung*, the *Times of India*, and the *International Herald Tribune* (see Frank Louis Rusciano and Roberta Fiske-Rusciano, "Towards a Notion of 'World Opinion,'" *International Journal of Public Opinion Research* 2 (1990): 305–322.; Rusciano, "First and Third World Newspapers on World Opinion: 'Imagined Communities' in the Cold War and Post–Cold War Eras," *Political Communication* 14, no. 2 (1997): 171–190. The Cumulative Index of World Opinion, referenced later in this paper, was used for all four newspapers in a media-marketing analysis (see Frank Louis Rusciano and John Crothers Pollock, "Does a Public Exist for World Opinion?" in *Proceedings of the American Association for Public Opinion Research*, 1995.

7. The notion of "negotiation" here does not refer directly or solely to the external negotiations which female representatives practiced to reach a documentary consensus. Rather, in keeping with our introductory statements, "negotiation" refers to the attempt to reconcile one's image of their nation (*Selbstbild*) with its international reputation (*Fremdbild*). The delegates' external compromises to reach a consensus are assumed to be reflective of these internal negotiations, but the two are not directly equivalent.

8. See note 6 on the components and prior usage of this scale.

9. Lucian W. Pye, "China's Quest for Respect," *New York Times*, February 19, 1996, A15.

10. Ibid.

11. Ibid.

12. The analysis suggests that a negotiation between just the United States and China is insufficient. The American newspaper pursued a clear agenda in its construction of world opinion vis-à-vis China's image. Our analysis suggests the United States' agenda need not concede with the agendas of other nations that would need to participate in a global consensus regarding an acceptable national identity for the Chinese.

13. Zhongyun, "Chinese Exceptionalism," p. 44.

14. Jisi, "China–U.S. Relations," p. 61.

15. This project consisted of telephone interviews conducted from the Hong Kong University of Science and Technology, and included 546 respondents in February 1997 and 1129 respondents in June 1997.

16. It should be noted, of course, that Chinese officials had often pointed out how Hong Kong's experience with democracy was relatively new; prior to a few years ago, the island did not have a freely elected government.

17. The symmetric λ for this relationship was .2987.
18. The η for this relationship is .5331.
19. This project consisted of telephone interviews conducted from the Hong Kong University of Science and Technology, and included 546 respondents in February 1997 and 1129 respondents in June 1997.
20. The percentages of those who responded "Strongly believe" or "believe" were combined as those who believe the statement to be true; the percentages of those who responded "Strongly disbelieve" or "disbelieve" were combined as those who believe the statement to be false.
21. These included 30 percent who answered "Chinese" and 28 percent who answered "Hong Kong Chinese"; similarly, the later figures include 25 percent "Chinese" and 24 percent "Hong Kong Chinese."
22. Patrick E. Tyler, "China Issue for the Post-Deng Era," *New York Times,* June 29, 1997, p. 15.

Chapter 5   The Indian/Pakistani Nuclear Tests: Brinkmanship without a Cause

1. Jaswant Singh, "Against Nuclear Apartheid," *Foreign Affairs* 77, no. 5 (September–October 1998): 52.
2. Ibid., 41.
3. Ibid., 51.
4. Samuel P. Huntington, "The Clash of Civilizations?" *Foreign Affairs* 72 (Summer 1993): 191.
5. Singh, "Against Nuclear Apartheid," 42.
6. Ibid., 48.
7. Ibid., 47.
8. Ibid.
9. Huntington, "Clash of Civilizations," 39.
10. Singh, "Against Nuclear Apartheid," 43.
11. Huntington, "Clash of Civilizations," 67–78.
12. Singh, "Against Nuclear Apartheid," 43.
13. Ibid.
14. Ibid., 51.
15. Strobe Talbott, *Engaging India: Diplomacy, Democracy, and the Bomb* (Washington, DC: Brookings Institution Press, 2004), p. 26.
16. Singh, "Against Nuclear Apartheid," 43–44.
17. Ibid., 49. It is interesting to note that Singh denies domestic political motivations for the test, arguing on the same page that such considerations would not have required "the range of technologies and yields demonstrated in May." While strategic reassurance might not have justified such revelation, however, stimulating feelings of national pride certainly did.
18. Ibid.

19. Talbott, *Engaging India*, p. 15.
20. Ibid., p. 31.
21. Ibid., p. 29.
22. All content analyses were reviewed or done by the author, to avoid intercoder conflicts of interpretation.
23. See Frank Louis Rusciano, *World Opinion and the Emerging International Order* (Westport, CT: Praeger, 1998), chs. 2 and 5.
24. The breakdown of references on India were positive 3.6 percent (5), negative 85.5 percent (118), neutral 4.3 percent (6), and no mention of India 6.5 percent (9).
25. The breakdown of references on Pakistan were positive 3.6 percent (five), negative 31.9 percent (forty-four), neutral 23.2 percent (thirty-two), and no mention of Pakistan 41.3 percent (fifty-seven).
26. The χ square value for references to India in world opinion was 10.15 with 6 degrees of freedom and a significance level of .11867; the χ square value for references to Pakistan in world opinion was 9.39 with 6 degrees of freedom and a significance level of .15257.
27. The χ square value for references to India in world opinion was 5.64 with 3 degrees of freedom and a significance level of .13063; the χ square value for references to Pakistan in world opinion was 2.33 with 3 degrees of freedom and a significance level of .50602.
28. Most of the comparisons, and analyses, focus upon India as the subject for world opinion. This decision was made because of the inclusion of an Indian newspaper in the analysis (no Pakistani newspapers were included in the study).
29. The significance level for the Pearson's r in this case was .182.
30. The Pearson's r for this relationship in negative stories on India was .251, with $p = .006$; the r for negative stories on Pakistan was .471, with $p = .001$. Stories reflecting positive or neutral opinions toward these nations tended to show the same pattern, but there were too few cases for a significant relationship to be established.
31. The Pearson's r for this relationship in negative stories on India was .299, with $p = .001$; the r for negative stories on Pakistan was .350, with $p = .020$. Again, stories reflecting positive or neutral opinions toward these nations tended to show the same pattern, but there were too few cases for a significant relationship to be established.
32. Huntington, "Clash of Civilizations," p. 191.
33. K. R. Malkani, "Living with the Bomb," *Hindustan Times*, June 30, 1998, p. 1.
34. Z. S. Afridi, "India Disturbs Asian Stability," *China Daily*, June 6, 1998, p. 4.
35. B. Hongwei, "India's Nuclear Tests Deserve Condemnation," *China Daily*, May 15, 1998, p. 1.
36. E. Arnett, "Delhi Able to Play Nuclear Trump in Game for Control of Kashmir," *London Times*, May 15, 1998, p. 21.
37. Ibid.
38. J. F. Burns, "Hindu Nationalists Move to Rule India's Atom Era," *New York Times*, May 16, 1998, p. 10.
39. Malkani, "India, China, and the Bomb," *Hindustan Times*, June 3, 1998, p. 1.
40. A. Ganguli, "From Babri to the Bomb," *Hindustan Times*, May 18, 1998, p. 1.

41. Malkani, "Living With the Bomb, p. 1.
42. Huntington, *The Clash of Civilizations and the Remaking of World Order* (New York: Simon and Schuster, 1996), p. 244.
43. Talbott, *Engaging India*, p. 134.
44. Ibid., p. 136.

Chapter 6   The War at Home: Identity Versus Values

1. It is arguable that world opinion was highly critical of the United States during the Vietnam War, but the Cold War context of that conflict entails ideological baggage that makes the discussion of world opinion more problematic.
2. See Frank Louis Rusciano, "Near and Distant Mirrors: International Media Perspectives on World Opinion after September 11, 2001," in *Framing Terrorism: The News Media, the Government, and the Public*, ed. Pippa Norris, Montague Kern, and Marion Just (New York: Routledge, 2003), pp. 159–179.
3. Indeed, if certain reports from within the Bush administration are to be believed, many were pushing for Iran to be the next target of U.S. military action after the intervention in Iraq was "completed."
4. Intercoder reliability was ensured through careful review of all cases among the principal researchers and their assistants.
5. Unfortunately, a similar analysis of negative, positive, or neutral references to Iraq was not possible because the distributions between the two newspapers were too different to provide sufficient cases for study.
6. See, for instance, Frank Louis Rusciano and Bosah Ebo, "National Consciousness, International Image, and the Construction of Identity," in Rusciano, *World Opinion and the Emerging International Order* (Westport, CT: Praeger, 1998); and Rusciano, "The Construction of National Identity—A 23-Nation Study," *Political Research Quarterly* 56, no. 3 (September 2003): 361–366.
7. Joseph Nye describes a more productive use of a nation's influence over world opinion as "soft power" in his book *The Paradox of American Power*. He notes how propagating our values can be a positive force, so long as we pursue it through persuasion, rather than through some combination of superior military or economic force. *The Paradox of American Power: Why the World's Only Superpower Can't Go It Alone* (New York: Oxford University Press, 2002), pp. 1–40.
8. Spain, however, withdrew its troops from Iraq after the Socialist victory in the 2004 elections.
9. Ibid.
10. President George W. Bush, transcript of address to a joint session of the U.S. Congress, Thursday, September 20, 2001.
11. Benjamin R. Barber, *Fear's Empire: War, Terrorism, and Democracy* (New York: W. W. Norton and Company, 2003), p. 62.
12. President George W. Bush, transcript of speech to the United Nations General Assembly, September 21, 2004.

13. Ibid.
14. Then chairman of the House Subcommittee on Terrorism and Homeland Security, to Georgia law officers, November 2001. Chambliss later became senator from Georgia.
15. Interview on Cal Thomas radio show, November 2001. Mr. Ashcroft's office later claimed that this version of his statement was incorrect.
16. Speech in November 2001.
17. James Caroll, "Warring with God," *Boston Globe*, October 21, 2003.
18. Samer Shehata, "Islam and Its Contemporary Relationship to the West," *The New Republic* symposium on Public Policy, November 13, 2003.
19. Pippa Norris and Ronald Inglehart, "Public Opinion among Muslims and the West," in *Framing Terrorism: The News Media, Government, and the Public*, ed. Pippa Norris, Montague Kern, and Marion Just (New York: Routledge, 2003), pp. 203–228.
20. Ibid., p. 214. The study classified Muslim nations as those countries that had a plurality of citizens following the Islamic faith and included Albania, Azerbaijan, Bangladesh, Egypt, Iran, Jordan, Morocco, Pakistan, and Turkey.
21. Pew Global Attitudes Project, "Iraqi Vote Mirrors Desire for Democracy in the Arab World," February 3, 2005, p. 1.
22. Ibid., p. 2.
23. Ibid., p. 3.
24. Norris and Inglehart, "Public Opinion," pp. 214–216. The first three issues were studied using simple agree/disagree statements. The gender equality index was summed from the following questions, with the less-tolerant responses coded lowest: "On the whole, men make better political leaders than women"; "When jobs are scarce, men should have more of a right to a job than women"; "A university education is more important for a boy than for a girl"; "Do you think that a woman needs a child in order to be fulfilled or not?"; and "If a woman wants a child as a single parent but she doesn't want a stable relationship with a man, do you approve or disapprove?" This scale was reproduced for the analysis presented later in this chapter of how these issues divide Islamic and Western nations.
25. J. Ann Tickner, "Feminist Perspectives on 9/11," *International Studies Perspectives* 3, no. 4 (November 2002): 333–350.
26. The ηs for the tables on divorce, abortion, homosexuality, and overall gender equality were .177, .073, .153, and .588, respectively. Although η is low on the abortion question, there are significant differences between the Western nations and U.S. conservatives, and the U.S. liberals and U.S. conservatives, as noted in the text.
27. The significance levels for divorce, abortion, homosexuality, and gender equality were .180, 1.000, .999, and .355, respectively.
28. Garry Wills, "The Day the Enlightenment Went Out," *New York Times*, November 4, 2004.
29. These results are based upon telephone samples of 1001 American citizens over the age of eighteen.

30. Benjamin R. Barber, *Fear's Empire: War, Terrorism, and Democracy* (New York: W. W. Norton and Company, 2003), p. 49. Garry Wills made a similar argument when describing Reagan's appeal as president in *Reagan's America: Innocents at Home* (New York: Penguin Books, 2000).

31. Sidney Verba and Gabriel Almond, *The Civic Culture* (Boston: Little, Brown, 1965).

Part III

Chapter 7   Addressing the Real Problem: Draining the Swamps of Despair

1. Antony Beevor, "Nobody Loves a Liberator," *New York Times*, April 13, 2003.

2. This threat level was later changed to "gathering threat," a more ambiguous phrase, conjuring up storm clouds rather than an actual storm, when no weapons of mass destruction (another amorphous term) were found.

3. It is notable, for instance, that the United States had formerly urged Russia to work toward allowing Chechnya to secede from the nation, but that after Chechnyan rebels committed terrorist acts, Putin became a U.S. ally in the fight against terrorism, even though the Chechnyan conflict had been going on for years and had virtually nothing to do with al-Qaida. Further, U.S. policy toward Musharraf had been to isolate him for seizing power in a coup over Pakistan's elected leaders. Our commitment to democracy in this regard ended when he offered the United States support in the war on terror in Afghanistan.

4. Benjamin R. Barber, *Fear's Empire: War, Terrorism, and Democracy* (New York: W. W. Norton and Company, 2003), p. 205.

5. J. Ann Tickner discusses this point in her excellent article, "Feminist Perspectives on 9/11," *International Studies Perspectives* 3, no. 4 (November 2002): 333–350.

6. James Kurth, "The Real Clash," *The National Interest*, no. 37 (Fall 1994): 3–15.

7. Francis Fukuyama, "Women and the Evolution of World Politics," *Foreign Affairs* 77, no. 5 (1998): 24–40.

8. Amin Malouf, *In the Name of Identity: Violence and the Need to Belong*, trans. Barbara Bray (New York: Arcade Publishing, 2000), pp. 143–164.

9. Allan Bloom, *The Closing of the American Mind: How Higher Education Has Failed Democracy and Impoverished the Souls of Today's Students* (New York: Simon and Schuster, 1987), p. 26.

10. James Baldwin, *The Price of the Ticket: Collected Nonfiction, 1948–1985* (New York: St. Martin's Press, 1985), p. 87.

Bibliography and Related Readings

Afridi, Z. S. "India Disturbs Asian Stability." *China Daily,* June 6, 1998, p. 4.

Arnett, E. "Delhi Able to Play Nuclear Trump in Game for Control of Kashmir." *London Times,* May 15, 1998, p. 21.

Asch, Solomon. "Group Forces in the Modification and Distortion of Judgments." In *Social Psychology,* edited by Solomon Asch. London: Routledge and Kegan Paul, 1952.

Avinieri, Shlomo. *Proceedings of the Conference on Europe in the New World Order.* Georgetown University: Washington, DC, 1991.

Bacova, Viera. "The Construction of National Identity—On Primordialism and Instrumentalism." *Human Affairs* 8, no. 1 (1998): 32–33.

Baldwin, James. *The Price of the Ticket: Collected Nonfiction, 1948–1985.* New York: St. Martin's Press, 1985, p. 87.

Baldwin, J. M. *The Elements of Psychology.* New York: H. Holt, 1893.

Barber, Benjamin R. *Fear's Empire: War, Terrorism, and Democracy.* New York: W. W. Norton and Company, 2003, p. 62.

———. *Jihad vs. McWorld.* New York: Random House, 1995.

Bartley, Robert L. "The Case for Optimism: The West Should Believe in Itself." *Foreign Affairs* 72 (September/October 1993), 15.

Becker, Jurek. "My Father, the Germans and Me." *German American Cultural Review,* Winter 1994.

Beevor, Antony. "Nobody Loves a Liberator." *New York Times,* April 13, 2003, A18.

Bell, Daniel. *The Coming of Post-Industrial Society: A Venture in Social Forecasting.* New York: Basic Books, 1973.

Beniger, James R., and Jodi A. Gusek. "The Cognitive Revolution in Public Opinion and Communication Research." In *Public Opinion and the Communication of Consent,* edited by Theodore L. Glasser and Charles T. Salmon. New York: Guilford Press, 1995, p. 258.

Berger, Peter L., and Thomas Luckman. *The Social Construction of Reality.* Garden City, NY: Doubleday, 1966, p. 160.

Best, Paul J., Kul B. Rai, and David F. Walsh. *Politics in Three Worlds: An Introduction to Political Science.* New York: John Wiley and Sons, 1986.

Bloom, Allan. *The Closing of the American Mind: How Higher Education Has Failed Democracy and Impoverished the Souls of Today's Students.* New York: Simon and Schuster, 1987, p. 26.

Bloom, William. *Personal Identity, National Identity and International Relations.* Cambridge: Cambridge University Press, 1990.

Bogart, Leo. "Is There a World Opinion?" *Polls* 1 (1966): 1–9.

Bruner, M. Lane. "Rhetorics of the State: The Public Negotiation of Political Character in Germany, Russia, and Quebec." *National Identities* 2, no. 2 (2000): 159.

Brzezinski, Zbigniew. "Power and Morality." *World Monitor,* March 1993, 23–28.

Bull, Hedley, and Adam Watson. *The Expansion of International Society.* Oxford: Clarendon Press, 1984.

Burns, J. F. "Hindu Nationalists Move to Rule India's Atom Era." *New York Times,* May 16, 1998, 10.

Canache, Damarys. "Looking Out My Back Door: The Neighborhood Context and Perceptions of Relative Deprivation." Paper presented at the annual conference of the American Association for Public Opinion Research, Fort Lauderdale, FL, May 18–21, 1995.

Caroll, James. "Warring with God." *Boston Globe,* October 21, 2003.

China Daily. "India May Increase Defense Spending." June 6, 1998, p. 1.

Conradt, David P. "Changing German Political Culture." In *The Civic Culture Revisited,* edited by Gabriel Almond and Sidney Verba. Boston, MA: Little, Brown, 1980.

Csepeli, Gyorgy. "Competing Patterns of National Identity in Post-Communist Hungary." *Media, Culture, and Society* 13 (1991): 325339.

Davis, J. A., and Tom W. Smith. *General Social Surveys: 1972–1982.* Chicago, IL: National Opinion Research Center, 1982.

Davison, W. Phillips. "International and Public Opinion." In *Handbook of Communication,* edited by Ithiel del Sola Pool and Frederick W. Frey. Chicago, IL: Rand McNally, 1973.

Deutsch, Karl. *Nationalism and Social Communication.* Cambridge, MA: MIT Press, 1966.

Doran, Michael. "The Pragmatic Fanaticism of al Qaeda: An Anatomy of Extremism in Middle Eastern Politics." *Political Science Quarterly* 117, no. 2 (2002): 185.

Doty, R. L. "Foreign Policy as a Social Construction: A Post-Positivist Analysis of U.S. Counterinsurgency Policy in the Philippines." *International Studies Quarterly* 37: 297–320.

Ebo, Bosah. "Africa and the West in the New World Information Order." Paper presented at the Northwestern University Conference on Communication and Development, Chicago, IL, 1983.

Fuentes, Carlos. Interview. By Bill Moyers. In *A World of Ideas,* edited by Bill Moyers, New York: Doubleday, 1989, p. 307.

Fukayama, Francis. "Women and the Evolution of World Politics." *Foreign Affairs* 77, no. 5 (1998): 24–40.

Ganguli, A. "From Babri to the Bomb." *Hindustan Times,* May 18, 1998.

Gergen, K. J. "Social Construction in Question." *Human Systems: The Journal of Systematic Consultation and Management* 3 (1992): 163–182.

Gilligan, C. *In a Different Voice.* Cambridge, MA: Harvard University Press, 1992.

Goldstone, Jack A. "States, Terrorists, and the Clash of Civilizations." In *Understanding September 11,* edited by Craig Calhoun, Paul Price, and Ashley Timmer. New York: New Press, 2002, p. 142.

Grader, Sheila. "The English School of International Relations: Evidence and Evaluation." *Review of International Studies* 14 (1988): 29–44.

Greenfeld, Liah. "Nationalism and Class Struggle: Two Forces or One?" *Survey* 29 (1985): 153–174.

———. *Nationalism: Five Roads to Modernity*. Cambridge, MA: Harvard University Press, 1992.

Hedges, Chris. "Top Leader of the Bosnian Serbs now under Attack from within." *New York Times*, January 4, 1996, A1, A8.

Herman, Edward S., and Noam Chomsky. *Manufacturing Consent: The Political Economy of Mass Media*. New York: Random House, 1988.

Hill, Christopher J. "World Opinion and the Empire of Circumstance." *International Affairs* 72 (January 1996): 109–131.

Hinckley, Ron. "World Public Opinion and the Persian Gulf Crisis." In *Proceedings of the American Association for Public Opinion Research*. Phoenix, AZ, May 16–19, 1991.

Hindustan Times. "Arabs Jubilant Over Tests." May 17, 1998, p. 1.

Hindustan Times. "PM's Statements on N-Tests in Parliament." May 27, 1998a, p. 1.

Hirsch, Fred. *The Social Limits to Growth*. Cambridge, MA: Harvard University Press, 1976.

Hongwei, B. "India's Nuclear Tests Deserve Condemnation." *China Daily*, May 15, 1998.

Huntington, Samuel P. "If Not Civilizations, What?" *Foreign Affairs* 72. 1993.

———. "The Clash of Civilizations?" *Foreign Affairs*, Summer 1993, 22–49.

———. *The Clash of Civilizations and the Remaking of World Order*. New York: Simon and Schuster, 1996.

Inglehart, Ronald. *The Silent Revolution: Changing Values and Political Styles among Western Publics*. Princeton, NJ: Princeton University Press, 1977.

Institut für Demoskopie Allensbach. "Germans Shun Extremists: No Signs of a New Anti-Semitism." *Allensbach Berichte*, January 1993.

Irish Times. "India Lights the Touchpaper." May 13, 1998: 1.

James, W. *The Principles of Psychology*. New York: H. Holt, 1890.

Jarausch, Konrad H. *The Rush to German Unity*. New York: Oxford University Press, 1994.

Jisi, Wang. "Chinese–U.S. Relations at a Crossroads." In *China—United States Sustained Dialogue: 1986–2001*, edited by Zhao Mei and Maxine Thomas. Dayton, OH: Kettering Foundation, 2001.

Jones, Roy E. "The English School of International Relations: A Case for Closure." *Review of International Studies* 7 (1981): 1–12.

Juergensmeyer, Mark. "Religious Terror and Global War." In Calhoun, Price, and Timmer, *Understanding September 11*, p. 36.

Kiely, Richard, Frank Bechhofer, Robert Stewart, and David McCrone. "The Markers and Rules of Scottish National Identity." *Sociological Review*, 2001: 33.

Kinzer, Stephen. "As Strife Recedes, Germans Breathe Easier." *New York Times*, March 18, 1993a, A13.

———. "Germany Ablaze: It's Candlelight, Not Firebombs." *New York Times*, January 13, 1993b, A4.

————. "Stepson of German Politics: Is Fatherland Proud?" *New York Times*, February 22, 1993c, A4.

Knudson, Tonny Brems. "International Society and International Solidarity: Recapturing the Solidarist Origins of the English School." Paper presented at the workshop *International Relations in Europe: Concepts, Schools and Institutions*, 28th Joint Sessions of the European Consortium for Political Research, Copenhagen, Denmark, April 14–19, 2000.

Kuran, Timur. "The Religious Undertow of Muslim Economic Grievances." In Calhoun, Price, and Timmer, *Understanding September 11*, p. 68.

Kurth, J. "The Real Clash." *The National Interest*, no. 37 (Fall 1994): 3–15.

Lewis, Bernard. "The Roots of Muslim Rage." *The Atlantic*, September 1990, p. 53.

————. *What Went Wrong: Western Impact and Middle Eastern Response*. New York: Oxford University Press. 2002, pp. 26–28.

London Times. May 15, 1998, p. 21.

Maier, C. *The Unmasterable Past: History, Holocaust, and German National Identity*. Cambridge, MA: Harvard University Press, 1988.

Malkani, K. R. "India, China, and the Bomb." *Hindustan Times*, June 3, 1998, p. 1.

————. "Living with the Bomb." *Hindustan Times*, June 30, 1998, p. 1.

Malkki, Liisa. "Citizens of Humanity: Internationalism and the Imagined Community of Nations." *Diaspora* 3, no. 1 (1994): 41–68.

Malouf, Amin. *In the Name of Identity: Violence and the Need to Belong*. Translated by Barbara Bray. New York: Arcade Publishing, 2000, pp. 143–164.

Mayall, James. *Nationalism and International Society*. New York: Cambridge University Press, 1990.

Mazrui, A. A. *The Africans: A Triple Heritage*. Boston, MA: Little, Brown, 1986.

McFalls, Laurence. "Culture Clash and the Current German National Identity Crisis." In *Proceedings of the American Political Science Association*. Washington, DC, September 2–5, 1993.

Mead, George H. *Mind, Self, and Society*. Chicago: University of Chicago Press, 1934.

Morgenthau, Hans J. "Is World Public Opinion a Myth?" *New York Times*, March 25, 1962, p. 23.

Mowlana, Hamid, and Laurie J. Wilson. *The Passing of Modernity: Communication and the Transformation of Society*. New York: Longman, 1990.

New York Times. "Mideast: Now a People's Peace." September 15, 1993, A26.

Noelle-Neumann, Elisabeth. *The Spiral of Silence: Public Opinion—Our Social Skin*. Chicago: University of Chicago Press, 1992.

Noelle-Neumann, Elisabeth, and Renate Koecher. *Allensbacher Jahrbuch der Demoskopie, 1984–1992*. Munich: K. G. Saur, 1993.

Norris, Pippa, and Ronald Inglehardt. "Muslims and the West: Testing the 'Clash of Civilizations' Thesis." In *Proceedings of* "The Restless Searchlight: Media and Terrorism." The Kennedy School: Harvard University, September 1, 2002.

————. "Public Opinion among Muslims and the West." In *Framing Terrorism: The News Media, Government, and the Public*, edited by Pippa Norris, Montague Kern, and Marion Just. New York: Routledge, 2003, pp. 203–228.

Nye, Joseph S., Jr. *The Paradox of American Power: Why the World's Only Superpower Can't Go It Alone*. New York: Oxford University Press, 2002.

Obasanjo, O. *Proceedings of the Conference on Europe in the New World Order.* Georgetown University, Washington, DC, 1991.

Pew Global Attitudes Project. "Iraqi Vote Mirrors Desire for Democracy in the Arab World." February 3, 2005.

Price, Vincent, and Hayg Osahaga. "Social-Psychological Perspectives on Public Opinion Research." In *Public Opinion and the Communication of Consent,* edited by Thomas L. Glasser and Charles T. Salmon. New York: Guilford Press, 1995. p. 178.

Pross, Harry. "On German Identity." *Media, Culture, and Society* 13 (1991): 341–356.

Pye, Lucian. "China's Quest for Respect." *New York Times,* February 19, 1996, A15.

Reich, Robert B. "What Is a Nation?" *Political Science Quarterly* 106 (1991): 193–209.

Rogers, Everett M. "The Rise and Fall of the Dominant Paradigm." *Journal of Communication* 28 (1978): 64–69.

Rostow, Eugene. *The Stages of Economic Growth: A Non-Communist Manifesto.* London: Cambridge University Press, 1971.

Rusciano, Frank Louis. "The Construction of National Identity: A 26-Nation Study." In *Proceedings of the American Association of Public Opinion Research.* Montreal, Canada, May 2001.

———. "Die Neuaushandlung der deutschen Nationalidentaet nach 1989." *Deutsche Umbrueche im 20. Jahrhundert.* Cologne: Boehlau Verlag GmbH and Cie, 2000, pp. 627–663.

———. "First and Third World Newspapers on World Opinion: 'Imagined Communities' in the Cold War and Post-Cold War Eras." *Political Communication* 14, no. 2 (1997): 171–190.

———. *Isolation and Paradox: Defining "the Public" in Modern Political Analysis.* Westport, CT: Greenwood Press, 1989.

———. "Media Observations on World Opinion during the Kuwaiti Crisis: Political Communication and the Emerging International Order." *Southeastern Political Review* 24, no. 3 (1996): 505–530.

———. "A World beyond Civilizations? New Directions in Research on World Opinion." *International Journal of Public Opinion Research* 13 (2001): 10–24.

———. "World Opinion on the Kuwait–Iraq Crisis: Does the Third World Have a Voice?" In *Proceedings of the Association for the Advancement of Policy, Research, and Development in the Third World.* Orlando, FL, November 18–22, 1992.

———. *World Opinion and the Emerging International Order.* Westport, CT: Praeger, 1998.

Rusciano, Frank Louis, and Roberta Fiske-Rusciano. "Towards a Notion of 'World Opinion.'" *International Journal of Public Opinion Research* 2 (1990): 305–322.

Rusciano, Frank Louis, Roberta Fiske-Rusciano, and Minmin Wang. "The Impact of 'World Opinion' on National Identity." *Harvard International Journal of Press/Politics* 2, no. 3 (1997): 71–92.

———. "The Transfer of Hong Kong to China: A Study of the Construction of National Identity." In *Proceedings of the World Association for Public Opinion Research.* Portland, OR, 2000.

Rusciano, Frank Louis, and John Crothers Pollock. "Media Perspectives on World Opinion during the Recent Bosnian Crisis." *Current World Leaders: International Issues* 40, no. 2 (1997): 56–72.

———. "World Opinion during Times of Crisis." In *Media Power and Politics*, edited by Doris Graber. 4th ed. Washington, DC: Congressional Quarterly Press, 2000, pp. 396–406.

Shehata, Samer. "Islam and Its Contemporary Relationship to the West." *The New Republic Symposium on Public Policy*, November 13, 2003.

Singh, Jaswant. "Against Nuclear Apartheid." *Foreign Affairs* 77, no. 5 (September/October 1998): 52.

Smith, Tom W. "An Experimental Comparison of Clustered and Scattered Scale Items." *Social Psychology Quarterly* 46 (1983): 163–168.

Sontheimer, Kurt. *Deutschlands Politische Kultur*. Munich: R. Piper, 1990.

Spinner-Halev, Jeff, and Elizabeth Theiss-Morse. "National Identity and Self-Esteem." *Perspectives on Politics* 1, no. 3 (September 2003): 515–532.

Talbott, Strobe. *Engaging India: Diplomacy, Democracy, and the Bomb*. Washington, DC: Brookings Institution Press, 2004, p. 26.

Talmon, J. L. *The Origins of Totalitarian Democracy*. New York: Praeger, 1960.

Tamir, Yael. "The Right to National Self-Determination." *Social Research* 58 (1991): 565–590.

Taylor, D. Garth. "Pluralistic Ignorance and the Spiral of Silence: A Formal Model." *Public Opinion Quarterly* 46, no. 2 (1983): 311–335.

Tickner, J. Ann. "Feminist Perspectives on 9/11." *International Studies Perspectives* 3, no. 4 (2002): 333–350.

Tyler, Patrick E. "China Issue for the Post-Deng Era." *New York Times*, June 29, 1997, p. 15.

United States Information Agency. "Global Media Generally Support Bush Gulf Peace Initiative, Mixed on U. N. Force Resolution." See "Dwindling U. S. Support for War." *Foreign Media Analysis*, December 11, 1990.

Verba, Sidney, and Gabriel Almond. *The Civic Culture*. Boston, MA: Little, Brown, 1965.

Vinocour, John. "The New World Order Is a Clash of Civilizations." *International Herald Tribune*, September 13, 2001, p. 1.

Waddel, Eric. "Language, Community and National Identity: Some Reflections on French–English Relations in Canada." In *Canadian Politics: An Introduction to the Discipline*, edited by Alain-G. Gagnon and James P. Bickerton. Lewiston, NY: Broadview Press, 1990, p. 61.

Wilcox, Clyde, Aiji Tanaka, and Dee Allsop. "World Opinion in the Gulf Crisis." *Journal of Conflict Resolution* 37, no. 1 (1993): 69–93.

Wills, Garry. "The Day the Enlightenment Went Out." *New York Times*, November 4, 2004.

———. *Reagan's America: Innocents at Home*. New York: Penguin Books, 2000.

Zaller, John R. *The Nature and Origins of Mass Opinion*. New York: Cambridge University Press, 1992.

Zhongyun, Zi. "Chinese Exceptionalism: Past and Present." In *China–United States Sustained Dialogue: 1986–2001*, edited by Zhao Mei and Maxine Thomas. Dayton, OH: Kettering Foundation, 2001.

Index

CPSIA information can be obtained at www.ICGtesting.com
Printed in the USA
BVOW03*0716200713

326353BV00003B/39/P